# "When Race Breaks Out"

# Questions about the Purpose(s) of Colleges & Universities

Norman K. Denzin and Shirley R. Steinberg
*General Editors*

Vol. 29

The Higher Ed series is part of the Peter Lang Education list.
Every volume is peer reviewed and meets
the highest quality standards for content and production.

PETER LANG
New York • Bern • Frankfurt • Berlin
Brussels • Vienna • Oxford • Warsaw

Helen Fox

# "When Race Breaks Out"

## Conversations about Race and Racism in College Classrooms

### THIRD REVISED EDITION

PETER LANG
New York • Bern • Frankfurt • Berlin
Brussels • Vienna • Oxford • Warsaw

Library of Congress Cataloging-in-Publication Data
Names: Fox, Helen, author.
Title: When race breaks out: conversations about race and racism
in college classrooms / Helen Fox.
Description: Third revised edition. | New York: Peter Lang, 2017.
Series: Higher ed: questions about the purpose(s)
of colleges & universities; vol. 29 | ISSN 1523-9551
Includes bibliographical references.
Identifiers: LCCN 2017000775 | ISBN 978-1-4331-3478-4 (paperback: alk. paper)
ISBN 978-1-4331-3974-1 (ebook pdf) | ISBN 978-1-4331-3975-8 (epub)
ISBN 978-1-4331-3976-5 (mobi)
Subjects: LCSH: College teaching—Social aspects—United States.
Racism—United States. | United States—Race relations.
Classification: LCC LB2331 .F635 2017 | DDC 378.1/25—dc23
LC record available at https://lccn.loc.gov/2017000775
DOI 10.3726/978-1-4331-3974-1


Bibliographic information published by **Die Deutsche Nationalbibliothek**.
**Die Deutsche Nationalbibliothek** lists this publication in the "Deutsche
Nationalbibliografie"; detailed bibliographic data are available
on the Internet at http://dnb.d-nb.de/.

Cover photo by Taro Yamasaki


The paper in this book meets the guidelines for permanence and durability
of the Committee on Production Guidelines for Book Longevity
of the Council of Library Resources.

© 2017 Peter Lang Publishing, Inc., New York
29 Broadway, 18th floor, New York, NY 10006
www.peterlang.com

Printed in the United States of America

In loving memory
of my mother and father
whose exasperation with
human stupidity and
injustice gave me cause for
hope

Like a camel on the loose, [race] has the capacity to do greater injury when we attempt to coop it up as opposed to when we let it run free. A classroom is an artificial cage for the animal of race, and race breaks out everywhere.

—Michael Eric Dyson

# CONTENTS

# ACKNOWLEDGMENTS

Many thanks

To my daughter Cybelle Fox for her splendid editing, research, advice, and enthusiasm for this project

To my daughters Elizabeth and Maria, and my stepchildren Sara and Jaime for their insights and their presence in my life

To my friends and colleagues in social justice work, whose questions and challenges to my ideas about race have kept me thinking, and whose kindness and company I could not do without:

Nehrwr Abdul-Wahid, Dan Adams, Marion Aitches, Patricia Aqui, Kanthie Athukorala, Janice and Gus Augustus, Nancy Barron, Ruby Beale, Teresa Brett, Dianna Campbell, Raymond Chauncey, Mark Chesler, Matthew Countryman, Louise Dunlap, Frieda Ekotto, Sandra Harris, Karen Henry, Chuck Hutchcraft, Yes Iman-Jihad, Said Issa, Margaret Jackson, Steve Jefferson, Fred Johnson, Ryung-wha Lee Kim, Michael Koen, Jeanne Koopman, Ann Larimore, Edith Lewis, Michael McConnell, Harry Mial, Sharon Miles, Barbara Monroe, Barbra Morris, Eliana Moya-Raggio, Jennifer Myers, Gail Nomura, Shari Saunders, David Schoem, Marla Solomon, Shirley Smith, Julie Steiner, Ralph Story, Sylvia Tesh, Pat Trammell, Victor Turner, Robert Walker, Tom Weisskopf, Osei David X, and the memory of Norman Hiza

To my research assistants from the University of Michigan's Undergraduate Research Opportunity Program:

Monica Austin, Nadia Grooms, and Rebecca Kinney

To my students, whose intelligence, sensitivity, and courage to think deeply about this painful and difficult subject keep me optimistic about the future of the human race

And to my husband, Jim Koopman, whose love sustains me

# INTRODUCTION TO THE THIRD
# REVISED EDITION

In 2012, when I was writing the Second Revised Edition of "When Race Breaks Out," Barack Obama had just been elected president for a second term. A slow, steady recovery from the economic crash of 2008 was by then underway, and despite the persistent social and economic divisions between whites and people of color, President Obama's calm, deliberative manner, his unending patience with lawmakers who opposed him at every turn, and his frequent evocation of hope, change, and unity had lulled many Americans into thinking that our nation had finally overcome the old racial divisions of the past. Journalists had begun to use the term "postracial" to describe the new reality of a black man in the White House. Most did not appear aware of the paradox—that Obama's visual blackness was proof that our country had moved beyond race. Students too seemed oblivious to the contradiction: "We're color-blind," they would say. "How can we not be? We elected a black president. Twice!"

It was true that the generation of students who had entered college only a few years prior to Obama's first election—the Millennials—were both more multiethnic than any previous generation and more socially progressive. Racial identity, gender, and sexual orientation, were, to them, "no big deal." But strangely enough, it was this attitude of openness and egalitarianism that made students—particularly white students—more impervious than ever to the serious study of race and racism. Classrooms were calmer than in previous years; students more politely disengaged from contentious discussions. Race rarely "broke out." Students of color sat in pained silence as their white peers confidently argued that there were no longer any significant barriers to advancement for people of color, no need for race-conscious policies, no need to consider race in explanations of economic inequality or to recognize racism, either interpersonal or institutional, on campus. And there was certainly no need to talk about racism within their generation. Their parents and grandparents might be racist, they said, but they, the youth, had left all that behind.

In such an atmosphere, I thought, teachers needed an approach that would engage this "postracial" generation in talking about race in ways that were the most intriguing and natural to them, yet at the same time, pushed their boundaries. If students could discover for themselves how central the idea of race remained in both institutions and personal interactions they would be more inclined to see it as a subject worthy of study. So as I revised the Second Edition I described an approach I had started to take in my own classes, one that built on students' fascination with popular culture. Even if they weren't willing to discuss race in any depth in class, I thought, they were engaging with it during their screen time. They were watching videos posted by their peers about all sorts of racial topics: ethnic identity, standards of beauty, stereotyping, interracial love, and marriage. They were listening to the provocative lyrics of hip-hop artists, and watching racially edgy video clips on Comedy Central. White youth were laughing at the "harmless" ethnic jokes posted by their friends, while youth of color were ranting about the ways they were stereotyped by their ignorant white peers. Even though they denied that racism was still a pernicious problem, Millennial students of all ethnicities were in fact primed to talk about race and eager to discuss it on their own terms.

How quickly times change. One rainy evening in 2014, a 17-year-old African-American high school student named Trayvon Martin was headed home from a convenience store where he had gone to buy an after-dinner snack. As he walked through the middle-class gated community where he and his dad were visiting, his hoodie pulled up over his head to ward off the rain, he was accosted by a Neighborhood Watch coordinator convinced that he was up to no good. A scuffle ensued, and within minutes, Travon had been shot dead. When the shooter, George Zimmerman, was acquitted of any wrongdoing a year later, the nation's racial divisions were brought into stark relief, and the idea that racism was no longer relevant began to crumble.

Suddenly, after a sixty-year hiatus, student activism reappeared on campus. And just as they had during the Civil Rights movement, young people of color were leading the way. In Florida, where the deadly encounter had taken place, hundreds of black and brown youth marched on the state capitol, demanding to talk to the Governor about changing the Stand Your Ground law, which made it legal for citizens to use deadly force when they feared for their life. George Zimmerman, a "white Hispanic," had feared the black teen he was hunting down. "But what about Trayvon's right to stand *his* ground," student activists asked. "If he had been legally armed and had shot the man who had been trailing him through the community, would he have been found not guilty? Hardly." As frustration mounted, students of color began to organize nationwide.

What brought youth of color out in such numbers? A young black organizer told me about his elation when he first came upon Dream Defenders, a Florida group that grew out of the verdict that exonerated George Zimmerman. When he dropped into a campus meeting, curious, but not expecting much, he was floored. "I'd never seen a more beautiful sight," he said. "I'm in a room surrounded by people who look like me, who have dreads, who have afros, who have braids, who have tattoos, people who society would write off as trifling, as unintelligent. And here they are having these really, really important discussions about social movements, about philosophy, about plans to represent our communities in a positive way. And among them were so many black and brown women who were so vocal and unapologetic about what they were saying. That was just a beautiful thing for me. I'm thinking, I don't know what this is, but I'm getting involved!"

As the youth movement began to build, killings of unarmed blacks, usually by white police, were being filmed by bystanders, who then posted their videos on social media. Community outrage spread as the death toll began to mount: Eric Garner, grabbed in a lethal chokehold while selling unlicensed cigarettes; Michael Brown, shot dead during an encounter with police about jaywalking; John Crawford, killed at an Ohio Walmart while holding an air rifle he had picked up off a shelf; Tamir Rice, twelve years old, shot by police within two seconds of arriving at the playground where he was sitting on a swing holding a toy gun. Black women and girls were among the victims too, activists pointed out: Tarika Wilson, shot dead in her own home while holding her baby in her arms; 7-year-old Aiyana Stanley-Jones, who had fallen asleep watching television on her living room couch, shot in the head as officers stormed into her house in a midnight

SWAT-style operation. Marlene Pinnock, a great-grandmother who was beaten within an inch of her life by police for wandering in and out of traffic lanes on a freeway; Aura Rosser, a mentally ill African-American woman armed with a fish knife, shot in the heart by police in my own hometown, Ann Arbor, when her boyfriend had only called the police to escort her out of his house. As the list of the dead grew, three black community organizers, Alicia Garza, Patrisse Cullors, and Opal Tometi, created the hashtag #blacklivesmatter, which rapidly grew into an intergenerational movement that swept the country, engaging people of every ethnicity in street protests and demands for social change.

By 2015, when I was asked to write a third revised edition to "When Race Breaks Out," the racial climate throughout the country had been transformed. Students of color were emboldened to demand more respect on campus, while other students reiterated their conviction that the protesters were exaggerating, or "playing the race card for all it's worth." As campuses grew more polarized, adults, too, took sides. Some cheered wildly when blatantly racist remarks were made on national television that had not been heard or accepted by the majority for generations. Whites publically sneered at "political correctness." Relieved of the burden of civility, crowds roared their approval of ethnic stereotypes, threats to ban whole groups of immigrants on the basis of their religion, and the branding of entire ethnicities as criminals. A white senator expressed his belief that people of color had not contributed anything to western civilization. David Duke, the former Grand Wizard of the Ku Klux Klan, declared his candidacy for the U.S. Senate.

It is in this racial cauldron that I have written the third edition of When Race Breaks Out. Since the protests began, the internet has exploded with new articles, blogs, websites, and videos about race. Selecting the best among them has been difficult, knowing that by the time this edition goes to press, more shocking scenes of violence will have been captured on cell phones, more hateful rhetoric will have been aired, more activists will have protested and many more perceptive analyses of racial events will have been written and circulated. Besides updating the Annotated Resources section, removing outdated pieces and adding new material that captures the spirit of these racially turbulent times, I can only encourage you, teachers and students, to use the power of the internet to find and critically analyze information about the new events from a variety of sources, and to use these resources to tap into the new curiosity, enthusiasm, doubt, and indignation about racial events that is now so evident among youth.

Among the new material you will find in this edition are resources on the white extremism that has developed and spread so rapidly during the Obama presidency, and how televised hatred is producing an alarming level of fear and anxiety among young children of color.

I have added explanations of terms that, if not new, have recently come into more popular usage: micro-aggressions, cultural appropriation, orientalism, intersectionality, environmental racism.

The section on the psychology of racism has been expanded, and includes the latest research on implicit bias, which over the last 30 years has proven that so many of us, including myself, hold preconceptions about identity groups that go completely unrecognized.

I have added new information about the histories, cultures, and personal experiences of Arab Americans and Muslims, Native Americans, Asian Americans, African-Americans, and Latino/as, including common myths about immigration and the rise of lucrative private detention facilities to detain the undocumented.

I've added pieces on how disproportionate school suspensions for black children begin in preschool, and how that pattern continues throughout the criminal justice system. There is new information from black police officers about the extent of racism in their departments, and an extensive, searchable website that contains arrest records for African-Americans state by state, showing that blacks in the United States face overwhelming prejudice within the criminal justice system.

In the section on the science of race I have added important work on genetics that shows even more clearly how race is an imprecise biological concept. You will find articles and videos that show how the idea of race continues to be misused in science and public policy, and how unscientific assumptions about race and biology run deeply through medical practice, from genetic testing, to diagnosis of disease, to the development of new, "race-specific" drugs and treatments.

Finally, you will find information on local and national activism, and how whites can be better allies to people of color.

The times may be frightening, but we live at a teachable moment.

Helen Fox
*July 25, 2016, Ann Arbor, Michigan*

# INTRODUCTION

Since the 1970s, a small number of dedicated university faculty have been promoting honest talk about race and racism in their classrooms. Some are white; many more are of color. Whether their academic backgrounds are in History or Psychology or Anthropology or Education or any other subject, they must somehow address great gaps in their students' knowledge: the histories of multicultural America, the psychology of racism and race relations, the sociology of racialized institutions, the biology and anthropology of scientific racism. Semester after semester, they have worked over this same ground, explaining how racist ideas and assumptions from our nation's past continue to be perpetuated, often unconsciously, by both whites and people of color. They have gained expertise moderating inflammatory—or painfully silent— classroom discussions, speaking from their own experiences and family histories and encouraging students to do the same. They have watched many white students turn from disbelief to astonishment to great sadness as they discover what whites have done to people of color in the past and how these practices continue to poison our relationships today. Patiently and gently, they have helped students of color face their own doubts and fears, their internalized hatreds, their daily encounters with racism. The experience can be an exhausting one for students, for it takes a great deal of energy to question the way one has been taught to make sense of the world and begin to see that other interpretations are possible. But for faculty, especially faculty of color, the work can be debilitating. For not only are they bringing out students' emotionally charged beliefs and feelings, but the very subject of discussion is the students' negative reactions to people, real and imagined, who look very much like the instructor standing before them. Handling this situation with compassion and grace drains the emotional and spiritual forces and threatens one's physical well-being. "It takes a lot of love to do this work," an African-American professor of Social Work told me. "I don't think I have enough love anymore."

In fact, this work was never more vital than it is today. The economic, social and educational gains of people of color over the last thirty years, the increasingly ethnic "look" of television shows and advertisements, the rise of Ethnic Studies departments and best-selling books by authors of color might suggest that Americans have more understanding of each other, more ability to interact and accept each other as equals. But today, as yesterday, our country's future leaders have little knowledge or appreciation of multicultural America. While scholarship on race and ethnicity has blossomed, requirements that students learn and discuss new information and insights into the American experience have not kept pace. Students can graduate from a major university without understanding, for example, why there are so many Spanish place names in California or why Japanese Americans still feel the effects of their parents' and grandparents' internment during World War II. Most cannot explain why "race" is no longer considered a scientifically valid concept, or how "racism" might be different from "racial hatred," or how the power to define terms and limit access to rewards helps maintain our country's racial hierarchy. While they may have heard of internalized racism, they are often not aware of the ways self-hatred is packaged as normal, even cool, by the popular media. Many do not understand why a Chinese American student would be uncomfortable being thought of as a "model minority" or how wearing a Cleveland Indians hat would offend anybody. Many feel frustrated, even cheated, when they discover they have to decipher the accented English of an international graduate student instructor. In classes where they do discuss issues of race, white students are astonished to learn the ways being white gives them unearned privilege and how that privilege has already boosted their test scores and future marketability. Most middle-class students, regardless of their ethnicity, have little sense of what it is to struggle for basic necessities and are shocked to learn of the depth and extent of poverty in their own country—not to mention what being poor can mean abroad.

Above all, students today are bewildered by the beliefs of their peers across the racial divide. Students of color cannot comprehend why whites seem so unaware of their own power and privilege. In their experience, white power is an elementary fact of American life: whites dominate Congress, control the media, and set the standards for university and professional success. From the music valued as "classical" to the literature called "Great Books" to food that restaurants choose to call "American," white culture sets the standards, frames the questions, and defines what is "normal." For white students to claim they do not feel powerful seems ludicrous—even dishonest.

Many white students, on the other hand, have no idea why students of color seem so angry. In their experience, there is no "white culture" that dominates everything. In fact, they sometimes feel a little disappointed at having to be some bland, "generic" form of American, for they have little sense of the rich mixture of European languages and cultures that make up their family histories. As individuals, they don't feel powerful, and this puts them on the defensive. *They* are not in Congress, they argue hotly. *They* have no say in what gets on television; *their* relatives never engaged in the slave trade. Their grandparents may be racist, but *they're* certainly not! Racist laws and institutions are a thing of the past. The playing field is level now, and anyone who works hard can succeed.

Students are not to blame for the degree and extent of their misunderstanding of each other and of history, for college campuses are only a mirror of the difficulties we all have in facing the issues that keep us apart. But how can we say that students with so little understanding of the American experience have mastered the subjects they came to college to study? If they have never developed the patience to listen to anyone with an accent, how can they practice medicine with immigrant patients or rise in international business? If they have never studied the role of the Chinese in the building of the railroads or learned of the contributions of Koreans and Japanese and Filipinos and Punjabis to the development of U.S. agriculture, how can they say they have learned American history? If they have no knowledge of cultural styles and values different from their own, how can they work effectively in multicultural teams in science and engineering? If they have never been asked to reflect about the privileges of being white and middle class or understood something of the psychological effects of internalized racism, how can they venture an opinion about drugs in the inner city or the improvement of elementary school performance? And if they have never discussed race at all in a college classroom, how can they even begin to see the ways the

American construction of race lies buried in every aspect of our intellectual and social life?

As black social critic Michael Eric Dyson says in an interview:

> [Race] does not simply belong in a class on ethnic studies or African-American culture. ... Race belongs in every American classroom and in every American subject matter precisely because it is like what they call in logic the suppressed premise of so many syllogisms of American democracy. Race is part and parcel of the very fabric of the American intellectual project and also at the heart of the American project of democracy and self-discovery. We would be well-served by being more explicit about it and therefore taking it into account rather than allowing it to inform our debates from a distance. [For] by letting it inform our debates from a distance we do not get a chance to theorize race, we do not get a chance to explore race, and we do not get a chance to deconstruct or demythologize racist power to hurt and harm us ... (quoted in Dobrin, 1997, pp. 170–171)

I want to encourage faculty, especially white faculty, to take up the task of bringing honest, informed discussion about race and racism into more college classrooms. It is our turn, our responsibility. None of us are experts. All of us fear saying the wrong thing, or not being understood, or not quite grasping the experience of others, especially once we begin to see how different that experience can be from our own. Few of us have kept up with scholarship on race, so we feel uneasy at the prospect of opening up a discussion before we are thoroughly informed. Once we start reading, we can easily feel overwhelmed with what we don't know about other histories and cultures and what might happen when the "suppressed premise" of race is let free in the classroom. We may be uncertain about how to evaluate the complex analyses and strong opinions of scholars across the racial divide. Even the language of that scholarship may be different from what we are used to: poetic, evocative, judgmental of ourselves and our most cherished institutions.

As a white instructor, I began to sort all this out for myself only gradually, learning from my first botched attempt to deal with a racial slur in an English classroom, my unwittingly insensitive comments to students of color, my anger and impatience with white students who made thinly veiled racial remarks about welfare cheats, or people who won't learn English, or football players who go for the big bucks instead of the hard work of studying. As I designed and taught more writing courses with themes of social justice I slowly made my way through new literatures and histories and scholarly discussions and found delight in my personal discovery of multicultural America. I learned from traveling both in this country and abroad, noticing how people interact with each other and what areas are contested, and how, and allowing these observations to inform my understanding of my own locale, my own interpretation of social and political life in America. As I revised my courses to include more information and better discussions about race I learned from the reactions and advice from my students, especially conservative white students and radical students of color. I learn from being forced to confront my blind spots, my resistance, the points at which my emotions take over from reason. And I learn by signing up for anti-racism workshops where I am asked to discard my role as teacher and became a vulnerable participant whose embarrassing emotions and deeply personal revelations are yet more grist for the mill.

Prompted by a student to design a course that would combine readings and discussions of present-day racism with active community involvement in antiracist activities, I spent a summer reading and accumulating stacks of potential course material as well as reviewing most of the videos on racism held by the University of Michigan's Film and Video Library. As I taught the first version of "Un-teaching Racism" I finally felt comfortable with my ability to address the issues and the strong emotions that came up. But as I thought more deeply about the teaching issues involved, I was curious about how other instructors approached these discussions. How safe do they try to make their classrooms? How do they handle outbreaks of emotion? What shuts discussion down? What should we be doing about resistant students, angry students, white students who are politically conservative? What should we consider success?

These questions soon became a research project that involved individual, one-to two-hour interviews of thirty-five University of Michigan faculty members across a variety of disciplines: English, Education, Philosophy, Economics, Mathematics, Women's Studies, Romance Languages, Public Health, Sociology, Psychology, and Social Work. Twenty-four were white and eleven were instructors of color: three were African-American, three Asian American, one Native American and four Latina. Some of these faculty were very practiced with these issues; others were new to them; a few had not dealt with them at all but were thinking it might be a good idea to do so. I chose these faculty members because I knew their interests and their work; they in turn suggested others who might like to contribute to this project. In addition, I employed three students from Michigan's Undergraduate Research Opportunity Program (UROP) to interview other students about their experiences with classroom discussions and the general racial climate on campus. In all, they heard from seventy undergraduate and graduate students, either in person or through an email survey. About thirty of these respondents were white (I say "about," since a few students did not answer or wrote "American" or "other" when asked: "What is your ethnicity, as you define it?"); forty identified themselves as students of color, mixed, or bi-racial. The students were about evenly divided between male and female (31 M, 39 F), while among faculty, women predominated (22 F and 13 M).

Through all these experiences and conversations I have learned how to put the uncomfortable subject, race, together with a familiar old friend, experiential teaching and learning. And along the way, I have discovered something unexpected: despite the grim nature of the subject matter, teaching about race and racism can be—well, fun. Once I had just the article or video that addresses students' most common misunderstandings and frustrations, once I had some conversation starters, some unusual discussion formats, some in-class writing assignments, and some role plays and simulations that promote debate and critical thinking, the class took off on its own.

I want this book to give you ideas about how you might approach the subject of race and racism in your classes. This is not a how-to guide, since there are no "right ways" to have these conversations, and no consensus about where we want students to go or how we should help them get there. Instead, I will tell you what I've learned about race, about teaching, and about myself. I will give you the best resources I've found, and describe some classroom exercises and writing assignments that address common questions and misunderstandings. I will let the faculty I've interviewed tell you some fascinating stories about times when "race broke out" in their classrooms, and I will tell you some stories of my own. In what follows, I prefer to think of my role as that of a guide rather than an authority dispensing expert knowledge. I have come to realize that all Americans are so deeply enmeshed in the society we have inherited that none of us can claim to be an objective authority on race relations. For how does one become an expert on all the ways one's own mind and heart have been molded by the stream of history?

# · 1 ·

# STARTING WITH OURSELVES

## Telling Our Stories About Race

My own perspectives about race have been shaped by the place where I grew up: the so-called "integrated" community of Hyde Park on Chicago's South Side in the late 1940s and 1950s. We lived next to the University of Chicago, and a few blocks away from what the adults—white adults, that is—called "the line," which separated "us" from the poorer blacks who had recently come up from the South for the jobs that were booming then in the stockyards and the steel industry. My mother had bought a cheap little row house with a garage full of rats that my uncle, a Chicago beat cop, tore down for us soon after we moved in. Our neighbors on one side were a Japanese family with three kids near my age who—I discovered much later—had recently relocated from a detention camp out West. On the other side lived a Chinese family who owned a small, steamy laundry where their kids had to go after school, and who were the first people I knew to own a television set. Next door down was another Japanese family, very civil and self-contained when my mother said hello to them on the street, and then a family of German Jewish immigrants, whose apartment was dark and smelled of cabbage.

That was about as far as my world extended until I went to elementary school and made friends with kids who lived closer to Lake Michigan and farther away from "the line," the daughters of university professors and lawyers and art dealers and importers. In my circle too were girls whose fathers were cab drivers, and whose mothers worked the night shift in the county hospital, or gave sulfur-smelling perms to old ladies in their living rooms. All these girls were white, of course. It's not that we deliberately excluded the "colored kids" or the "Japanese kids" (so we told ourselves), it was just that the Chinese and Japanese kept pretty much to themselves, and the colored kids lived behind the line so most of them didn't go to our school. That was the logic of racism of those days, the everyday, "subtle" racism of our progressive, educated, University of Chicago community. The blatant segregation that accounted for "the line" was never spoken of, nor were the wartime detention camps or the Chinese Exclusion Act—the reasons for the cool reticence of Asian families in interactions with whites, the distance they maintained in neighborhood relations. Most of my friends were Eastern European Jews whose parents or grandparents had been immigrants, or Protestants whose families didn't mention their origins, so it seemed like they had been around a long time. We were German and a little Scotch-Irish, my mother told me, but that was a long time ago, in my great-great grandparents' time. She and my father both had issues with religion in their young adult years and had become atheists, so we weren't Protestant, really, but more to the point, we were not Catholic. Catholics were a special caste in Hyde Park, shunned and separate. At a time when science was elevated to the status of a religion, especially among academics, being a practicing Catholic was retrograde—or lower class.

When I was in third grade, I announced to my mother and older brother that I could tell the difference between Protestants and Catholics just by looking at them. My brother, who knew everything, protested this: "Catholic is not a race," he said. "Anyone can be Catholic. You cannot tell the difference." But I could. The Catholic kids in my school were skinny and dressed in worn-out clothes. They said "ain't" and used what my brother called "double negatives." They didn't put their hands up first in class. Catholics were not as good as we were, not as smart. We knew this in our family—in fact, our own cousins were Catholic, and we knew very well how we were supposed to think about *them*. We lived this. Why were we supposed to pretend it was invisible to us?

It's funny how our ideas about people are formed so firmly and illogically in childhood. Our world is so small, our elders so powerful, and the unspoken and unacknowledged so charged with mysterious meaning that the world we construct can stay with us, deep and unquestioned, long after we grow up. I traveled the world and learned to appreciate the beauty of Hinduism and Buddhism before I rethought my ideas about Catholics. My feelings about blacks were more complicated, though, since little was explicitly said against them, but at the same time, the idea of a barrier that kept some kind of dark tide at bay was made to seem normal. My relationships with "colored people" as a young child were distant and benign, so it puzzled me when I learned that whites considered them dangerous. My own experience—another powerful determinant of our internal logic—belied that idea. Growing up as a "latch key child" I had the freedom to wander after school, climbing trees and scouting for alley cats, and this unfortunately made me vulnerable to human predators. But in all my encounters with strangers I was never bothered by "colored" men; it was whites who were unpredictable and dangerous, and it was white men I finally learned to avoid by crossing the street. I remember being questioned by a policeman after the scariest of these episodes, and even though I was only nine, I could hear the disbelief in his voice as he asked me about my attacker: "He was a *white* man? Are you *sure*?" I despised that policeman. How could he do his job if he thought that white men didn't hurt little girls? Forty-three years later, when a serial rapist was murdering women in Ann Arbor, I was relieved to hear on the evening news that a survivor had described her attacker as black. While this information terrified some of my white female acquaintances still further, I felt strangely invulnerable. My innermost emotional logic was assuring me that a black man would leave me alone.

As far as I could tell in a community that almost never mentioned the word "race," the adults in Hyde Park—the white adults, anyway—were proud of their enlightened attitude, their "tolerance of people of all colors and creeds," not like those awful white Southerners we saw on television spitting and shouting racial epithets at black children while police dogs snarled and lunged on their leashes. In contrast to the contested schools of the South, Hyde Park High was, I suppose, a model of peaceful integration. It was about half black and some small percentage Chinese, Japanese, and Korean when I entered in 1956 and nearly 80% black when I graduated in 1960. My mother taught gym and health classes there, and she was proud to do what she could to help the black students "better themselves." All black students fell into the potentially "upwardly mobile" category in her mind, regardless of whether they lived in the stately mansions of the oldest and wealthiest Chicago black families a little to the north of us, or in the impoverished tenement apartments just behind the line. In her health classes, she used to teach a lesson called "My Dream House," in which students were to cut out magazine pictures of spacious suburban living rooms and gleaming kitchen appliances and paste them into scrap books "to give them something to aim for." Even before

I got into high school she used to bring those scrapbooks home and show me proudly how far her students had dared to dream. Never mind that our own house was tacky. Our washing machine spewed blue sparks over the wet basement floor ("Stay back, you'll get electrocuted!" my mother would yell as she sloshed clothes from wringer to tub); our shower stall was a flimsy tin box in a corner of the basement with a little dressing room she had fashioned from a plastic curtain pinned over a clothes line and an infrared lamp jerry-rigged from the ceiling. She kept a rat trap in the potato bin and a blackjack in her underwear drawer—by God, we were living our American dream, and if her students dreamed big enough, they could live one too.

Just as our "integrated" neighborhood maintained its blatant segregation by outright refusal to sell "white property" to blacks, our high school guarded the status quo with an ingenious system of tracking: "Regular" classes, by unspoken definition, were for blacks and a few seriously delinquent whites; "Accelerated" classes were predominantly white with a sprinkling of black and Asian faces, and "Double Accelerated," a track created especially for the college bound, was almost exclusively white. Many blacks were struggling with basic skills, of course, as they had just come up from the segregated South. My mother told me that the grades in our school fell in an inverse bell curve; many students excelled, many failed, a few were in-between, and this reflected the changing neighborhood. These disparities seemed normal to her, because it took time for a people to "better themselves." But the black students who had to play catch-up were doomed to the worst teachers who had little expectation they could ever become literate, and the capable and gifted blacks who excelled in the "Regular" classes were dismally underchallenged. Nevertheless, blacks seemed to accept their separation with quiet dignity. As Eldridge Cleaver said of the period in *Soul on Ice:* "… we lived in an atmosphere of novocain" (1968, p. 3). Except for an occasional fist fight, always within racial groups, corridors were calm and orderly. Lunch tables were segregated by tacit agreement, much like today's high school and college cafeterias, and while relations were cordial across racial lines, friendships were rare.

The only exception to this benign racist order was the school's a cappella choir. Our director was a brilliant teacher, a fine musician and composer, and, as we later came to realize, an alcoholic gay man struggling to live with the shame and ridicule imposed by 1950s society on "sexual deviance." Jerry Ramsfield was probably in his late thirties when I knew him. He had a blond wave, blue eyes that were watery and distant in the way of alcoholics, and a gentle, unassuming manner. His classroom reflected the racial makeup of the school: in my senior year the choir was about 20% white, 80% black. We sang in Latin, Hebrew, Standard English, and the language of Southern black spirituals; we performed in local synagogues, on television, and before huge, enthusiastic audiences in our own auditorium. In Mr. Ramsfield's classroom, all students were—I want to say—equal, but that word somehow implies that inequality was an option for him, or that he had a conscious goal of making his classroom safer or fairer than the world outside. But I think it never occurred to him to respect anyone less than anyone else—race, class, age, all were irrelevant to him. He never raised his voice. He could make a roomful of sixty teenagers pin-drop quiet by tapping his ring very softly on the blackboard.

One day Mr. Ramsfield asked if some of us would come with him to rehearsals of a church choir he had been directing in his spare time. They were giving him a chance to try out some of his own compositions, he told us, but they were a small choir, just getting started, and they needed more voices. My mother studied the address. "It's in a colored neighborhood," she said, frowning. "But all right, I guess you can go." About six of us, black and white, piled into Mr. Ramsfield's car and he drove us deep into the heart of Chicago's South Side. We were a little disappointed when we got there, for the choir consisted mostly of older folks, and Mr. Ramsfield's compositions were atonal and difficult for everyone. But the choir received us graciously and seemed happy enough to have our young, strong voices mingling with theirs. As we were lining up for lemonade and cookies afterward, I heard a commotion and a familiar voice, and there, to my horror, was my mother, striding across the practice hall. "Get your coat, we're going home," she said sternly, grabbing my forearm and pulling me toward the door. No time for thank you's to the church ladies, no polite excuses to the dark, handsome teenagers crowding around the punch bowl. Mortified and stunned into silence, I followed her out to the car.

Looking back, I can see that Mr. Ramsfield's invitation had put my mother in an awkward position. She couldn't just refuse to let me get into the car with the black tenors and basses and go into the black neighborhood where who knows what might happen, for then she would have had to admit what she and everyone else tried so hard to deny. There had been many messages about tolerance in our upbringing: "Everyone is the same on the inside, despite the color of their skin." "Never demean or ridicule, for people can't help what they look like." Mr. Ramsfield had rejected the implicit racism in that nice, liberal talk and taken integration a step further, living what he believed and encouraging us to do the same. My mother had tried to practice tolerance. But she could not escape the experience of her own early years when racism was officially sanctioned and slurs and insults much more commonplace. Despite her yearning for a gentler, fairer world, her fear got the better of her, fear that I would find a black boy attractive, fear of where it all might lead. Later that night she slipped a long letter under my door, describing those fears in detail: Blacks were cowardly. Black culture was inferior. Blacks had never contributed anything to the world. Black boys wanted white girlfriends in order to raise their status, but they would never be any better than they were. Furious and ashamed, I tore the letter into pieces so small, even the garbage man wouldn't be able to read them.

I left Hyde Park for college a few years later. I felt strange for a while in the all-white environment of the University of California but I was too caught up in my new life to reflect on where I had come from, too busy trying to make up the deficiencies in my education—for in the inner city, even "Double Accelerated" classes are scant preparation for college. When I thought about the past at all, I felt cynical and disgusted with the hypocrisy of my "model" neighborhood. It would be a long time before I realized how much of Hyde Park I carried with me—its idealism, its sense of dignity and possibility, and its strange, contorted rules about race.

\* \* \* \* \* \*

When I went to India in the Peace Corps, I was quite sure I was going to a Caucasian country. This is what I had learned in my Anthropology class at Berkeley: There are "Five Races of Man": the Caucasians, who originated in the Caucasus Mountains and spread out toward Europe on one side and down through Turkey to India on the other; the Mongoloids, which included the "Orientals" of China, Japan, and Korea, the "Eastern Asiatics" of Burma, Thailand, Laos, Vietnam, and Indonesia, and the American Indians, who had crossed the Bering Strait from Siberia and migrated down through the Americas; the Negroid peoples, who came from Africa; the Australoids, who lived in the Australian desert and in scattered pockets throughout the Pacific; and finally, the Bushmen of Southern Africa, who were thought to be so different they didn't fit into the other major categories. I was certain that this idea was correct, first because it was presented to us as scientific, and therefore unassailable, and second, because it gave authority to my growing vision of equality and human dignity: that people of all races were endowed with the same human capacities and strivings, that all spoke languages that were equally complex, and though some of their social systems might be exotic or "primitive," they all could yield clues about human nature and were therefore worthy of serious study. It was a relief to think about race that way, actually. My previous training in this area had been so subtle, so fraught with innuendo and shame, that it was good to have it out in the open.

Whoever had organized the Peace Corps predeparture training had invited, among other "thought-provoking" speakers, a black man who did not sound at all like my white professors at Berkeley. This man spoke in the politically charged language of the newly formed black radical movement— personal, provocative, and unabashedly ghetto. "I think you're all going over to do good deeds in India because you feel guilty about being white," he said, shaking a finger at us from the podium. A moment of intense confusion spread through the audience of new college graduates. No one had ever suggested to us that we should feel guilty about being white. But even if we should, how would going to India make us feel better about ourselves? Obviously, this man didn't have his facts straight. Hands started going up, cautiously at first, so as not to embarrass him.

"Indians are Caucasians," we told him. "Anthropologists classify. ..." Our speaker let out an incredulous, bitter laugh. "You think you're going to a country full of *white* people?"

"Caucasians can have a variety of skin tones," we ventured.

"Aw, come on. You learned that in *college?* You'll see when you get over there, you ain't goin' to no Caucasian country!"

We glanced over at our Hindi language instructors, who were standing along the wall of the auditorium, listening with amused interest to the exchange.

"It's the facial features and hair that differentiate Indians from Negroes and Orientals," we told him. Of course the evidence before us did not particularly validate our claim. Not only were our Indian instructors different colors, but some of them had fairly broad noses, like Africans. Some had straight black hair like Orientals; others had wavy hair, like Europeans. We turned back to the speaker who had given up on racial classification and was now talking about black power and the change that was coming in America. He seemed overly emotional, even angry at us. We didn't understand this, but we did not take it personally. We knew we were good people. Our parents were proud of us. President Kennedy had told us we were the hope of the world. "Ask not what your country can do for you," Kennedy had said pointedly. "Ask what you can do for your country." We listened respectfully as our speaker finished his talk. We knew we needed practice listening to unusual ideas. After all, we were going to the ends of the earth!

Although I never seriously entertained the speaker's thoughts about guilt, his talk did get me thinking about the Five Races of Man. If racial categories were so set and scientific, what accounted for the variation within them? I thought back to my high school corridors, full of "Negroes" of all shades, from deep brown to nearly white, some with curly or wavy hair, others with straight, shiny hair that frizzed up after swim class. Noses and lips and body shapes came in all varieties too, not just the "Negroid type" of my college textbooks. I had heard that Negroes and whites and American Indians had gotten mixed together somehow back in the days of slavery. But regardless of their actual heritage, everyone knew they were all supposed to be called "Negro." There was always some slight identifying characteristic, something vaguely African about them.

Racial identification could be confusing, though. A sister of one of my high school friends had "frizzy" hair, no different from Negro hair, but the family came from Germany and her siblings' hair was thin and straight. I had puzzled over this intensely when I was about fourteen. Could this sister be adopted? She was just as fair-skinned as the rest of the family. I looked carefully at their mother's hair. It was curly, to be sure, but not so tightly curled as her daughter's. There was one important clue, however: none of the family seemed embarrassed about this child's looks. They acted like she was just as sweet and rambunctious and lovely as her sister. So that meant she must be white. In the 1950s, everyone knew that Negroes could not be thought of as beautiful. No woman with even faintly brown skin had ever won a Miss America beauty contest. Beautiful skin was described as "fair" or "pale" or "pearly white" by the soap commercials. No models in magazines, no stars in the movies were any color but white. And I knew what Negro kids went through to get themselves ready for school—the lye-based hair straighteners the boys joked about sometimes, the skin lighteners, the painful hair combing sessions.[1]

Thinking back, I remember how incredibly important it was, for whites at least, to be sure of a person's race. While conservatives wanted this information in order to keep the boundary lines intact, liberals were more conflicted. We weren't going to use racial information to openly promote discrimination, but still we had to know, in the privacy of our own minds, how to classify people so we could think about them the way we were supposed to. Of course you couldn't just ask, "What are you?" as some so bluntly do today. In those days, you had to be polite, and it wasn't polite to mention race.

W. E. B. Du Bois (1965, p. 215) wrote poignantly about the "double consciousness" of American blacks, who must live with the "sense of always looking at one's self through the eyes of others, of measuring one's soul by the tape of a world that looks on in amused contempt and pity." I would add that many liberal white Americans like myself have lived—and continue to live—with a double consciousness of our own. Like openly racist whites, we have been taught to gaze on people of color and judge them, but our judgments are always informed by two conflicting points of view. Subtle, unspoken messages urge us to look at people of color with some mixture of contempt, pity, amusement, embarrassment, and fundamental sense of difference. But at the same time, overt messages—the presidential speeches, the homilies of teachers and parents, the movies about interracial comradeship, the television advertisements by international conglomerates—are all about respect and harmony and friendship and love and the fundamental similarity of all people. And this is why we so often send signals of exclusion, even while we sincerely believe, in our conflicted hearts, that "color doesn't matter."

No wonder I have felt so awkward about discussions of race and racism in my classrooms. Everything I have learned about race growing up has been profoundly contradictory. Strong, unspoken messages about how to be racist shamefully contradict the ways I have been taught to be a good person. This makes me embarrassed when I hear my white students demean and judge people of color, even obliquely, in discussions of drug addiction or prison reform or immigration or affirmative action. It makes me distressed when students of color—always in the minority in my classrooms—have to listen to white students reveal their biases and ignorant stereotypes. My own family's struggle to become middle class has made me sensitive and proud; I am shocked when a student uses an expression like "trailer trash" or when someone says "low class," instead of "lower class," implying that poverty and struggle are somehow immoral. Because I am so caught up the whirlpool of conflicting messages, so powerless to stop the ways I myself am influenced, I feel hurt and angry when I see students of color succumb to the subtle, pervasive judgments of their intelligence and character and learn to fear interactions with whites. I am ashamed that my society refuses to see how it simultaneously promotes white supremacy and pretends it doesn't exist. I am impatient—and I hate being impatient—with people who don't get it. And yet, the more I learn, the more I recognize that I am just beginning to get it, myself.

\* \* \* \* \* \*

In his book, *The Courage to Teach* (1998, p. 2), Parker Palmer says, "we teach who we are":

> As I teach, I project the condition of my soul onto my students, my subject, and our way of being together. The entanglements I experience in the classroom are often no more or less than the convolutions of my inner life. Viewed from this angle, teaching holds a mirror to the soul. If I am willing to look in that mirror and not run from what I see, I have a chance to gain self-knowledge—and knowing myself is as crucial to good teaching as knowing my students and my subject.

Yet Palmer doesn't say very much about race in his reflections on his own teaching, even though he clearly works with diverse populations and with a subject—education—that includes everyone. His silence on how he learned to think about race no doubt reflects his upbringing, as it does for most whites who consider themselves compassionate, caring people. That silence of white teachers and students about their experiences with race is frustrating and galling to people of color. How is it that whites have no stories about how learning about race has affected our engagement with our students, our understanding of our material, our values and beliefs, our soul? Why are bookstores full of stories about the ways people of color have been affected by race relations yet carry nothing, or nearly nothing, about the experiences of whites? There are books about whites as onlookers, yes. There are stories of whites who fight for social justice. There are books about whites as brutal perpetrators of racism. But there is very little, either in the popular press or in the field of education, about how whites learn about race and how that affects us as human beings, as teachers, and as participants in race relations today. We need to tell those stories, not necessarily as public confessionals, but to ourselves, privately, perhaps by writing from time to time in a journal, perhaps on long walks alone. These are not easy things to think about or tell. As I have struggled with this writing I have become gloomy and irritable. I have not slept well. But I am a better teacher for it. At this moment, even without students around me to tell me so, I know I am capable of more honesty, greater compassion, and a clearer, more certain vision.

# Note

1. An anthropology book written in my undergraduate days speculates that "Negroes" could "look forward to" a future innovation that would make it possible for people to "change their skin color whenever they like, by simple injection. A colored woman could thus turn white with less effort than it takes to have her hair straightened, waved, and set. This would be particularly effective for those with narrow features and dark skins" (Coon, 1965, p. 317).

# · 2 ·

# INSIDER'S GUIDE PART I

## Race, Ethnicity, and Identity

How can we open up honest discussions of race in our classrooms when the subject has been so fraught with emotion, denial, and taboo? The prospect is a good deal easier when we have some familiarity with the territory—an overview of the latest scholarship, the terms and concepts, the contested areas where people disagree. When I began to get serious about discussing race in my classroom, I began reading about race in many disciplines: Anthropology, Sociology, English Language and Literature, American Culture, History, Psychology, Public Health, and Education. From this reading, I put together summaries of the historical background and central concepts for myself so I would feel more competent to address students' questions and correct common misunderstandings. As I taught more courses and listened to more students and community people talk about their perspectives, I added quotes to illustrate some of these ideas. Some of these quotes come directly from student and faculty interviews or discussions with community members; some are quotes from authors who express a concept especially well. Others I have created myself, informed by voices of my students, my friends and colleagues, my relatives—anyone who had an opinion about race that was widely shared. You can use these definitions,[1] summaries, and quotes both to expand your own background knowledge and to start discussion among your students. In addition (or instead) you can consult the "Annotated Resources" section to find materials for classroom use that are particularly helpful for students. All these sources are thought-provoking, accurate, and easily understood by undergraduates.

* * * * * *

One of the first things students admit to being confused about is the difference between race and ethnicity. In a conversation about race at the University of Michigan, Manning Marable, an African-American scholar, explained the difference.[2] Race, says Marable, is an idea that has been (and continues to be) imposed on people in order to make it easier to exploit them, whereas ethnicity is something that groups of people create for themselves out of shared historical experiences. These definitions and their historical background help students understand how this came about:

race—a biological concept now discredited by most anthropologists as a way of categorizing human beings because it is based on superficial, vague, and inaccurate characteristics ("red," "yellow," "black," or "white" skin; "straight" or "kinky" hair, etc.) and because it has been used over the past 200 years to create a bogus hierarchy of cultural, moral, and intellectual worth that has often justified unequal treatment. There is now wide agreement among scientists that there is much more variation within "racial" groups than across them. The "black" racial category, for instance, includes people whose ancestors were European, Native American, Asian, and Latin American as well as African. Even within Africa, people differ more than any other "racial" group; they may have broad or slim noses, short or tall stature, full or thin lips, and skin color ranging from light tan to ebony. In the United States, the "white" category has become more inclusive over the years, as Jews, Irish, and Italians, once reviled with such terms as "black," "savage," "bestial," "simian," "low-browed," and "groveling," have gradually been accepted into the prestigious "white" category. Mexican Americans have been legally considered "white," yet treated as racially inferior to other whites. "Asians" have been grouped together by the U.S. Census Bureau only since 1990. People from India, whose color ranges from pale white to ebony, were all classified as "Caucasian" by anthropologists in the 1960s. And after September 11, 2001, previously "white" Arab Americans found themselves on the lowest rung of the racial hierarchy, despised, shunned, and vulnerable to attack. "The fact that Americans believe that Asians, blacks, Hispanics, and whites constitute biological entities called races is a matter of cultural interest rather than scientific substance. It tells us something about American culture—but nothing at all about the human species" (Fish, 1995, p. 56).

**ethnicity**—a combination of cultural affinity, geographic roots, language, religion, sense of shared history, and, to some extent, ascribed "race." The quotes that follow express views of several mature, reflective students of various ethnicities when asked to discuss their own ethnic origins:

I used to say I was just an American mongrel, because our family is such a mishmash of European cultures. But now that I'm getting interested in genealogy, I call myself Celtic, an old name for the peoples of Ireland, Scotland, Wales, and the Cornish coast of England. Of course, if I wanted to go really far back, I could call myself African, I suppose, since the human race originated in Africa. But ethnically, I think I have more affinity with people like the present-day Irish. It's hard to tell really, it was all so long ago.

My parents were Korean, but I was adopted by a white American family and I don't know much about my birth family's heritage. I was raised in a white suburban milieu and never hung out much with Asian or Asian American students. So right now, at least, I see myself as ethnically white American. I've only rarely heard Korean spoken and have no particular interest in learning it. That shouldn't seem strange, really, when you consider that many of my friends who come from Polish or Irish or German backgrounds can't speak those languages either.

I'm Jewish. I know that's a religion, not a race or ethnicity, but for my community it's shared customs, beliefs, and even language—we all learned a little Hebrew as children, and many of our grandparents speak Yiddish. I guess it's more accurate to say we're Eastern European Jews, because there are Ethiopian Jews, Dutch Jews, French Jews, even Chinese and Indonesian Jews who have different cultural and language backgrounds.

I'm bi-racial African American and white. I can't say I'm one or the other exclusively, because that would be like one of my parents doesn't exist. I love both sides of my family, and I appreciate my cultural ties to both communities. There's a lot of pressure to be exclusively black. I realize that people who don't know me might think I'm arrogant for choosing to be mixed. And I understand that many of my friends don't really have a choice. Society brands them as black and implies in so many ways that they are losers, just because they don't like the way they look. I hate that, and I want to work to end that kind of stupidity and injustice. But I reserve the right to honor all my heritage. I think everyone should.

I'm a Cuban immigrant with French parents who was raised in Ohio. I've been told that I'm not Hispanic, since I don't speak Spanish, but I've also been told I'm not white. It's difficult to figure out where I fit in.

When you're biracial, people sometimes choose for you—or don't accept my answer. I'm told I'm half black and half Iranian. But how can you be half? I'm double: fully black and fully Iranian.

White students who have been raised in mostly white communities may naively assign ethnic categories to their new friends of color. "You're not really black," they might say; "I don't see you as Korean;" "I didn't know you were into the Hispanic thing." "Boston? No, where are you really from?" Other whites may hesitate to mix with students of color because they "don't know what to call them." They figure—rightly—that assumptions or mistakes on their part will be considered offensive and that they need to somehow educate themselves before entering the "minefield" of race relations. But without information about what this terminology is, why it can be so highly charged, and why different people in the same ethnic group may hold strikingly different opinions about it, many white students find it more convenient to claim that they "don't see color" or to avoid the subject altogether. Of course this strategy causes even more frustration for people of color. They point out that whites can avoid the subject of race since they are the majority, the "norm." Whites can claim their features as "All-American," their music as "classical," their language "standard," and their race as "human," denying all the while that they are prejudiced. Yet many people of color say they are tired of trying to educate whites, tired of revealing their own feelings and life experiences to people who may not even care. To move beyond this initial reluctance to interact, both whites and people of color need to learn some of the history and origins of racial and ethnic terminology. The following will help by giving them a little historical background and an introduction to the various points of view they may encounter without relying on students from all the different ethnic groups to do the educating. Discussion techniques and exercises to help students explore their own identities and reflect on their values and assumptions can be found in Chapter 8.

**White**—A category that came into use in late-seventeenth-century America to distinguish pale-skinned people, primarily of English origin, from African slaves, and later, to denote their legal and social superiority to Indians or "redskins" and the so-called "yellow races." In 1790, Congress passed the Naturalization Act limiting naturalized citizenship to "whites," and this remained the law until 1954. As immigrants from various European countries began coming to the United States, efforts were made to reserve the "white" category for those who had arrived before them; thus, Poles, Jews, Irish, Slavs, Italians, Catholics, Hispanics, and others could be referred to (and treated) as "nonwhite" until they allied themselves against blacks and/or became middle class. Today, "[t]he U.S. Office of Management and Budget's Directive 15 classifies a White person as a person having origins in any of the original peoples of Europe, North Africa, or the Middle East. Until recently, persons from India were considered White in the US census. ... In Britain, Middle Eastern and North African people would not be considered White, and Asian Indians have never been considered so" (Bhopal & Donaldson, 1998, p. 1304). Thus, "white" or "whiteness" is a social construction, not a biological fact.

Some common views on being white are expressed here by white students and instructors:

In my town, we don't think of ourselves as white. We just think of ourselves as Americans. I never really thought about why that would upset anybody.

—white undergraduate

I never answer on surveys when they ask you your race. I consider it an offensive question, or at least an unnecessary one. To me, a person's color is unimportant. It's their personality, their ability, the content of their character that counts. We're all members of the human race, so let's get over this false, divisive terminology.

—white graduate student

I don't see color. Seriously. I have lots of friends from different backgrounds and we all just treat each other the same. I don't get it when people say it's impossible to be colorblind. I mean, if you see color, aren't you the one who's racist?

—white undergraduate

The "white" category is much too limiting to describe me. I love other cultures, especially African—their music, their beads, their cool accent. Sure, I copy it! Even though my hair doesn't look so authentic in dreads, I love the style! Being white is so boring, don't you think?

—white high school student

I went to a private high school, so race wasn't an issue for me because, I'm ashamed to say, there were no other races to discriminate against. Most of what I learned about minorities came from the media.

—white undergraduate

I'm uncomfortable being white, especially when I'm with my friends of color. I'm ashamed of what my ancestors have done. But I don't have any choice. Everywhere we go, people see me as white and give me respect and privileges I don't really deserve.

—white undergraduate

I don't feel guilty about being white. I can't change whatever my ancestors might have done. Let's face it, the world has never been a place where everyone was nice to each other. Every family tree has some pretty despicable characters. I prefer to focus on the present.

—white instructor

I don't feel guilty but I do feel responsible—not for the past, which I can't change—but for the present. I wish we didn't have to think in terms of race, but since people of color are still judged by it, still excluded and hurt by it, we need to study it and learn how to do better in the future.

—white instructor

**Caucasian**—While "Caucasian" may sound scientific and therefore more dignified than "white," students should be aware that the term is now considered inaccurate, as it describes an extremely heterogeneous population, from Norwegians and Swedes to Pakistanis, Indians, and Bangladeshis, most of whom are believed to have "originated" in the Caucasus region of Central Europe. Ronald Takaki, an Asian American scholar, reminds us that regardless of its meaning, the term "Caucasian" is most commonly used as a euphemism for persons of European descent with all the privileges that category affords. In a U.S. Supreme Court ruling in 1923 that upheld the denial of citizenship to Asian Indians, the court argued: "It may be true that the blond Scandinavian and the brown Hindu have a common ancestor in the dim reaches of antiquity, but the average man knows perfectly well that there are unmistakable and profound differences between them today" (Takaki, 1998, p. 299).

**Anglo**—used in some Latin@ communities to refer to European Americans who are not overtly racist. A Mexican American colleague says, "In my home community if I call someone 'white,' especially 'whiteboy' or 'whitegirl,' that means they're really bad—in the Klan or something. Anglo is a more neutral term."

**People of Color**—a political term meant to be inclusive of all peoples who have been demeaned and excluded by whites over the course of history. Most commonly used in the United States, the term may sound strange to visitors and immigrants. Quotes by two immigrants, one recent, one more distant, describe a common change in perspective as newcomers learn the "racial rules" of their new country:

I was startled when I arrived from China to hear myself referred to as a "person of color." In China, I'm Chinese. Our color is the norm. In fact, if you compare my actual skin color to a white person's I'm a little lighter than most of them.

—Taiwanese undergraduate

I really like the term "people of color." It suggests that all the ethnic groups that have experienced prejudice and racism from the white majority can become allies and work together for social justice. When I first came to the U.S. in the 1940s, you had to accept the terms the whites decided to call you. They called us "Orientals" as if we were mysterious and evil. They called Native Americans "redskins" to distinguish them from the blacks, who they thought were the lowest of the low. They called Mexicans "wet-backs," even if their families had been here since the mid-1800s when California was part of Mexico. Calling ourselves "people of color" is a way to reclaim our dignity.

—Japanese American community leader

**African-American/Black**—Although the history of Africans in America is widely accessible these days, high school history texts still downplay its scope, its violence, and the moral paradox it presented to the Founding Fathers. "Americans seem perpetually startled at slavery," writes James Loewen in *Lies My Teacher Told Me.* "Children are shocked to learn that George Washington and Thomas Jefferson owned slaves. ... Very few adults today realize that our society has been slave much longer than it has been free. ... In 1720, of New York City's population of seven thousand, 1,600 were African Americans, most of them slaves. Wall Street was the marketplace where owners could hire out their slaves by the day or week" (1995, p. 142).

Without enough knowledge of history or of how that history continues to affect Americans today, many white students are confused and sometimes put off by the depth of the emotion that some black students carry with them. Here, students with African heritage talk about the terms they use to identify their ethnicity:

I am not an African American, I'm black. I refuse to be called American until the day that this country treats me with same value and respect as everyone else. Unfortunately, I don't expect that day will come in my lifetime.

—black undergraduate

I'm not "African American." I'm an African in America—"othered," kept back, never accepted. That's been the status of my family for generations.

—black graduate student

My mother calls herself Black—capital B—my aunt won't hear of anything but African American, and I prefer to be called an American of African Descent, which stresses the American-ness of my experience. We are an extremely diverse community that values our individualism and our independent thinking. This is one of the reasons we are so tired of being singled out in the classroom and asked for the "black point of view"—as if we all think the same way or live the same experiences.

—American undergraduate of African Descent

Call me African American or black, it makes no difference to me. I'm proud of my heritage—which, by the way, includes Irish and Cherokee, as well as African. But

I've never been anything but black. All my family is black, all my neighbors are black, all the teachers I've ever had were black. I'm never going to be anything but black, so get used to it.

—black undergraduate

I hate these discussions about ethnicity where we're supposed to dig into our roots. The story of my ethnicity is incredibly painful. Why do you think so many African Americans have white ancestry? It was not a story of love affairs and peaceful intermarriage.

—African American undergraduate

**Arab American**—Cultures of many Middle Eastern, Muslim, and/or Arabic-speaking countries are represented by this large category: Egypt, Lebanon, Jordan, Saudi Arabia, Yemen, Palestine, Iraq, Iran, Afghanistan, Syria, Oman, Qatar, and the United Arab Emirates. Mostly Muslim, but also Christian, Chaldean (Iraqi Christian), and Jewish, many Arab Americans are less concerned about the terms used to identify them (as long as they are not pejorative) than about being stereotyped as terrorists and oppressors of women.

You may think I am oppressed because I wear a headscarf and dress modestly. But in my culture, this has nothing to do with oppression of women. It has to do with respect—respect for our customs, respect for our privacy, respect for our family values.

—Arab American graduate student

I've heard some people say that depicting Arabs as terrorists in American movies is okay because it's based on reality. Well, it's true there are a few extremely militant, possibly deranged people from Arab countries who threaten to blow up airplanes or who do blow up airplanes. But there are millions more peace-loving, family oriented, warm, funny, caring people who also speak Arabic and practice Islam. The problem is that most Americans have almost no contact with real Arab Americans, so they begin to believe that we're all dangerous, or that Islam is a violent religion. Of course that's as silly as thinking that all Christians are terrorists because the Ku Klux Klan is Christian or because the neo-Nazi skinheads talk about Jesus sometimes.

—Arab American law student

**Hispanic**—This term for people of Spanish and sometimes Portuguese descent has been common in the United States since the Nixon administration and covers more than twenty different nationalities. Like all terms for ethnicity, it is contested and political, preferred by some and not by others, changing as the social context changes. The authors and students below express their views about the term:

I don't like the term Hispanic. Call us Latinos if we're men, Latinas if we're women. It's more respectful and more accurate.

—Latina graduate student

"Hispanic" ... is Eurocentric and denies the fact that the people being labeled are not just of Spanish origin. Nor do they all speak Spanish. "Hispanic" denies our indigenous or Indian roots. It also denies our African roots, from the thousands of slaves that were brought to Latin America. (Martinez, 1997, p. 12)

Don't lump us together. We are Cubans, Puerto Ricans, and Mexicans, we are Spaniards and Colombians, Argentines, and Chileans, Nicaraguans, Salvadorans and many more. Learn our national origins and ethnic roots. Find out our personal preferences in the ways we refer to ourselves and our cultures. It can be confusing, even for us, but if you listen and show genuine interest in our languages and cultures, we won't be offended by your questions. And don't assume that we reject the term "American." Some of us are very devoted to the United States, very patriotic!

—Puerto Rican student

I am an American, even though I'm a citizen of Brazil. A lot of people here in the U.S. don't understand how that's possible. But they sometimes forget that America includes a lot more than the United States: Canada, Mexico, Central America, South America—it's all America.

—Brazilian student

Latinos ... were, are, and will always be perpetual alien residents never fully here— strangers in a native land. We are of a different variety simply because, unlike previous immigrants, most of us didn't come to America; instead, America came to us. Ours isn't just another immigrant's story, simply because assimilation may never be fully completed. ... We may eat American food, buy American merchandise, and greet Americans daily with a "Buenos días, mister" but at the core we'll always remain untouched. (Stavans, 1995, p. 200)

**Chicano/a**—a term created by Mexican American activists in the social protest years of the late 1960s and 1970s. Chicano/a authors explain the origin of the term and the history of violence between the United States and Mexico that is rarely presented from the Mexican or Mexican American point of view in standard U.S. textbooks. Passed down orally, through families and neighborhoods, these emotional memories continue to affect Chicano-Anglo relationships today:

In 1846, the U.S. incited Mexico to war. U.S. troops invaded and occupied Mexico, forcing her to give up almost half of her nation, what is now Texas, New Mexico, Arizona, Colorado and California. ... The border fence that divides the Mexican people was born on February 2, 1848 with the signing of the Treaty of Guadalupe Hidalgo. It left 100,000 Mexican citizens on this side, annexed by conquest along with the land. The land established by the treaty as belonging to Mexicans was soon swindled away from its owners. The treaty was never honored and restitution, to this day, has never been made. (Anzaldúa, 1987, p. 7)

From early on, the Chicano psyche has been belligerent. Silent resistance, a refusal to accept their new status, always colored the lives of Mexicans north of the Rio Grande. (Stavans, 1995, p. 62)

In the past, Chicano often meant lower-class, with a negative connotation. During the 60s, young Mexican Americans started to use "Chicano/Chicana" as an affirmation of pride and identity and to say, "We're not Mexicans or Americans. We're a combination—a special population with our own history and culture." (Martinez, 1997, p. 13)

**APA: Asian Pacific American**—Asian Pacific Americans or APAs are the fastest growing ethnic minority in the United States, even though they comprise only 5.6% of the total U.S. population. They are Chinese, Filipinos, Japanese, Vietnamese, Korean, Asian Indian, Laotian, Mien, Hmong, Cambodian, Pakistani, Bangladeshi, Sri Lankan, Indonesian, Malaysian, Thai, Nepali, Tibetan, Fijian, Samoan, Native Hawaiian, and many others—especially when we distinguish between different ethnic groups within national contexts (Punjabis, Bengalis, and Tamils from India, for example). First to arrive in the United States were the Chinese miners in the 1850s, hoping to strike it rich in the Gold Rush. Later, APAs came from Korea, Japan, India, and the Philippines to build railroads, cut sugarcane, reclaim swampland, work on farms and ranches, and open small businesses. Temporary sojourners at first like many European immigrants, they gradually made homes here; some APAs have lived in this country a lot longer than many European immigrant families. But because of the 1790 Naturalization Act, which remained in force until 1954, immigrants from many Asian Pacific countries were not allowed to vote and were prohibited from land ownership in some states. And because of their "racial uniform" it has never been possible for them to become "mere individuals, indistinguishable in the cosmopolitan mass of the population" (Park, quoted in Takaki, 1998, p. 13).

APA students and faculty express some of the pain of exclusion and marginalization their families have felt for many generations:

We are Asian *American*, not "Asian." God, I get so tired of explaining that.
—Asian American student

I prefer to be called "Filipino-American" rather than Asian American. Asians come from so many countries and are so incredibly different in language, culture, and historical experience. When you care enough to find out where our ancestors came from, we appreciate that. One thing though—don't just blurt out, "Where are you from?" to someone who looks Asian. Their family may have been here longer than yours! It's a touchy subject, but approaching it with some thought and sensitivity shows your respect.

—Filipino American student

I don't know how many times it's happened to me—I go into a store and someone slows down their speech, or talks to me like I'm deaf. My family has been speaking English for three generations. And yet, we're still not considered "real Americans."

—Japanese American student

My dad is seen as white, or at least a "normal American" in his workplace, and I think he's proud of it. But to me, it's scary. As our family becomes more American, does it mean we're becoming less Indian? I'm afraid our language and culture will be lost within two generations.

—Indian American student

I hate the hyphen. It seems like a small thing to some people, but to me, it is a constant reminder of our history of marginalization. I prefer to see it written "Asian American."

—Korean American student

My daughter had to explain to her white friends why yelling, "You ignorant immigrant" at a taxi driver who looked Asian was offensive. They told her to lighten up.

—Japanese American instructor

**Native American/Indian/First Nation**—Like other groups who become part of America involuntarily, Native Americans' relationship to whites has been marked by violence and pain, the extent of which has only begun to be recognized by the white majority. U.S. government-sanctioned genocide reduced the population from tens of millions to 200,000 by the beginning of the twentieth century. Unemployment, the root cause of poverty, is 50% on many reservations and up to 90% on some. The suicide rate for Native Americans is 70% higher than the rate for the general population (Winik, 1999).

This passage from Mary Crow Dog's story of her life, *Lakota Woman*, illustrates a small part of what happened: the attempt to "civilize" Indian children by educating them in boarding schools:

It is almost impossible to explain to a sympathetic white person what a typical old Indian boarding school was like; how it affected the Indian child suddenly dumped into it like a small creature from another world, helpless, defenseless, bewildered, trying desperately and instinctively to survive and sometimes not surviving at all. ... Oddly enough, we owed our unspeakable boarding schools to the do-gooders, the white Indian-lovers. The schools were intended as an alternative to the outright extermination seriously advocated by generals Sherman and Sheridan, as well as by most settlers and prospectors over-running our land. "You don't have to kill those poor benighted heathen," the do-gooders said. ... "Just give us a chance to turn them into useful farmhands, laborers, and chambermaids who will break their backs for you at low wages." ... The kids were taken away from their villages and pueblos, in their blankets and moccasins, kept completely isolated from their families—sometimes for as long as ten years—suddenly coming back, their short hair slick with pomade, their necks raw from stiff, high collars, their thick jackets always short in the sleeves and pinching under the arms, their tight patent leather shoes giving them corns, the girls in starched white blouses and clumsy, high-buttoned boots—caricatures of white people. When they found out—and they found out quickly—that they were neither wanted by whites nor by Indians, they got good and drunk, many of them staying drunk for the rest of their lives. (1991, pp. 28–30)

A lot of people—white people (though I don't really like that all-purpose term)—are interested in Native American spirituality and ritual these days. They come into the shop to buy a dreamcatcher or some Indian art, and they ask around to see if they can get in on a sweat lodge ceremony. But at the same time they have no problem putting down our people when they see fit. I don't get it. Do they have so little awareness of what they're doing? Do they have so little knowledge of the pain that comes with our history?
—Native American store manager

Indians were already an old culture in this land 2000 years ago. ... The native peoples had cities as large as any in Europe. They had governmental systems that lasted five times longer than our own. ... The Indians had wars, they enslaved people, but they were further ahead than most of the world in learning how to get along with each other. ... Indians' criteria for greatness or success is different than Anglo criteria. Ask Indians who is the most successful, and we'll often point to the poorest person, the one who gave himself to everyone else.
—Senator Ben Nighthorse Campbell, Northern Cheyenne (R) Colorado (quoted in Winik, 1999, pp. 7–8)

At Thanksgiving, the elementary school used to ask me and my husband to come into the classrooms to give the kids the Indian point of view. We did that for several years and it went well. But after a while I began to wonder why they didn't ask us to come any other time of year. We have a philosophy of life and a relationship to nature and our community that would be very beneficial to these young people. But when I suggested that, they just stopped calling us.
—Native American parent

A Native American student explains how students of other ethnicities can begin to get to know the community today:

"Native American" and "First Nation" (which is used in Canada) are respectful terms that should remind people that North America was not just an empty expanse when the European settlers arrived. It's cool to know us by our tribal names—like Odawa, Sioux, or Choctaw. If you start going into it you'll find there are over 500 different tribes and 175 languages still spoken! Inside the community, though, most of us just call ourselves "Indian." We're very unpretentious people. If you want to get to know us a little, take a look at some of the movies made by Indians, like *Smoke Signals*. Or come to a pow wow and get accustomed to our chanting and drumming, our style of dancing, and our regalia. Don't say 'costumes.' Costumes are for Halloween.

\* \* \* \* \* \*

Now that students have an overview of the major ethnic groups and some idea of why ethnic relations are so emotionally complex, they should be ready to take on the even more difficult area of modern-day prejudice and racism. First, they should be aware that even the term "minority" is loaded with emotional and political meaning. The next three definitions, "minority," "model minority," and "voluntary/involuntary minority," explain why, and offer some "insider" views of these terms.

**minority**—A term used to denote low numbers and/or less power vis-à-vis the majority (i.e., women are a numerical "majority" but a "minority" in terms of political power). Students and authors speak candidly about the emotions and thoughts the term brings up for them:

> When you refer to me as a "minority student" it gives the impression that I'm "less than" something. I'm not a "minority," I'm Kevin Chang, first year student at the University of Michigan. Why can't we just all be individuals?
> —Kevin Chang

> As long as we are treated as outsiders, we need the term "minority." It makes the point that racism is still a problem in this country.
> —Korean American student

> People of color may be minorities in the U.S., but in world terms, they're the majority by far! Using that term reflects a kind of global provincialism.
> —white instructor

> By the middle of the twenty-first century the so-called "white" ethnic group will be a minority in the United States. We'd better figure out how to get along before that happens.
> —white undergraduate

Mexico is sinking
California is on Fire
& we are getting burned aren't we? ...
but what if suddenly the continent turned upside down?
what if the U.S. was Mexico? what if 200,000 Anglo-Saxicans were to cross
the border each month to work as gardeners, waiters, musicians, movie
extras,
bouncers, baby sitters, chauffeurs, syndicated cartoonists, feather-weight
boxers, fruit-pickers, & anonymous poets? what if they were called waspanos,
waspitos, wasperos or waspbacks?
what if we were the top dogs?
what if literature was life?
what if yo were you
& tú fueras I, Mister?
(from *Califas*, Guillermo Gómez-Peña, 1993, p. 71)

**"model minority"**—Term used by whites to compliment Asian Americans
on their attainment of educational and occupational success and/or to pointedly
contrast that success with the level of achievement of other minorities. Asian
American students and an instructor express a variety of reactions to the term:

> I don't mind when they call us a "model minority." At least it isn't a negative image.
> A lot of us do get high grades because our parents forced us to study when we were
> little. We can be really competitive. The other day I got the highest grade in a class
> of 200 students and I yelled out, "Asian power!" Some of the white students were a
> little PO'd but hey, they could study harder.
>
> —Chinese American undergraduate

> I'm not sure how I think about the term "model minority." It's good that other people
> recognize our hard work and achievement, but it's sad that they still view us as a
> "minority." That sounds so exclusionary. Why can't we just be part of the mainstream?
> —Japanese American undergraduate

> To be referred to as a model minority seems to me like we are being petted and told
> "good dog."
>
> —Taiwanese American undergraduate
> (quoted in Oyserman and Sakamoto, 1997, p. 445)

This term "model minority" just continues to create biases. People who don't know
us tend to assume that Asian Americans are naturally smart or that we've had it easy
in this country. They don't realize that there are a lot of Asian Americans who are
still living below the poverty line. Some are on welfare. Others have suffered huge
economic setbacks because of discrimination. When my father came over, he was a
trained physician but they wouldn't let him practice in this country, so he and my

mother started a small grocery store. Can you imagine what it's like for a doctor to spend his life selling oranges? Consequently, he pushed me and my brother very hard. We had to work in the store after school and all the rest of the time we had to study. We didn't have much of a childhood.

—Korean American instructor

Regardless of the positive connotations of the term "model minority" it is STILL a STEREOTYPE. This means that there are certain expectations of Asians based simply on their appearance. I think this is b-s-, and I try with all my ability to avoid being labeled.

—Korean American undergraduate (quoted in Oyserman and Sakamoto, 1997, p. 445)

**voluntary/involuntary minority**—Terms used by Nigerian American anthropologist John Ogbu to distinguish between immigrants who voluntarily left their homeland for a new life in another country and those who were incorporated into a society against their will by conquest, colonialism, or slavery. Though both groups "are subjected daily to cultural and intellectual denigration," says Ogbu, voluntary immigrants interpret the racism they experience as only a temporary setback to their goal of making a home for themselves in their new country. Because "they tend to compare their present status in the U.S. with their former selves and/or with their peers 'back home' … they usually conclude that things are better for them or their children here." Thus, they push themselves educationally and economically to surmount the barriers of racism and exclusion (Ogbu, 1989, pp. 13–16).

Involuntary minorities, on the other hand, "do not have a homeland situation of former selves and peers to compare their present circumstance." African Americans, Native Americans, Native Hawaiians, Puerto Ricans, Chicanos, and other groups whose ancestors were conquered or colonized by the United States can only compare their situation to that of the dominant group. Their poorer schools and neighborhoods, their tenuous economic prospects, and their lower social status all lead them "to believe that (1) job and wage discrimination is more or less institutionalized and permanent, and (2) individual effort and hard work are important but not enough to overcome racism and discrimination" (Ogbu and Simmons, 1998, p. 172). This causes "the community, families, and students [to be] skeptical and ambivalent about the role of education in getting ahead" (p. 173).

Interestingly, this effect is not confined to U.S. minorities. Studies around the world have found the same striking differences between groups that are voluntary minorities in one country and involuntary minorities in another. Finns in Sweden, Koreans in Japan, and Maoris in New Zealand all are involuntary minorities and are doing poorly, compared to their much better educational and economic performance when they immigrate voluntarily to other countries (Ogbu, 1989).

Students who have come this far in their thinking have probably brought up the term "political correctness" in their discussions—or if they haven't, they are thinking it. Like many other charged terms, "PC" has different meanings to people of different political persuasions.

**politically correct (PC)**—Term used on U.S. campuses since about 1990 (Herbst, 1997) to mean an imposed or self-imposed sensitivity and/or a progressive political stance toward socially marginalized groups. Students and faculty express different views on political correctness (now sometimes simply called "bias") that bring out frustrations and emotions on all sides:

> It has become so necessary for instructors to be politically correct in their teaching styles that the classroom and the real world have become two different universes. Instructors have to cater to hypersensitive individuals and use "proper" terms for everything. By proper, I mean "African American" instead of "black." Most blacks have no clue as to what Africa is like and have never met a true African person. Let's face it, whites are white, blacks are black.
>
> —white undergraduate

> As professors we have a certain amount of power in the classroom. We should use our power to enforce rules of behavior, to let students know very clearly the ways they can interact with each other. They have to act decently, politely, with some degree of sensitivity, even if it is forced or fake at first. The important thing is to establish an atmosphere of respect that is safe for everyone. Call it political correctness if you want. I call it basic human decency.
>
> —white instructor

> Political correctness is a kind of emotional manipulation that people indulge in when they don't have the courage to face differences of opinion and point of view. For example, a white student might say that it's very difficult to know what to call people from different ethnic groups because the terminology keeps changing. Then someone else, maybe a person of color, maybe a white person, will say something like, "Unfortunately, that opinion is often expressed by white people who want to avoid having to learn anything about people of color." End of conversation. The person who expressed a perfectly valid opinion decides to shut up and the conversation goes nowhere. The underlying problem is lack of trust—on all sides.
>
> —white instructor

Unfortunately the class is so PC that honest discussion about race is difficult. When I can't see where white students are coming from, I tend to distrust them. I've had bad experiences in the past with whites I believed were my best friends—all of a sudden they came out with something really stereotypical or exclusionary. It's not their fault—they have learned it from their families and communities. But it's been unbelievably hurtful. I'd rather know what I'm up against right from the start.

—biracial African American and white undergraduate

I occasionally get comments on my student evaluations that say the class is "biased" or that "the instructor doesn't treat all students fairly." While I care about all my students, I'll admit I favor points of view that don't get a fair hearing in a society that suppresses and denies its racism. I'm not going to stop teaching that way, but it worries me a little when I come up for review.

—white professor

# Notes

1. Some of these definitions were worded with the help of Herbst (1997).
2. January 1992. Informal presentation at the University of Michigan's Center for Afroamerican and African Studies.

# · 3 ·

# INSIDER'S GUIDE PART II

## Discrimination, Racism, and Race Hatred

The following definitions and examples are focused on racism and other forms of discrimination and hatred. As in the previous chapter, some of the quotes come directly from published texts, formal student interviews, and student writing; others I have created from memories of ideas, feelings, and opinions I have heard expressed in the classroom, in private conversations, or in all-white public environments. Many of the quotes show how people express their prejudice and racism—sometimes unconsciously or subtly, sometimes quite openly. Other quotes try to capture the experiences and points of view of people who are targets of racism. You can use this "insider information" to educate yourself the way I did when I began to tackle this subject. You'll feel more competent to answer students' questions, steer them in the right direction when they get off track, and, most importantly, you'll be prepared to give your students specific examples that link abstract concepts to real life.

I have also used this guide, or parts of it, to open up the topic of racism in the classroom, or to prepare students for discussions of race-related topics in various disciplines. I might start with the first three definitions in this chapter, prejudice, discrimination, and "reverse discrimination," since these terms are commonly misunderstood. After students have read the definitions, I ask questions that help them think more deeply about each quote: "Have you ever heard this attitude expressed?" "Is discrimination (or prejudice) always wrong?" "Is discrimination by people of color against whites as destructive as discrimination by whites against people of color? Why or why not?" You might want to limit discussion time for each example so students will stay open to new information as they work their way through the definitions in this chapter. You'll probably find that this information is a lot to give students all at once. Go slowly and be sure to ask questions that promote discussion as you go along. More ideas for discussion and other, more creative ways of addressing these topics can be found in Chapter 8 and in the Annotated Resources section.

\* \* \* \* \* \*

**prejudice**—an attitude, either positive or negative, toward a category or group or toward individuals on account of their group membership.

> I'd hire an Asian any day because they're really hard workers.
>
> —white employer

> Can't you find a nice Jewish boy to go out with?
>
> —Jewish grandmother

> Mexicans just want to come up here so they can take our jobs.
>
> —white food service worker

> The bomber was a devout Muslim? It figures.
>
> —non-Muslim American

> We give all our employees a drug test before they come to paint your house.
>
> —white manager of Latino workers

> White people can't be trusted. Deep down, they're all racist.
>
> —African-American undergraduate

**discrimination**—behavior that denies people equal treatment because of their membership in some group (Herbst, 1997).

> This all-male academy succeeds because our students learn without distractions. Believe me, we will fight to keep it this way.
>
> —male administrator

> Yes, our admissions policies do favor children of alumni. It's a kind of "thank you for your support," a way of increasing loyalty to the school.
>
> —white administrator

It may not be fair, but we discourage white students from joining the multicultural council. We need a space where we can just be ourselves.

—Latino undergraduate

Racial profiling at airports is just common sense.

—white undergraduate

I have been followed so often in stores—it doesn't seem to matter if I'm dressed up or wearing jeans. What's ironic is that most people who steal from stores in this area are not African American.

—African-American professor

I am a professor, I have written many distinguished books on African American history and literature. I make a six-figure salary. But when I try to hail a cab, I get passed up again and again.

—African-American professor

I've been told that Asians are not suited for management positions because we're not "dynamic" enough. But that's just discrimination based on stereotypes. Look at our cultures, our history, you'll see fighters, orators, leaders—both men and women.

—Chinese American professor

**reverse discrimination or reverse racism**—terms that emphasize the irony of trying to create a more egalitarian society by giving preference to one racial group over another. The often unstated assumption is that racism is a thing of the past and the playing field is now more or less level.

I'm against affirmative action because it discriminates against white males. Sure, minorities have been disadvantaged by racism in the past, but two wrongs don't make a right.

—white male undergraduate

When I told the bus driver that I had no change, he just glared at me. But when an elderly black lady was fumbling with her purse, he laughed and waved her on. That's reverse discrimination.

—white undergraduate

In my law class we learned that some theorists actually propose that black juries should discriminate in favor of black defendants because racism is so pervasive in our society that blacks will never get justice from the white-dominated judicial system. Isn't that reverse racism?

—white undergraduate

The next three definitions deal with stereotyping—from the unthinking generalizations people often make about groups they don't know very well to ethnic "jokes" and "othering" of "exotic" groups, to the vicious slurs of outright racists. I try to reassure students by saying that we all probably have incomplete or incorrect information about some ethnic groups, that none of us intends to hurt anyone by our ignorance, and that this is a chance to think about the generalizations and negative judgments we might be making without realizing it. I then read the quotes aloud to the class or give them a printed copy of these next three definitions. Then I ask questions like, "What group or groups are stereotyped here?" "Why do you think this stereotype is so common?" "Can you think of other examples of stereotypes that you've heard or seen?" "When are stereotypes humorous and when are they painful?" "Is it harmful to stereotype your own ethnic group?" "What can we do when we hear our friends making remarks based on stereotypes?" When you get to the examples of derogatory stereotypes, you might want to avoid reading some of the quotes aloud even if no students from the targeted groups are present—racial slurs carry astounding power. I ask my students to read silently, and then tell them that while whites have often demonized people of color, there have always been whites that have repudiated this practice—in all historical eras. If students bring up the derogatory stereotypes that some people of color have used against whites or that people of color have used against each other, I acknowledge this, and then ask students to move on to the discussion of different types of racism that follows, where this point will be examined in more depth.

　　**stereotype**—a set of traits that come to characterize an identity group, often based on inadequate knowledge or understanding of that group.

> You flew on Qatar Airlines? Wasn't that kind of a scary experience?
> > —one white undergraduate to another

> Hi, Noriko, glad—to—meet—you. Uh … do you speak English?
> > —white undergraduate

> This university needs to show its commitment to minority students by offering more remedial help.
> > —white administrator

> White people at this university are so ignorant about what it's like to be poor.
> > —Vietnamese American undergraduate

> I come from a family of English teachers, so Standard English was the norm at home. But I had to learn to speak the Black vernacular in order to be accepted as authentically black—by both my black and my white peers.
> > —African-American undergraduate

"I am Chinese," remarks Chester in David Hwang's play *Family Devotions*. "I live in Bel Air. I drive a Mercedes. I go to a private prep school. I must be Chinese." (quoted in Takaki, 1998, p. 4)

**orientalizing, exoticizing**—stereotyping, often fueled by the media, that depicts Asians, Arabs, immigrants, and sometimes other people of color as bizarre, violent, crazed, deviant, oppressed, pleasantly exotic (to whites), or foreign, no matter how many generations their family has lived in the United States. In advertising, for example, Asian and Asian American females are often pictured as mysterious, submissive, and sexually available to white males. Asian males are depicted in movies as Kung Fu experts, or wise old masters who seldom speak, or sly, devious criminals. Arab-looking individuals, even children, are cast as terrorists.

I prefer to date Asian women. I'm really tired of loud-mouthed, pushy females who have an opinion about everything. Asian women are quiet. Low maintenance. I don't need an intellectual equal as a partner; I get enough mental stimulation at work. When I come home I want a woman who's ready to please me, not argue with me.
—white male

Asian models are all so slim and sexy and gorgeous—I don't know why Asian American women complain about it. If being mysterious and exotic were such a bad thing, why would they agree to be portrayed that way?
—white male undergraduate

I feel sorry for Yasmine. She has to wear a scarf all the time, even when it's hot. She says it's her choice and that she's honoring her religion, but I find it hard to believe that.

—non-Muslim female undergraduate

Other students tend to exoticize me sometimes. They ask me to say certain words because my accent is "so cute" and then they repeatedly ask me to teach them to curse in Spanish or to make them some authentic Mexican food. This, you might say, is showing their curiosity towards my culture, but after a while it gets ridiculous and insulting. I've been asked if there are trees in Mexico and why we like to live in such degraded conditions.
—Mexican undergraduate

**derogatory stereotype**—a set of negative traits that ridicule and demonize an identity group.

"Jew, Jew; Two for five; That's what keeps; Jew alive" (Folk rhyme)

Why are Muslim terrorists so quick to commit suicide? Because you can't wash the smell off a donkey. LOL
—e-mail from the Chief of Staff of the Los Angeles County Sheriff's Department

He held his head up in the glare of the lamp—a head vigorously modeled into deep shadows and shining lights—a head powerful and misshapen with a tormented and flattened face—a face pathetic and brutal; the tragic, the mysterious, the repulsive mask of a nigger's soul. (Conrad, *The Nigger of the "Narcissus,"* 1976, pp. 26–27)

Chinese immigrants to California in the late 19th century were depicted in a magazine cartoon as "a bloodsucking vampire with slanted eyes, a pigtail, dark skin, and thick lips. Like blacks, the Chinese were described as heathen, morally inferior, savage, childlike, and lustful. Chinese women were condemned as a 'depraved class,' and their depravity was associated with their physical appearance, which seemed to show 'but a slight removal from the African race.'" (Takaki, 1998, p. 101)

In "An Open Letter to Mr. Edward Zwick," Hala Maksoud, President of the American-Arab Anti-Discrimination Committee says in part: "The 20th Century Fox Movie, *The Siege,* is packed with stereotypes of Arabs and Muslims as violent, unscrupulous and barbarous. It portrays Arabs and Muslims as a homogeneous, threatening mass who are repeatedly referred to as 'those people.' Even when 'those people' are incarcerated behind barbed wire, they do not elicit any sympathy, because they all look alike and different from the rest of 'us.' Furthermore, a clear and direct link is made between Islamic religious practices and terrorism. Indeed, images of a Muslim washing his hands before prayer, as hundreds of millions of Muslims do every day, precedes acts of terror in the film. This firmly reinforces fear of Muslims in the viewer's mind. ..." (www.hri.ca/urgent/thesiege-1101.shtml)

The following are definitions and examples of six types of racism discussed in current literature, along with some related terms. I have students read them over and then ask questions that help them think critically about them: "What do you think of this definition, these examples?" "Have you heard people saying these kinds of things?" "Where have you read things like this?" "Has a group you belong to (religion, gender, class, ethnicity) ever been a target?" "What do you do to try to avoid being a target?" "How is racism similar to or different from religious persecution?" "Why do some people feel that whites are the only group that can truly be racist?" "What can we do as individuals to stop racist words and practices?" "What could we accomplish by joining with others?"

Discussion of these concepts can be tricky. See later chapters for how instructors in a variety of disciplines handle these conversations, and ideas on how to get beyond students' tendency to blame the victim, to treat the subject superficially, or to clam up.

**"traditional" or "old fashioned" racism**—an open and unapologetic belief in the superiority of the white "race" based on notions of biological, cultural, and/or moral inferiority of other "races." While this form of racism is less socially and officially sanctioned than it was before the Civil Rights Movement and other ethnic identity movements of the 1960s and 1970s, it is still alarmingly prevalent—and rising. In fact, in 2016, the Southern Poverty Law Center reported 892 extremist groups across the country; their numbers grew by 14% in 2015 alone. Hate groups include the Ku Klux Klan, racist Skinhead group anti-immigrant "Patriot" militia organizations, and many others. An interactive hate group map can be found at http://www.splcenter.org/get-informed/hate-map

We believe in Hitler's ways. But that don't mean we worship him. He was smart, but he was a homosexual. I think what he did with the Jews was right, mainly. They was coming into Germany, buying up the businesses, treating the Germans like slaves. I think he killed *more* than six million. That was just all they could find.

—Member of the Nazi Low Riders, Antelope Valley, CA
(quoted in Finnegan, 1998, p. 288)

God is calling white men and women to take a message to their brothers and sisters. The time for remembrance is upon us. It is our responsibility to warn our brothers and sisters that Satan's plan for world domination, one-world government, racial amalgamation, etc. is setting its sights on us.

—Thomas Robb Ministries
http://www.christianidentitychurch.net/our_mission.htm

"I won't have a Filipino in my house when my daughter is around," said one of the women. "Is it true that they are sex-crazy?" the man next to her asked. "I understand they go crazy when they see a white woman." "Same as the niggers," said the man who did not like Filipino servants. "Same as the Chinamen, with their opium." "They are all sex-starved," said the man of the house with finality. "What is this country coming to?" one of the women said. (from the memoir, *America Is in the Heart* by Carlos Bulosan, 1996, p. 141)

**ethnic slur**—derogatory term used by any ethnic in-group to put down an ethnic out-group: spic, gook, redneck, frog, white trash, chink, jungle bunny, hula girl, mick, russky, kraut, sand nigger, etc. Ethnic slurs by the dominant group are meant to keep a subordinate group in its place (e.g., "wetback," "nigger"). Slurs by the subordinate group are a way of "talking back" to the more powerful group (e.g., "gringo," "cracker," "honky") and thus have less power to hurt (Herbst, 1997).

**one-drop rule**—the idea that having any black ancestors—that is, having "one drop of black blood"—defines people as "black." This social "rule" was originally established to increase the number of people who could be considered slaves. As racial tensions grew increasingly hostile after the end of the Civil War, a great deal of anger and ridicule was directed at anyone suspected of circumventing the one-drop rule by "passing" for white. For example, before the 1920 presidential election, Warren G. Harding was accused of passing by elderly whites who claimed they knew his father was "a mulatto with 'thick lips, rolling eyes and chocolate skin'" (Appling, 1998, p. 20). Ironically, when African-Americans suggest that Beethoven, Dostoyevski, Abraham Lincoln, and Thomas Jefferson should rightly be called "black" using this same rule, their claims are dismissed as absurd.

**rule of hypo-descent**—"According to hypo-descent, the various purported racial categories are arranged in a hierarchy along a single dimension, from the most prestigious ('white') through intermediary forms ('Asian'), to least prestigious ('black')" (Fish, 1995, p. 58). Children who result from interracial unions are often categorized by others as members of the less prestigious race. In other words, the child of a "black" parent and a "white" parent is seen as "black," no matter how light their skin. Interestingly, other cultures may see different features as more important. In Togo, West Africa, African-American Peace Corps Volunteers have had the unsettling experience of being called *yovo*, a term meaning "white" or "foreigner." For the Togolese, the manner of dress, the way of carrying one's self, and the country one calls home are more salient characteristics than skin color.

**racial hatred**—stereotyping, resentments, slurs, ignorance, and hatred of any "race" for any other. Some whites and people of color assert that only whites can be racist because whites as a group have the power to make and enforce legal and cultural rules that keep the racial hierarchy in place (see "institutional racism"). Others point to the anti-Korean and anti-Chinese racism in Japan; racism against indigenous people by Latin Americans who claim to have no indigenous "blood"; and Arab anti-black racism in Sudan and Mauritania, where Arabs still keep black slaves.[1] All agree that racial hatred (as opposed to racism) can be practiced by any ethnic group.

> I've been ordered to get glasses of water for neighboring restaurant patrons. I've been told to be careful mopping the floors at the television station where I was directing a show. Even with my U.S. passport, I've been escorted to the "aliens only" line at Kennedy International Airport. I've been told I'm not dark enough. I've been told I'm not White enough. I've been told I talk American real good. I've been told, "Take

your humus and your pita bread and go back to Mexico!" I've been ordered to "Go back to where you belong, we don't like *your* kind here!"
—Filipino-German American (Arboleda, 1998, p. 1)

Unfortunately, too many young black kids today are saying they hate all white people—even when they've never met a white person in their lives! That's a real problem. But that's not the same as racism. Racism equals prejudice plus power—the power to make the rules and set the standards, to control the corporations and the banks and the police force, to set the curriculum and to make up the IQ tests, to choose to put money into poverty programs or to spend it on the military.
—black community activist

**"symbolic" or "modern" racism or "racial resentment"**—a more subtle form of racism that became more prevalent in the United States in the 1980s, symbolic racism claims the moral and cultural, rather than biological, superiority of whites, and avoids racial epithets or crude put-downs. Widespread among both conservatives and liberals, it is based on the belief that targeted groups violate "traditional American" moral values embodied in the Protestant ethic such as hard work, self-reliance, obedience, and discipline. It is rooted in early-learned fears and stereotypes that can be self-righteously ethnocentric:

The main reason Puerto Rican kids don't succeed in school is that their parents don't care about education.
—white Education major

They discovered down in Florida that when people feed the alligators, they lose their ability to forage in the wild. Welfare does the same thing to humans. If you keep giving handouts, you're not helping anyone.
—white undergraduate, referring to an analogy made by white legislators in the U.S. House of Representatives, March 24, 1995

People are ready to call anything racism when it is going to benefit them. I'm sorry, but I'm tired of hearing it. It's just a way for them to slack off and not do the work.
—white undergraduate

We're not allowed to say this in the current atmosphere of political correctness, but don't you think the reason there are so many black men in prison is that so many black men are criminals?
—white graduate student

While these attitudes and behaviors are called "modern" racism, their roots are very old. Frederick Douglass observed: "[W]hen men oppress their fellowmen, the oppressor ever finds, in the character of the oppressed, a full justification for his oppression. Ignorance and depravity, and the inability to rise from degradation to civilization and respectability, are the most usual allegations against the oppressed" (quoted in Gates and West, 1997, p. 2).

code words—modern forms of racism must somehow accommodate egalitarian values and the belief that racism is a thing of the past, so words with no overt racial connection are used to refer euphemistically to stigmatized groups. "Inner city youth," "at-risk student," "illegal," "those people," and "unqualified" are some examples. Other code words refer obliquely (and positively) to whites and sometimes to so-called "model minorities": "taxpayers," "home-owners," "family values," "working families," "deserving poor," "middle-class families." As Cornel West points out, "In this age of globalization, with its ... information, communication, and applied biology, a focus on the lingering effects of racism seems outdated and antiquated. ... Yet race—in the coded language of welfare reform, immigration policy, criminal punishment, affirmative action and suburban privatization—remains a central signifier in the political debate" (Gates and West, 1997, pp. 107–108).

dog whistle politics—coded racial appeals to white voters that tap into their fears of immigrants, Muslims, and "criminally prone" black men, manipulating them to support policies that benefit the wealthy. "Dog whistle politics explains how politicians backed by concentrated wealth manipulate racial appeals to win elections and also to win support for regressive policies that help corporations and the super-rich, and in the process wreck the middle class" (Lopez, 2014, pp. xii).

aversive racism—another modern form of racism, more subtle than symbolic racism, that is practiced, often unconsciously, by whites with strong egalitarian values. "Aversive racists ... sympathize with the victims of past injustice; support public policies that, in principle, promote racial equality and ameliorate the consequences of racism; identify more generally with a liberal political agenda; regard themselves as nonprejudiced and nondiscriminatory; but, almost unavoidably, possess negative feelings and beliefs about blacks" (Gaertner and Dovidio, 1986, pp. 61–62).

"People like to say that they're not racist, as if there is no racism in them," says social psychologist Raphael Ezekiel. "I find that not a sensible thing to say. We live in a society that is racist. Therefore, we have within our own souls at one level or another some racism. ... If one lives next door to a cement factory, inevitably one inhales cement dust and the cement dust becomes a part of one's body. If one lives in a racist society, one inhales racism and that becomes part of one's soul. ... If one wants to be an effective fighter for social justice it's not enough to say, 'I hate racism.' You have to spend the time and effort to get acquainted with the racism you do have inside your-self, so you can take account of it. It's like the Leadbelly song, where he says, 'You got to say, Good morning, Blues.' You've got to say good morning to the racism in you, so you understand where it can trip you up." (quoted in "Roots of Racism," Fall, 1997)

**institutional or systemic racism**—the network of laws, practices, norms, and values that effectively prevents equal access to education, jobs, legal ser-vices, earnings, and respect across ethnic groups. Since the Civil Rights Era, institutional racism has been much reduced because many laws made with conscious racist intentions were struck down. What remains is a system of discrimination that is largely invisible to and/or denied by whites, especially those in power. The following are some examples offered by perceptive white students to show how they unwittingly help perpetuate past injustices in insti-tutional contexts.

> My high school offered AP classes that boosted my GPA to 4.2, so when I applied for college I was able to beat out students from inner city and rural high schools who got all As. That, of course, made me a better candidate for a top law school.

> My parents made a point of staying in Detroit when other white people fled to the suburbs. They like that liberal image. But they sent me to one of the best private schools in the state, where I had maybe two black classmates. Even though that makes me uncomfortable, I would do the same for my kids.

> I have confidence in the health system because people of my race have never been singled out as guinea pigs for experimentation. That means I won't hesitate to go to the doctor for regular checkups and follow their advice when I get really ill. I wish everyone felt the same level of trust that I do.

> When I have kids I'll be able to send them off to school, knowing that they will not be automatically placed in a lower reading group or a special education class because of their color or class. And I know that if my kids are like me they'll get all kinds of special dispensations from high school teachers who'll decide they're "promising" kids, even if they're little delinquents.

> I cannot imagine the police requiring me to give a blood sample for DNA analysis because a murderer of my race, age, and approximate height is loose in the commu-nity. What an uproar there would be if people from my race and class were treated that way!

**implicit bias**—favoring one identity group over another without being con-sciously aware of doing so. Everyone, even the most fair-minded people, can be biased toward society's dominant and historically most favored groups: whites, males, straight and cis-gendered people, upper middle and upper class, fluent Standard English speakers, and so on. Thirty years of implicit bias research has validated this unsettling idea, explained in detail by the Kirwin Institute for the Study of Race and Ethnicity: http://kirwaninstitute.osu.edu/wp-content/uploads/2015/05/2015-kirwan-implicit-bias.pdf. Students and instructors can take the test online at https://implicit.harvard.edu/implicit/takeatest.html

I was so sure I could not be biased I took the test three times. Even then I questioned the validity of the methods—until I reviewed the research.

—white antiracist educator

I knew I was biased against white males since I've had some bad experiences with them on campus. But biased against black males too? That was a surprise.

—African-American male undergraduate

I was discouraged to read about how pervasive implicit bias is. How can we ever get rid of religious intolerance if we're not even aware of our own biases?

—Muslim undergraduate

Police departments are starting to do anti-bias training for all officers, at least in my area. It turns out that you can reduce biased behavior just by knowing you're affected by implicit bias.

—African-American County Sheriff

**internalized racism**—anxiety, self-doubt, and in extreme cases, self-ha-tred felt by some members of stigmatized groups because of the pervasiveness of derogatory stereotypes, ethnocentrism, and other forms of racism. Several professors of color explain:

Internalized racism is what really gets in my way as a Black woman. It influences the way I see or don't see myself, limits what I expect of myself or others like me. It results in my acceptance of mistreatment, leads me to believe that being treated with less than absolute respect, at least this once, is to be expected because I am Black, because I am not white. (Yamato, 1992, p. 67)

It was only recently that I realized that in all my years of working for tenure, I had been accepting the idea that I should adapt myself to the white norm. We are taught very early on that the white style is the default, the background against which people of color are projected.

—Asian American faculty member

Internalized racism feeds on ignorant stereotypes that are pervasive throughout society and on the persistence of poverty among ethnic groups traditionally despised by the majority. An African-American scholar describes some of the conditions in impoverished communities of color that help self-hatred to flourish:

> Where there's work, it's miserably paid and ugly. Space allotment at home and at work cramp body and mind. Positive expectation withers in infancy. People fall into the habit of jeering at aspiration as though at the bidding of physical law. Obstacles at every hand prevent people from loving and being loved in decent ways, prevent children from believing their parents, prevent parents from believing they themselves know anything worth knowing. The only true self, now as in the long past, is the one mocked by one's own race. (DeMott, 1995, p. 37)

Anyone whose group has been stigmatized can suffer from self-hatred so internalized, so "normalized" it is sometimes hard to recognize:

> She sure looks better since she got a nose job.
>> —Eastern European Jewish male, referring to a classmate from his own ethnic group

> I just like light-skinned black girls better. It's just a preference. Just like some guys like tall girls.
>> —African-American male undergraduate

> She's lucky she's got good hair.
>> —African-American woman referring to a biracial friend with long, wavy hair

> He looks like an FOB ["fresh off the boat"]—no style. And that ridiculous accent! Why can't they learn to speak English properly over there?
>> —Indian American student talking about an international student recently arrived from India

As students of color begin recognizing and questioning the internalized racism that they have been carrying with them, the emotions that surface are sometimes overwhelming. Two students write about their experiences:

> As I held the child in my lap, I was repulsed by her dirty clothes, her nappy hair, the smell of urine. What does this say about my people? What does this say about *me*? I began to dread my volunteer service at the day care center. It became harder and harder to get up on Friday mornings.
>> —African-American undergraduate

I was silent in this class most of the semester because I was thinking about all the ways I have been taught to hate the Chinese part of myself—my looks, my Chinese name (which I almost never use). I was appalled when I realized that all this time I've hated my father, too—his accent, his stupid stories about his childhood, his strange ideas sometimes.

—biracial Chinese/European American undergraduate

Though many examples of internalized racism exist in literature and in academic texts, I prefer not to spend much time on the issue when teaching white students. It is too easy, even for the most well-meaning whites, to shift the problem away from the ways their group is implicated in the racist society we all inhabit and onto the effects of racism on target groups. While developing sympathy and understanding of other people's pain is a worthy goal, it is even more important for white students to understand the ways they have benefited from being part of the group that calls the shots. The literature calls this "white privilege" (McIntosh, 1992), even though it should be obvious that not having to suffer ridicule, exclusion, and judgments based on superficial physical characteristics should be a given rather than a privilege in a society that values egalitarianism.

**white privilege or "unearned" privilege**—pervasive and systemic ways that being white confers unearned advantage in U.S. society. White privilege is often blatantly obvious to targeted groups but nearly invisible to whites until its various manifestations are pointed out. When asked to consider ways that they were privileged in their own lives, some perceptive white students offered the following:

I can come late to class or have trouble expressing my thoughts in writing without anyone assuming I am unqualified to be in college.

I can sit on my front steps and have a beer without anyone thinking I am unemployed, lazy, or an illegal immigrant.

When I intern in an international corporation—and later, when I achieve my goal as a manager—I can be certain that the company culture will reflect the styles, language, values and norms I was brought up with.

When I approach an cash machine at night, no one will assume I am there to rob them.

I can choose not to think about race and racial problems—because I can easily believe that I don't have any.

The final two definitions, ethnocentrism and Eurocentrism, refer to the all-too human practices of seeing the world from one's own point of view, and then passing that point of view along as "normal and natural," or "the best," or "the smartest" way of doing things—especially if one is a member of the powerful majority.

**ethnocentrism**—the often unconscious practice of seeing and judging other groups through the lens of one's own cultural styles and values. In the quotes below, teachers and other authority figures are judging members of other groups by their own cultural norms without knowing enough about the values, cultures, and histories of the groups they view negatively:

> It really bothers me that Lei May is so quiet. I think she needs help developing her self-esteem.
> —African-American middle school teacher

> When an African produces writing of the same caliber as Shakespeare, I'll "diversify" my syllabus. Until then, we'll stick to the Classics.
> —white professor

> Why do you see them driving Cadillacs when they hardly have enough money to pay the rent?
> —white undergraduate

> If they'd only read to their kids. I know Native Americans come from an oral culture, but since the brain develops most during the first seven years they really need to provide an optimum environment at home.
> —white kindergarten teacher

**Eurocentrism**—the idea that Europe is the center of all that is worthy to study, imitate, or aspire to. Researchers have been surprised and troubled to find that Eurocentrism has subconscious effects on people on every continent. In a study that asked 400 first-year college students in twenty cities around the world to draw a world map from memory, students "greatly enlarged the size of Europe and shrank the dimensions of Africa." Researchers concluded this was not just the result of the "badly skewed Mercator projection" that mapmakers have used until recently to draw a round earth on a flat sheet of paper. "If the Mercator projection alone caused the size bias, then North America and Asia should also appear larger than life. ... But that did not happen: Europe was the only continent consistently exaggerated" (Monastersky, 1992, pp. 222–223).

Here, three white U.S. professors give a variety of reasons why their courses are Eurocentric:

> My reading list? It's writers I've read and enjoyed over the years. Yes, I know, they're all white males. But they're the ones I know best.

> I teach a course called "Great Ideas." We cover Galileo, Locke, Freud, Marx, Einstein, and Dostoyevsky. I've never had more than a few students of color sign up for my classes. The ones I've had have been very good—superior, I'd say. But I don't understand why this curriculum doesn't appeal to more of them. These ideas should be available to everyone.

> The unique source of the American ideals of liberty and equality is Europe, not Asia or Africa or the Middle East. It is European institutions we all should be studying, European authors we should be reading. We don't have room in the curriculum for a study of all the world's cultures. As a specialty, yes, I can see it. Diplomats need to know about foreign ways of thinking, languages, history and so forth. But this should not be our core curriculum.

# Note

1. For more on issues of slavery in contemporary Africa, see Cotton (1998).

# · 4 ·

# CLASSROOM CONFRONTATIONS

I firmly believe that you cannot change your perceptions of people who come from unfamiliar cultures while having safe and superficial chitchat. It is only when you get uncomfortable and passionate that the true work towards reform can begin. Sometimes, in order to be heard, in order to make progress, you have to be raw and honest.

—African-American undergraduate

The challenge in this conversation is to get below the social niceties to the real divisions between us. And that involves to a certain extent normalizing the fear, suspicion and not knowing. The classroom has got to feel like a safe enough place that students can say what they think, even though they sometimes wish they didn't think those things. And then I think there can be a conversation. Often it's heated, often it's angry, but there's a commitment to stay with it and to work it through. It may not reach a resolution, but it may reach a sharing.

—Charles Behling, University of Michigan Program on
Intergroup Relations[1]

When we open up discussions about race and racism, topics that have long been taboo for well-meaning whites and a thorn in the side of communities of color, it is only natural that strong emotions will surface. "One thing I wasn't quite prepared for when I first started doing this was that students bring a lot of anxiety and anger and frustration and sense of injustice into the classroom," says a Philosophy instructor. Not only are students of color frustrated and upset about the daily indignities of racism, "there are a lot of angry white students who think they didn't get into Harvard because of affirmative action. The stakes are pretty high for them and they take it very personally."

Sometimes students' emotionally charged views emerge as soon as a race-related issue is introduced by a text or lecture or discussion topic. But more often, the confusion and hurt smolder under a thin veneer of civility. "There is very little honest dialogue around race," observes a white graduate student who grew up in an African-American community. "The political environment is so charged as to make every talk about race seem scripted. There is a great deal of distrust on all sides." "We worry so much about being politically correct that we make ourselves uptight and uncomfortable," adds an African-American sophomore. "Students don't want to offend," says a white faculty member. "They don't understand—as I think many of us don't if we're honest—what those boundaries of offense are."

Given our country's history, it is perhaps only reasonable that such tension still, prevails. "Think about it this way," writes a perceptive white undergraduate. "What we know as 'black' culture started evolving when the European slavers started taking Africans sometime during the sixteenth century. In America the slave trade stopped about 250 years ago. Blacks have been citizens, in the electoral sense of that word, for about 160 years. That citizenship has been forcefully protected and given teeth for about 30 years. Hardly more than a generation. One generation between Bull Connor and the fire hoses and living together in college dorms.[2] When people ask, 'When are we all going to get along and live like color doesn't matter?' I always marvel at how stupid these questions are. We don't even know each other! It's like the first real dance you went to as a kid. Boys on one side, girls on the other. We stand and stare at each other, aware of the fact that we are different, but not knowing exactly how, or what that means. We're scared to go over and talk to each other, for fear of what our own group will say." (Miller, 1998, pp. 12–13).

But other students, particularly students of color, suspect that beneath white students' naive goodwill and their careful, "politically correct" comments lie all manner of racist assumptions and beliefs that they hesitate to voice or even acknowledge. An African-American senior says, "If I am in a class that is comprised of mostly whites I always feel that they try and contain their true feelings for my sake—especially when we are discussing anything that has to do with African Americans." A Puerto Rican student adds, "In the classroom people are more afraid of sounding stupid by telling how they feel about other people of different ethnicities. Thus, they remain quiet most of the time or deviate from the subject or agree with a non-racist view just so they won't look bad." Even when white students are not consciously suppressing racist beliefs and feelings, they often remain silent because they believe they have nothing to contribute to the discussion. Race, to many whites, is an attribute of other people, people of color. And racism is something that people of color experience, regrettably, from ignorant whites—someone in their parents' or grandparents' generation perhaps, or someone in another part of the country without a college education. Since so many white students have grown up in residentially segregated communities,[3] it is not clear to them how they, too, are participants in race relations. They do not see their own views on affirmative action or poverty or educational attainment or health outcomes or police practices or political representation or the distribution of wealth as racist or even racially biased. Even when they are interested in learning about how they and their society have been affected by racism, they believe their role is to listen and try to make sense, internally, of this new view of the world. They may be doing a lot of thinking in their silence, but their thinking is not evident to students of color, who may be angry and even frightened by this apparent stone wall. "At the beginning of this class," writes one of my African-American students, "I could see that I had a certain ire about white people, and I didn't know where it came from. They irritated me because ... while some of the people of color were pouring out our hearts [about experiences with racism] the rest of the class was silent. As a result of this ... I decided not to put my feelings and thoughts out in the air and just did what the others were doing—sitting quietly."

Sometimes, however, the careful treading around an issue is disrupted when an outspoken student voices an opinion and the exchange that follows escalates into a loud, threatening display. A white graduate student instructor describes what happened in her first year of teaching a sophomore-level class in Philosophy where most of her students were white:

On this particular day we were talking about affirmative action, and someone took the position that colleges that were primarily African American—Morehouse, for example—were totally racist. That was the start of it. Then someone else said, "What about those black fraternities on our own campus? It's ridiculous that they should be allowed." And that pushed a lot of buttons for people. One of the two black students said, "Well I'm in a black fraternity, and I'll tell you why!" And a white student jumped up and yelled, "Well, I think you're a racist for joining one!"

We were in one of those small basement classrooms with the little windows up by the ceiling, and it was very hot and tense. And these were two very large, loud men. I think they were standing on chairs at this point. I was thinking, "Oh, God, what am I going to do?" The whole class was getting into it, egging them on. I kept trying to say, "Look everybody, be quiet, hold on," but my voice was really weak and scared sounding. Finally they stopped shouting and sort of looked at me. It was just luck that it was close to the end of the class, so I was able to say, "OK, here's where we've come in the discussion so far. You've raised some points on this side and some points on that side. Here are some of the questions you still have to think about and now we're all going to go home and next time we'll continue." So then in the next class before we did anything else I gave this big lecture on respect. No yelling, no name calling, no making fun of people, no rolling your eyes or reading the paper while other people are talking. But in addition to personal respect, you also have to respect other people's positions. You can't just dismiss their arguments; you have to listen to what they say. So after that, things were much calmer. It must have been a sort of catharsis. I was wondering what students would say on the course evaluations at the end of the semester. But it was really weird; they didn't even mention this altercation. They just said, "We really got to debate the issues; it was a really heated debate. It was great."

Although this instructor remained uncomfortable with emotional outbursts and tried successfully in later years to manage her classes in ways that would avoid them, some faculty welcome opportunities to get down deep, to "the real divisions between us." Sandra,[4] a white English professor, says:

I've been teaching for twenty-nine years, and in just about every class I've had, there's been a confrontation. I know that's probably my teaching style. I encourage it. Let me give you an example. Recently I had a kid in an Introductory Composition class who was a classic small town, God-fearing conservative, and he had written a really racist paper. I don't remember what the unifying idea was supposed to be; each paragraph was about a different thing. But in every one of them this kid, Jarret was his name, managed to say something racist. Things like, "Don't get me wrong, I don't have anything against black people personally, but you know, they're lazy, they're stupid, and if they really wanted to make it in the world they'd get off their butt." Well, he didn't say 'butt,' but that was the gist of it.

There were two black students in that class with very different personalities and different class backgrounds: Tyrone, an angry kid from inner city Detroit, and Denise, a middle class sorority girl whose interests ran to getting the right diet, how to keep your abs flat, how to know if you've got the right man, that kind of stuff. She was into being raceless, if you know what I mean. For most of the semester she appeared as if she didn't notice she was black. She had really adopted that persona. So when Jarret read his paper to the class, Denise tried to deal with it by deflecting the discussion to correctness issues. She was clearly using it as a strategy to defuse the tension: "Oh, I have a comment" (you know, trying to break in). "On page three, on the third line, you need a comma."

But Tyrone wasn't having any of it. He was standing up, ready to fight! Or rather, he *looked* like he was ready to fight. You know, I think it makes white instructors uneasy when they have that kind of explosiveness from a student who has grown up in inner city black culture. They don't understand that even though someone like Tyrone might use a threatening tone of voice or even jump up out of his chair, he isn't ready to physically fight; he is ready to *contend*.[5] And to try to make him calm down or to suddenly intercede—or more than intercede, intervene: "Now we're going to go around the table and take first Jarret, then Denise, then Tyrone"—that would have been like a slap in the face to this person. For me to do that would be to completely shut him down.

So when something like that happens, I jump right in. I don't try to be neutral or play the moderator, especially in the first confrontation of the semester. I'm real clear about my own politics. I say something like, "Tyrone's right! That *is* a racist statement!" But at the same time, I want to know what Jarret has to say about this. I want to know what he was thinking when he wrote this. But what I don't do is tell Tyrone that we're taking turns. Instead, when I see that other people want to speak (and I know they want to speak because they're shouting) it's, "OK! Jarret! Jarret has something to say!" I just shout over all the uproar. I want be sure that everyone who wants to can get into the discussion. When it's just two people arguing, the class gets real uncomfortable. So I throw my two cents in, kind of simultaneously, and that gets people hopping. And sometimes, when we'd leave the class, we'd all still be talking, taking it out in to the hall.

While Sandra is clearly comfortable with this style of open confrontation, other instructors are frightened by the prospect of a class out of control. A white professor who teaches a graduate course on Health Politics says:

I'm very worried about what I might stir up. If I stirred up things that I was unable to handle and made deep problems in people's lives, I would think I was responsible. But also, I'm hesitant about making some special deal in class about people's race, that they would have a perspective on life that would come out of the fact that they're white or black or Latino ... I think there are other aspects of who we are that may be more critical than our gender or our race. On the other hand, white people do have the privilege of not having to think about their race. It's a huge privilege! We never have to assume that someone's treating us in a special way because of our race. It's out of our ken. We "have no race" because we're the majority. And occasionally I get a little glimpse about what that might be like, but most of the time, I don't know, I think about my inability to talk about race with any kind of authority.

Despite fears of losing authority or control, some instructors who are initially hesitant plunge in anyway and discover that the openness and depth of the emotional exchange have benefits that far outweigh the anxiety they may continue to feel throughout the semester. June, a white instructor of English Composition and Literature, was dissatisfied with "all these little polite arguments" that went on in her classrooms:

> I was disappointed in how I had been teaching. It was a personal challenge for me to try to get some real conversations going. I had my chance when I found myself with an Advanced Argumentative Writing class with a lot of strong personalities—about ten students out of twenty-five who were comfortable with open conflict and didn't think much about it.
>
> There were three black students in that class, which doesn't sound like many, but it was a first for me. I had taught composition for years at Michigan and almost never had an African American student in my classroom. One of these students was a real big man in the Black Student Union on campus. On the surface, he was very political—he wore his hair in an Afro and always came dressed in a dashiki and beads—but underneath, he was unsure of his opinions and seemed afraid of offending anybody. Then there was this other black guy, a fraternity type, who wasn't going to have anything to do with the Black Student Union. He had this gorgeous girlfriend who used to walk him to class—a black girl, always dressed to the nines. The rest of the students were white. Scrubbed-looking. Some of them were athletes; others were headed for business or law school. About half of them were Jewish, and after a while they all began sitting next to each other, so this created a pretty strong dynamic. Then there were three young white women who came from small Michigan towns. They were scholarship students from blue collar backgrounds and they were working umpteen hours a week as well as going to school.
>
> And then there was Gloria. The first day, when she walked into the classroom, I couldn't figure out her race. It's hard to explain the color of her skin. It was like she was black but her skin was light. And for her, that was a big issue. She said that people used to tell her all the time, "Oh what pretty hair you have, what beautiful skin you have." And that made her really angry, because the reason she looked like that had to do with a tragedy in her grandmother's past. And this had caused the whole family a lot of pain, which was made worse by all the attention Gloria got for being pretty. So most of the time she was into looking severe, somewhere in between an intellectual and a nerd. After the semester ended, we used to sit outside and eat lunch together sometimes, and she would tell me about her life. Every story she told me had to do with her past and with other people's perceptions of her.
>
> Her family was very poor—I don't even know if you could say they were working class. She had been a scholarship student at a prestigious private high school and one of only two African Americans there. She hated that school, even though she was grateful for the doors it opened up for her. She once said something that really stuck with me: "Do you believe that I was friends with this black girl only because we had the same color skin? I didn't even like her! And I don't think she liked me. Have you ever been friends with someone just because they had white skin like yours?" She was real smart and extremely articulate, but she was unhappy with her college experience because she felt that professors set up their classes so that nobody ever got to say what

they really thought. And that was making her crazy. Her grandmother had always told her, "You gotta get along with white people. You gotta pay attention to what they want." But she had never had that kind of temperament, even as a child. And so by the time she got to my class, she was boiling. The first day, oh man, I knew it was going to be a nightmare.

I had set up a little get-to-know-you activity. Everybody was supposed to say something about themselves that would help other students remember who they were. Students were saying things like, "Well, I went to Israel this summer for three weeks." Or, "I'm going out for water polo." And all this time, Gloria was lying way back in her chair with her feet spread out, just staring at everybody. People were beginning to notice her even before she spoke because she looked so disgusted. And when it was her turn, she said—in a kind of husky drawl—"Well, my name is Malcolm. And you'll find out why soon enough." There was dead silence. It was the first serious thing that anyone had said. Nobody asked her any questions, the way they had the others. And at the end of class, she just got up and strolled out the door. Her body language was so exclusive, so dismissive of everybody. I knew she was dismissing me, too.

Every day after that she came into class ready to pounce. The first time I let them choose partners to share their papers with, she chose the black student leader. And immediately, she started ripping his paper to shreds. "You're trying to suck up to whites here? What's your deal here? Are you a white lover?" She would never whisper; everything was public. The poor guy was speechless, he was so into not rocking the boat. When he finally replied, he tried to couch everything so politely: "Well, have you thought about such and such?" And she wasn't having any of it. Oh, he was mortified by her. He thought she would ruin everything for him.

One day, one of the Jewish girls, Tanya, brought in a personal experience piece that she wanted to read aloud for the whole class to critique. It was a typical freshman essay about how adversity can make you stronger. She had been in a car accident that had resulted in some scars on her face, so she'd had a number of plastic surgeries to repair the damage. Looking at her there was no way you would know that she'd ever had any kind of disfigurement. She was a beautiful girl, flawless skin, dark eyes, perfectly formed features. Nevertheless, she had been really shaken up by the possibility that she could lose her good looks so easily. She was on the verge of tears as she read it aloud, because this was the worst thing that had ever happened to her. And most of us were trying to take her seriously, even though it was kind of hard because she was so pretty.

But Gloria was incensed. And when Tanya was finished, she launched into a diatribe: "How could you possibly take yourself so seriously? How could you waste the time, not only of me, not just of black people, but do you think that everybody in this class has had a life like yours, that they could have six plastic surgeries? You need a reality check, girl!" I mean, Gloria was on the verge of tears too. Her cousin had just died in a gang fight. Another family member had been raped as she was leaving work on the night shift at a downtown hospital. All this was happening thirty miles away in Detroit while kids on campus were consumed with football games and frat parties and water polo.

So that was the flash point. Right then, two of Tanya's friends started screaming at Gloria, "You've been judging us all semester! You don't bother to figure out what anybody else thinks! What do you know about how Tanya feels? Is it her fault that her Dad has money, that her Dad could pay for this? Is that her fault?" And Gloria said, "I know all about you kind of people. I've been around people like you all my life. I'm sure I understand."

And then, the interesting thing was that the black fraternity guy who came to class dressed to kill, who never wanted to say anything controversial and certainly had never wanted anything to do with Gloria, all of a sudden came out on Gloria's side. "Well, you'll have to admit this is kind of superficial," he said. "I mean, can't you see that this is kind of insulting to some of the others in this class? Couldn't you have put this in perspective before you put this in our face?"

So now it wasn't just Gloria shaking things up anymore; the whole mode of communication kind of shifted, and everyone got into it, even the ones who had started out so polite. So for the rest of the semester, there was a lot of shouting. A *lot* of shouting! People would come down the hall and open the door to see what was going on. And even though my stomach was in knots, I have to admit, I felt exhilarated. "This must be right," I thought. "People are really looking at each other and talking to each other and arguing about what somebody's writing. That's engagement!" But on the other hand, my whole white Southern upbringing was that you don't have confrontations! I had tried to play it that way at first. But when I started doing my usual thing of, "Okay, now, just a second," there was this dead silence. And people were looking at me and trying to raise their hands for me to recognize them. And I thought, "I'm just going to die if I sit through the semester with people looking at me to raise their hand!" I really was scared of shutting it all down.

I had one student who was so courtly—if you can use that word for a kid of nineteen or twenty. He had been taught to be low key no matter what, and he was really determined to stick to his upbringing. In the middle of the semester he came in to my office and told me how frustrated he was because he had things he wanted to say but he couldn't, because everyone was shouting. So I said, "Well, do you want me to say, 'Charles wants to say something now?'" Well, no, he said, because that would be embarrassing. So I said, "What can I tell you then? You don't want me to intercede." And so even he stopped trying to raise his hand and got in there with the rest of them. Sometimes things would get so heated, people would be jumping up out of their chairs to make a point. So then I would try to calm things down by rephrasing what they were saying so they'd see me as a kind of moderator: "Oh, so you think such and such." But the first time I did that, Gloria looked at me and said, "What is *that*!? You mean you think we didn't hear what she said?! Get outta here, talking trash like that!" And then the students who were arguing with her would say, "Yeah, Gloria's right!" It was wild.

One of the reasons I let it go on at such an emotional pitch was that I was so fascinated by what they were saying. Even though I've taught about issues of race and class for years, I think I'll never get through working on these issues in myself. For one thing, I don't think I have ever fully understood the extent to which white people are held responsible by black people for history. That was a big issue in this class. The white students had been pretty isolated, either in prep schools or small towns, and hadn't had much contact with black kids. They knew about black people being angry at white people but they didn't quite understand why. They would say things like, "It's not my fault that black people were slaves. My ancestors didn't even come over here until World War Two."

One of Gloria's big deals—she had a huge screaming fit one day—was about how groups that have been targeted in the past can have so little understanding of how oppressed groups feel today. "You're Jewish and you don't think it's okay to hold people responsible for what happened in the past?" she yelled at them. "Don't you have someone who was killed in the Holocaust? Don't you think that people should know what happened to you and take some responsibility for seeing that it never happens again?" And they were just blown away! I think they had never really made that connection, even though several of them had been in Israel and Europe the summer before and had toured the concentration camps. They just sort of said, "Oh," and sat there, thinking.

It was even harder for some of the working class kids to make these connections. One girl talked extensively about this, how she didn't accept being held accountable because her ancestors had never had any position of authority so they couldn't have done anything to anybody. "I'm not rich," she said. "I don't know anybody who's rich. I don't know anybody with any kind of power. What do you want me to do?" And Gloria said, "I want you to go to a movie with a black guy if he asks you—and be happy about it." And the girl said, "Wow, I don't even know a black guy at this university!" And Gloria says, "That's my point!" You know, it was so fascinating to watch them and take in what they were saying and see the ways they were looking at each other. I just couldn't bring myself to manipulate their discussion, to play chess pieces and "facilitate."

Of course it wasn't total anarchy. They would listen to me. They would move from small groups into the large group and back again when I asked them to—slowly sometimes, still arguing, but they would get there. They certainly wrote some superior papers. I had given them complete freedom to write arguments on whatever topics they wanted, and many of them chose to write about their lives, what had affected them, and what they thought about things. And because of the openness, some of the kids who had been really isolated got to find out what people from other groups really thought of them and their values. Like Robert, the guy who was in the black student association, he said he had never been around whites until he came to the university. And actually he became quite good friends with a white guy in the class, and they often chose to be partners to give each other feedback on their writing. Robert had written a paper about interracial dating and how he would never go out with a girl who wasn't black. And I think this was the first time he ever really knew what a white person thought about his ideas, or that anyone would say that it was racist to think he'd only have a black girlfriend. He had to examine these ideas that he'd absorbed from his friends at the Black Student Union and to defend these arguments for the first time. But all these topics were relatively tame. Sometimes, the discussion got into issues that are really taboo, at least among white people. Like some of the conspiracy theories—all the Jews in Hollywood who are trying to keep black people out of the entertainment business, that kind of thing. And I can tell you it was a revelation to the Jewish students that all three of the black students—who were so different from each other—all three of them believed that Jewish people were trying to shut them down. Maybe if it had just been Gloria who had said that, they wouldn't have paid so much attention. But that was something brand new to them, that black people in general felt there were ethnic groups who were actively trying to keep them back.

Occasionally I did feel I had to intervene when someone said something beyond the pale, but I never did it in front of the class. Stacy, one of the white girls who came from a working class family, said something so inappropriate one day that I asked her to come talk to me about it in my office. She must have been fed up with Gloria's constant putdowns and dismissal of everyone's arguments, and in fact, she was right to call her on it, but the way she phrased it was really racist. She said, "I used to think my grandparents were bigots because of the way they talked about blacks, but you, Gloria, you're just exactly the way black people are!" So I called Stacy in for a chat and I asked her, "Why don't you tell me more of your ideas about black people and where you think those ideas came from?"

So Stacy started telling me about growing up in a tiny town in Michigan where the residents were proud of the fact that there were no black people for miles around. Black people knew better than to even drive through that town, she said, because they knew it would be dangerous for them. Since the town was too small to have a high school, she had been sent to a consolidated school district where teachers taught the students to treat everyone as equals and not be racist. But this was still kind of hypothetical because the school was uniformly white.

Every Sunday after church Stacy's family would go to her grandma's house for dinner, and her grandma, who always wanted to tell them what to think about everything, would go on about how blacks are dumb and lazy, and how they're poor because that's the kind of people they are, and that you should never feel sorry for them because everybody makes their own life. Stacy didn't really question this until she was a high school senior, when she had to start looking for scholarships because her family didn't have enough money to send her to college. That's when she started thinking, "If we make our own lives, why don't we have enough for me to go to college? Other people have money to go to college, what's the matter with my parents? What's the matter with my father?" But at the same time she still blamed blacks for causing all the trouble, and the contradiction—which she still wasn't seeing very clearly—continued to be confusing for her. "This is one of the things I hate about college," she told me. "It's making me love my family less than I used to. Especially my grandparents." So I said, "You might consider writing a paper about that." And she said, "No, no! That would be like I was blaming my poor grandmother, and she can't help it, she's of another generation. I don't want anybody criticizing my grandparents!"

I think Stacy also wondered why I had called her in to my office for her racist remarks while I never intervened when Gloria was on her verbal rampages—which were probably on and off racist. I didn't really feel guilty about it, but I had to think why that would be okay—when on the other hand it wouldn't be okay—to treat them differently. And what I finally told Stacy was that people like Gloria, people who were minorities, people who had been marginalized in our culture, had been silenced all their lives. And that white people—regardless of their class background—had never been silenced. I said that while it was important to be truthful in class and say what she really thought, repeating those derogatory stereotypes about blacks seemed like ganging up on them when there were only three blacks in the class and twenty-one whites. I said it seemed kind of thuggy. She was kind of taken aback at that because she was a really nice girl. She didn't want to be thuggy. So we left it at that. She wasn't resentful. But then she wrote a few really shallow essays before she was able to get to the heart of the internal conflict she was having.

Near the end of the semester Stacy announced with great emotion that she had a paper she wanted to read to the whole class. She had turned her conflict with her grandmother into a philosophical issue about how to decide what is good and what is evil, using her grandmother as an example of how complicated that notion is. Her conclusion was that it's tempting to blame someone like her grandmother and to call her a bigot, but that's an easy way out. It's a dangerous thing to simplify, or to quantify, abstract notions like good and evil; the best you can do is to always be challenging your ideas any time you are tempted to put a label on them. At the end, I bet there were a dozen people who were crying. And Gloria was just transfixed. In fact, I think that was the first time that Gloria had ever paid attention to anything anybody wrote. She usually went, "Mm hm. Yeah." You know, "You're boring. This subject is boring." She was so good at communicating that! So after Stacy finished she looked directly at Gloria and said, "Are you going to say something?" And Gloria said, "I really appreciate your honesty. I don't like your grandma. I think your grandma's a bigot. That's her problem. But I really like you. I appreciate your honesty and your courage." That did it; Stacy started crying along with the rest of us.

What was so thrilling to me about that class was the depth, the honesty, and the real thinking that was going on. Their arguments weren't just random shouting or name calling. They were arguing about perspective: about what's important in life, what's worthy to be thought about, worthy to be written about. And the interesting thing was all these different perspectives that people were coming from were grounded in race and class. And you could see the allegiances shifting as the semester went on. The working class white students started saying they had more in common with people like Gloria than with the affluent students, and how their views on race might have something to do with the way they themselves are stigmatized. They all started thinking about how class had shaped their way of looking at the world and who they were. And for these nineteen and twenty year olds, it was a revelation! All of a sudden, they were saying, "Oh my God, you mean everything I think is important comes from what class I am and what color I am?" Of course, people like Gloria understand that pretty early on, which was why she was so frustrated and lashed out so much in class.

On the last day of the semester I decided to let each of them make a closing statement. I told them they could each say anything they wanted, and no one could ask questions or comment on it, just like in a law court. And in her closing statement, Gloria said, "One of the reasons I've been so hard to live with is that I had to learn years ago what it seems like you're just thinking about now. And it makes me mad that I didn't get to be a little girl as long as you did." That was important for her to say, and important for other people to hear.

And then, one of the really quiet working class students—she came from a single parent home in a small town and her mother was a waitress, so she was having a pretty hard time with all this stuff; she was having a pretty hard time in general, scraping pennies together—she started out crying, and by time she had gotten midway into her closing statement, a whole bunch of us were trying not to cry. She said she was glad she was in the class even though she hadn't said much—because she doesn't like people to know what she thinks about things. And then she turned to Gloria and said, "But Gloria, people like you don't understand what it's like to be white and poor. Everything in the world makes you feel like you're not as good as other white people. It makes you feel so low. You think you are the only one with problems just because you're black." And then, turning to Tanya, she said, "People like you make me mad too, because you think nobody in the world has problems and that it's nothing to go out and buy a party dress for a hundred dollars." And everyone, including Gloria, was moved that she had finally said something and that her statement was so truthful and open, and Gloria even called her up after class because she wanted to ask her some questions, and they went out for pizza together—maybe only that one time, but it was interesting that they took it upon themselves to continue that conversation.

Several years later, Tanya—the one who had got so much criticism about her plastic surgeries—called me up to say goodbye before she graduated. She wanted to tell me that that English class had been the best class she had ever taken at the university, despite the fact that it had also been the most difficult. She said it was the only class she'd had where people could say what they really meant. It was the only class where people had really begun to listen to each other.

*  *  *  *  *

Classrooms like these stir up many of our hopes and fears about real dialogue, deep reflection, and critical thinking about race and class. If only all students could come this far and be so moved by their new understandings of each other. If only all students were willing to risk saying what is on their minds. But on the other hand, what if the students had not come together at the end? What if the students of color had become even more hurt and embittered in the process? What if the white students had gone away with their prejudices even more deeply entrenched than before?

Instructors who choose to let students confront each other so freely and honestly need to feel a deep conviction that "getting real" is the only way that healing can begin. It doesn't matter what the assignments are, or what subject matter is involved, or whether the instructor decides to stay in the background or jump into the conversation. As long as the instructor believes, deeply, "This must be right!" her conviction will be felt by everyone in the room—even when, as Michael Eric Dyson says, the "animal of race" breaks out of its artificial cage and runs unfettered and free.

# Notes

1. The University of Michigan's Program on Intergroup Relations (IGR) is a social justice education program on the Ann Arbor campus jointly sponsored by the College of Literature, Science and the Arts and the Division of Student Affairs. www.igr.umich.edu
2. While the history of black and white relations is the most well known, we might also add that it has been only 165 years since the United States took over half of Mexico, 125 years since the final suppression of the Plains of Indian tribes by the U.S. army, 115 years since the forcible annexation of Hawaii and Puerto Rico, and only 60 years since Asian immigrants were finally allowed to become U.S. citizens.
3. About 92% of white Michigan undergraduates grew up in neighborhoods that were predominantly white, and 83% went to predominantly white high schools (Michigan Student Study, 1994).
4. Names of instructors and students in Chapters 4 and 5 are pseudonyms.
5. See Kochman (1981): "Whites consider 'fighting' to have begun when violence is imminent, that is, before violence has actually occurred. ... [Signs include] the intensity of the anger that is shown and the presence of insults. ... Significantly, while blacks consider ... these signs relevant in setting the stage for fighting to occur, they do not consider them sufficient to conclude that a fight has actually begun. This is because for blacks, the boundary between words and actions is clearly marked. ... Fighting does not begin until someone actually makes a provocative *movement*" (pp. 45–66).

# · 5 ·

# HAVING A "CIVIL CONVERSATION"

Passionate confrontation can be a powerful learning experience when the instructor feels that conflict around racial issues is normal and ultimately productive, and that emotion is not a fearful thing, but a force, an energy, for cutting through falsehoods and fears. But confrontation is not for everyone, nor is it the only way instructors can help students move toward a greater understanding of each other. A Social Science professor with white, Native American, and African-American ancestry says:

> I truly believe in people being civil to each other in the classroom. I think that if someone is domineering or disruptive, that has negative emotional fallout for all of us, myself included. And that is very hard to overcome; it will affect the dynamics of the class. So I differ from some of my longtime colleagues in this kind of work in that I do not think that a disruptive conflict is necessary in order to have the class go forward. I want to maintain civility in the classroom, even at a possible cost—and I want to stress *possible*—that people will not speak their minds fully. I'm not convinced that speaking one's mind totally fully contributes positively to creating a dialogue. I've had students say remarkable things in the classroom when they became trusting enough to say those things. And I think that can only happen when the class has a history of being able to talk together, even if it's very tentative.

A white instructor of Introductory Composition agrees. "We tend to think that the highly charged moments are the most significant," says Andrea,

> but it's sometimes just the opposite. Students aren't always ready for direct confrontation or even much overt personal discussion of race, especially in their first year. Even though I think students sometimes shy away from conversations about race in unproductive ways, I don't blame them sometimes; first year students have so much on their plate. They're away from home for the first time, dealing with the demands of college level course work, all the while trying to make friends, trying to fit in somewhere. Once I had an African American student who told me, "You know, there's something really nice about not having to go outside your comfort zone." And that made me think, yes, students really need the privacy of their own thoughts sometimes, and a feeling of safety in how we talk about things together.

Andrea tries to model a level of comfort around racial issues that convinces her students that talking about race is a perfectly normal and reasonable thing to do:

> I might refer to myself as a white woman, just in passing. That simple act says something very powerful to students. It's like, "Look, I can call myself a white woman in class! Did anybody melt?! Did anybody die? No!" And from there, I can move right on to something neutral, like how to use specific examples in an essay. You know, I've never had a student say about one of my classes, "That class is too political, too heavy-handed." And my class is *very* political. But I think there are ways to enact the politics in the classroom that are as effective as talking in political terms. And that can be done in moments that are not highly charged.
>
> My experience has been that students respond to each other in just the right ways a good deal of the time. However, if someone says something offensive, or that could be interpreted as offensive, I go back to it and try to frame it in a way that doesn't impute any bad intentions on the person who said it. I've never had anyone in my class who was downright mean or mean spirited. But people come out with things sometimes without being aware of how they sound to others. White students might talk about "they" or "those people" when referring to African Americans, for example. They don't say that to intentionally exclude anyone. But to many people of color, those words can sting. It's yet another way of placing whites at the center and everyone else outside the circle of importance or power—or even outside of what's considered normal. But usually I wouldn't go into all that. I might just say—in a perfectly ordinary tone of voice—"It's more inclusive to say 'African Americans' instead of 'them,'" and leave it at that. Or if a white student uses a catch phrase like "unqualified minorities" when talking about affirmative action, I might rephrase it, putting a somewhat different slant on it. I might talk about people with lower test scores but who were top students in their high schools, for example, which is in fact more accurate, and doesn't reinforce the idea that minority students are somehow unqualified. I try not to put words into their mouths, but I do want to give them

ways to talk to each other that are a bit more sensitive and that get them thinking about the generalizations they're making. It's really important not to just let a racially insensitive comment go by. But I'm not going to lecture them about it; I just mention it and move on. And if there's a way of bringing the comment or the issue into the subject we're talking about, so much the better.

Andrea's light touch, her way of assuming the best of every student, her sense of balance between defusing emotional tension and dealing directly with issues as they arise seem to come from a conscious decision about how best to approach issues of race with her first year students. Other faculty say that their preference for a low-key style stems more from their family or cultural background than from a deliberate decision to avoid confrontation. These instructors are just as dedicated to bringing multicultural perspectives into the classroom and may even assign angry and provocative texts by authors of color. But when discussion gets heated, they find themselves "putting on the brakes" because they were trained as children to be conciliatory and now are "just that way." Scott, a white instructor of Literature and Composition, reflects on how his "genteel" upbringing has molded his teaching style:

> The classroom is who you are, and I'm pretty darn congenial. I have manners, and I think that my students take some of that from me. My mother was a sort of socialite. We "entertained." We lived in a suburb of Buffalo, and it had its own little symphony. When they played, we would have the orchestra members over to our house, and I would be the one to take their coats upstairs to the bedroom. The conductor used to give me a quarter to take his coat. I think we aspired to things like garden parties. I had my picture in the paper when I was in kindergarten wearing a little smock that someone had made. And so I have grown up with certain social graces deeply embedded in me—the idea that if there's no conversation, you say something light and entertaining so that conversation will begin. And I notice that I do that in my classroom. When the Jewish kids from the East get together with the black kids from Detroit and they're angry or outspoken, the kind of manners I have been taught and the kind of rules of conduct that I implicitly model keep some of that down. So I'm not going to have blow-ups to any major degree.
>
> I think I approach everything indirectly, whether it is a story or a poem or any other issue. I don't know if I'd want to talk about race any differently. I'm averse to putting race or racism right on the table as the piece of meat you're going to carve. It seems too blatant, too direct of an approach. I know other instructors who just put it on the table, and I'd be happy to be a student in their classroom. I'd be a good participant. But to lead a class that way, I couldn't do it. So I can't say that I've had students arguing much about race in my class, even though it's brought up in the readings quite often. In my Composition classes I have a series of assignments that implicitly invite students to write about race, culture, and community. I have one assignment that comes from a reading by Michelle Cliff that asks them to "write something about

fire."[1] Cliff uses it as a metaphor—fire is something you have a strong feeling about. But if you think about it, fire could be other things, like a change from one energy state to another. So they might also write about change, or crossing borders. A student from the inner city might write, for example, "It's when I cross the borderlands between Detroit and the suburbs that I realize the impoverishment of my own neighborhood." They're not explicitly writing about race, but they do.

I have another assignment called "Who is your mother?" It comes from a piece by Paula Gunn Allen [1988] that identifies Native American tradition as a forerunner of modern white feminist activism and principles. And Gunn Allen is calling that "a mother." So the paper is modeled on that and asks students to inquire into who their "mother" is. And I say, "Well, you can write about your mom. That's actually one way of doing this. But also, you might think about the other forming agents in your life." So students will begin to write, not really knowing what they're writing about. And this is my trickery, because it gets students to uncover another layer. They might start out by saying, "My mother is my community." So then in group discussion of that idea we ask, "Well, what is it about your community that formed you?" And then race might come up—or it might not. The student might not be ready for it, either as an individual or as a writer. So that's what I mean by indirection: if race comes up, OK, and if it doesn't, I'll let it go. I really believe that students learn when they are ready. So I'll try to create an environment that will help them be ready. And if they grasp that opportunity then they do, and if they don't, then they don't. I realize that's very trusting and somewhat naive—the idea that if they don't get it in my class, they'll get it somewhere else. But that's the way I learned, myself. The environment may be ripe in one place, and so that is where you grow. And if you aren't ready to grow just yet, it might happen later.

Scott is also aware that his preference for indirection and low-key discussion is somehow connected with his general discomfort with the subject of race that so many instructors share:

I'm very race conscious. I notice black people, I notice Latino people, I notice Native Americans. Somewhere I'm sifting through a variety of stereotypes and contexts. I acknowledge that this is working on me in hidden ways, ways that would make me uncomfortable to think about and that I'm allowing to stay under the surface. I know this has an effect on me, and I know my students are affected by it as well. And I think, yeah, this undercurrent of race needs to be brought more to the surface in the classroom. But you only bring to your students that which you're prepared to deliver. So when someone brings the subject up I might just sit quietly, not trying hard enough to move the discussion forward. That communicates to my students, "It's okay not to talk about this."

I'm sure there's some denial on my part, and some self consciousness about being white. Maybe it is because I'm unsure of who I am even at the age of forty-three. And I'm a person who would say I know myself pretty well. But there are hidden pockets, and race is one of them for me, that are still somewhat mystified. I don't want to dig into them too deeply. But I do question myself, and this is what I've come up with. When I was a kid I used to drive into the inner city. I wrote about that once, "Time to time I drive in the ghetto" was the title of it. It was the sixties and there were riots, and the black area of Buffalo was like an open wound. A lot of attention was being paid to it by the media and I was very curious about it. I had just got my driver's license. I think I still feel like that, in the classroom when I bring up the subject of race, I'm a white guy still driving through someone else's town, someone else's neighborhood. I feel a little self-conscious. So then I think, "Maybe I'm bringing this up because I have this burden that I need to let go of and this is my way of doing it." And I don't know if I should be doing that. Maybe by bringing it up I'm stirring the soup when it should just be simmering. But on the other hand I think it's really important to have these conversations.

Scott is aware of his contradictions: that he can be more honest than most about race even while he allows his deepest feelings to remain inaccessible to him; that he excites racial tensions through the readings he chooses but pulls back from addressing race directly in discussion; and that his indirect style tends to "get him off the hook" sometimes, while at the same time, it is also an important and valid expression of his teaching philosophy. But he is willing to live with that. Race relations in this country *are* contradictory, he says, so being perfectly clear and up-front about one's feelings and politics may leave some of the deepest and most interesting complexities unaddressed.

Even more than open discussion, Scott says, whites and people of color need to get to know each other better as human beings, and this has to happen naturally, outside the classroom. "Maybe that's why I still drive into the ghetto sometimes," he tells me with a smile. "That's fun. And it's scary. Go to a big inner city park on a Sunday and it's packed with black people having a good time and you will be among the few white people there and you'll also be from out of town. Last weekend I was in Detroit and I said to myself, 'Let's try this, let's go.' I wasn't invited. And I didn't stay. I wouldn't have stopped to picnic. But still, I don't know. I think we need more interactions."

\* \* \* \* \* \*

Personal style, upbringing, ease or discomfort when dealing with race all affect the ways instructors approach classroom discussions. But in addition, the academic discipline itself may privilege a style of inquiry that directs the conversation away from the personal and emotional and more toward a kind of detached intellectualism. Two white Philosophy instructors talk about this style and how they modify it for discussions of racially charged issues in their classrooms.

"The accepted pedagogical style in Philosophy is that it doesn't matter who you are or what your personal feelings are on the subject," says Connie:

> What matters is your reasons. If your reasons are good, you win, and that's the end of it. That style is of course a very impersonal way of relating to the issues. There's a place for that, but with the subject of race, students come into the class with a lot of emotions, and if they can't give voice to them they just get frustrated. Many of our white students are very disturbed about the way the cafeteria is segregated, for example; this is something that they mention all the time. "Why don't people sit together?" they say. "That's ridiculous!" They are intimating, of course, that it's the students of color who are self-segregating, rather than themselves.[2] But the fact that they want to voice their frustrations about situations they've witnessed can be used very productively. The best discussions I've had around these issues are those in which students have been able to say what's on their minds.

Emma describes how she structures her class so that students learn to argue in the manner of philosophers while still having a chance to talk about their experiences and express their feelings:

> One of the things I try to get students to understand right away is that in Philosophy it's very difficult to come to a final conclusion about anything. The challenge is to evaluate the strengths of our own views, because every view has its strengths and weaknesses. And that's hard for students who have strong feelings on a subject. So what I do is try to help them articulate their point of view and their reasons for believing it, and then push them to figure out how they're going to respond to the objections to that point of view.
>
> I use the board a lot. Everything anyone says goes up on the board. Usually a problem will emerge from the lecture I give at the beginning of class. So I ask for their opinions: what do they think about this issue? And here is where I encourage them to talk about personal experiences because it's often what's happened to you personally that affects your opinions about moral issues like race. Usually there are a few students who start the discussion off because they're pretty sure they have "the answer." But I try to make sure that no answer is the obvious answer. As students offer their opinions, I put the arguments in favor on one side on the board and the arguments against on the other—I sometimes draw little stick figures. Or I'll end up drawing a kind of map of where one might stand on an issue and let students' ideas and opinions occupy different places on the map. Then I'll challenge them: "How would you answer this position over on the other side of the board?" And in order to answer, they have to really listen to that position, and understand what it means. One of the things about moderating discussions in Philosophy classes is that you can play the role of devil's advocate. When the consensus seems to be moving in one direction, I try to move it in the other direction to get them to see the other side.

Connie says, "Although I come at this work from a framework of justice and anti-oppression, the goal is not to convince everybody that a particular point of view is correct":

I think it's important not to make the more conservative students feel like they shouldn't have said what they said, or that the experience they described doesn't count here. But then I might give some historical context that I felt was lacking, or refer to readings that go beyond those ideas and assumptions. My class is designed to look at many different points of view on an issue, so there are always many opinions I disagree with. But my job is to present the different sides and give students the opportunities to criticize each position.

Of course some students learn to critique their own arguments better than others. The ones who can't or don't want to explore the opposition do poorly in the class, because their grades are determined by the papers they write, and these papers must deal very carefully and specifically with the objections to their arguments. So when a student brings a draft to my office I immediately start playing the devil's advocate. I keep pushing them to think about one objection after another until finally they are questioning the nature of truth. At that point of course they're pretty frustrated. They say, "How can I write this paper? How can I say anything, if everything can be questioned?" And then I say, "No, that's good! This shows you're really thinking!" Once they've got that frustration, once they say, "Wow! There are so many things to consider!" then they're really seeing the complexity of the subject.

One of the tricky things about arguing philosophically about issues of race is that the dynamics of the group are really affected by the backgrounds and personalities of the students. My classes are about 90% white, sometimes more, and that means that there is a very small group of people of color, not all of whom agree with each other, of course. Some of these students are right up front; they call the others on their assumptions and challenge the facts that they're presenting. In that case, I can sort of step back a little bit and just try to manage the discussion. But more often than not there are students of color who don't say much and you can tell that they're not feeling very good about the kinds of arguments that some of the white students are making. But this can be tricky because students sometimes give an argument that seems purely factual, but underneath, they are insinuating something else—sometimes quite consciously, as a matter of fact.

Say if a white student argues, "Well, where I went to high school, only five people got into Ivy League colleges and none of them were white, and I got much better grades than any of them," they're not just reporting a personal story, they're purporting to show that students who are getting in on affirmative action programs are clearly not as smart as they are. To many students of color or any recipient of an affirmative action program, that doesn't feel good. Actually, in Philosophy graduate programs, women of *any* color are there because of affirmative action, so I know from personal experience how this feels. It's awful to hear that. Even when no one actually comes out and says, "Look, I know you don't have a mind, but I'm sure you can't help it," you sort of understand that's what's being implied. And it's hard for me as an instructor to know what to do with that kind of argument when it comes up in class. You don't want to deny students the opportunity to speak from their experience, but on the other hand, when you know how implications of that experience can alienate other people, it's hard to know how to respond to that. It's something I still struggle with.

"Strong emotions do surface sometimes," says Emma, "but not always from the students who are targets of racism or sexism":

In one of my classes a white male student was being very rude and interrupting people. He was angry and frustrated because he'd had enough of feeling victimized by the idea that people like him are always to blame. The situation was tense and there were a number of students who were getting very pale and upset and finally one of them burst into tears and left the room. So at that point, I said, "You know, I think this is an important discussion and I think we have to have it, but it might be good if we take a break for five minutes so everyone has a chance to re-gather themselves. And I left to find out if the student was okay. When I came back, I said, "I would like to pick up the discussion where we left off—is that okay with people?" And they said yes, and after that the discussion was much calmer.

In cases like that I do enforce civility. I tell the disruptive student, "You're interrupting, and you need to wait your turn. You'll have time to state your point of view, but this isn't the time to do that, and I expect you, as I expect every person in the class, to respect the others." I end up being very authoritarian about that. In a lot of ways I am a very accessible, friendly teacher, but about that, I really exert my authority. On occasion, I've even said, "It's now time for you not to say anything, and if that's a problem then you can go; I'll talk with you after class or in office hours."

This doesn't mean that Emma requires that discussion be unemotional. "I'm not opposed to people jumping up and getting angry and frustrated in a way that's not abusive to other students in the class and when it is in some loose sense, their turn," she says. "I don't require that people put their hand up and be called on. What I would be opposed to is if people were outright rude or offensive to another student or were not allowing another student to talk. I just need to have that sense of civility in the classroom so that some don't jump all over others and everyone has their space or opportunity to speak."

Both these instructors feel that students who have been the targets of racism do have legitimate need to let go of their emotions at times during a discussion. Emma says:

I would have more tolerance if someone in a racially subordinate position says, "Stop, I can't deal with this right now; this person's opinion is just so misguided to me I've got to interrupt." I think that's a legitimate interruption. If students of color are getting frustrated because white students don't seem to have any understanding of where they're coming from, I'd ask them explicitly if they would talk about their personal experience—because I think students are very respectful on the whole of other people talking about their experience. It won't always enlighten everyone, but these stories, these perspectives, are so desperately needed in our classrooms! When students of color are willing to speak about their experiences, I just want to make sure it happens, because I feel that students who have had less exposure to communities of color are really impoverished; they don't have much of a sense of what is involved.

Now the hard part is when the white students in the class start to make judgments too quickly about what those experiences mean. They say things like, "Oh, you're being too sensitive," or "That incident wasn't about race, things like that happen to everybody!" And that annoys students of color, because they want to be able to evaluate their own experiences. So then, what I try to do is push down to more description: "Can you tell me more about what happens, in more detail, with more nuance?" And then I can cast it into hypothetical terms up on the board: "Would it be racist if it looked like this?" Or, "If the experience were a little different, like this, then what would it mean?" That way, we can have a discussion about how the experience could be interpreted that doesn't put the student on the spot as much. Their life isn't being analyzed. They've had a chance to speak their experience, they've had a chance to enrich the discussion, but they don't end up being the target of analysis.

Our own role as facilitators is to stake out what we think some of the issues are. I'm always about making the issues more complex, making the set of options more nuanced. And students of all backgrounds get to where they think that's fun. In a class of about forty students, I'd say I have about three quarters actively engaged in the discussion.

Connie adds, "Discussion about moral problems like race does amazing things for people. You get this sense that people often just read things and form opinions one way or another without really examining why. Once people start challenging each other intellectually, they grow, they shoot out rapidly. It's sort of an old-fashioned liberal idea, I guess, but I think they're better citizens when they've examined why they hold the opinions that they do." "It's really a passion for me," says Emma. "I really get charged by this; I come out of class sometimes just panting and exhausted, but I love it."

While Philosophy courses are about assessing various arguments and objections, in many other disciplines students know that they need to learn the professor's "expert take" on the subject matter. Many white students find this difficult to do in courses that take a progressive stance on race, where the analysis they are expected to learn calls their own motives and behavior into question. Eric, a white professor of Economics, deals with this kind of student resistance by approaching the subject of racial justice through an analysis of class:

> I'd rather guilt trip people about their economic privilege than about their racist attitudes. I personally believe that if the difference in unemployment rates were much lower between blacks and whites, negative racial attitudes would be enormously less. So in my classroom we don't discuss issues of personal prejudice. We talk about structural ways that political economies take advantage of racial differences. Most of my students know that rewards for employment tend to be racially distinguished: whites have a higher median wage and higher employment rate than blacks and Hispanics. And because they're hard workers themselves, they tend to think the reason for the wage discrepancy has to do with effort: if you want a job you can have it. But a lot of clever work has been done recently by people in political economy that implicates not the bad attitudes or poor performance of minorities or the bad attitudes of whites, but rather, it implicates the system. In a capitalist society, to achieve equilibrium you need a certain amount of unemployment. And this makes it possible to pit groups of workers against each other by divide and conquer mechanisms—which sounds a little dramatic, but it's the term they use in the literature. It turns out that contrary to popular belief, working class whites don't benefit economically from racial inequality. Where inequalities are greater, wages for both whites and blacks are less.[3]
>
> I tell my students that the "racial differences" that we're talking about are not differences in ability or talent or hard work; they are a direct consequence of the amount and kinds of resources that are available to the different racial groups. For example, the good schools they went to in the suburbs are really enormously subsidized, not just by blacks, but by truck drivers. People who can't get into this university are actually paying taxes that subsidize this place. And students react to this information quite differently than if you try to guilt trip them into feeling bad about their attitudes. If they thought that only personal prejudices accounted for the economic impoverishment of blacks, then of course they'd be sorry. But that doesn't get us very far in changing the system.
>
> My classes are quite diverse ethnically, but privileged economically. So my students generally like the idea that people should be able to make a lot of money because they themselves expect to rise very high in the salary structure. Of course, even if they never bring up race directly, this argument has an underlying racial component because they're well aware that the racial composition of the people at the top doesn't look like the racial composition of the people at the bottom. In fact, students who are sometimes most resentful of these arguments are the Asian students who very often come from fairly modest economic backgrounds. They've worked very hard and now they're going to go to business school and start out at around double the income of their parents.
>
> People like the idea that they deserve privilege. If they're advantaged by racial differences, they want to think that in some sense they deserve it. So I give a strong argument in favor of garbage collectors being paid at least as much as doctors. I ask them, "Would you rather spend your days collecting garbage or being a doctor?

Would you rather be wrestling with garbage cans out there in the snow, or be in a nice, clean doctor's office?" And then they say, "Well, didn't the doctors have to go to school?" And I say "Well, which is harder, going to school or being in a typical working class job?" And they find all that quite incredible, because they think they work very hard and therefore deserve higher rewards. And then you suggest that no, they don't deserve it; it's just the way the system is structured. I actually think a lot of people find this more plausible than the stories they've been told, which is that the garbage collectors don't work hard, or they're too lazy to succeed. And they know the doctors spend an awful lot of time on the golf course.

\* \* \* \* \* \*

In classes where discussion of different perspectives is key, experienced instructors agree that setting ground rules (or "group norms") at the beginning of the semester before emotions have a chance to erupt helps keep conversations civil and to some extent "safe" for everyone. Some instructors simply talk to the class about their expectations. For example, one little speech I've made in Introductory Composition classes goes like this: "The issues we will be discussing can be sensitive and emotional. You don't have to agree with what I think. Everyone's contribution and perspective is valuable in this class, as long as you give reasons for your opinions and listen carefully to the opinions of others. Of course I know you are all mature enough not to get into personal attacks so I hardly need to mention that using ethnic slurs (I might then have to define the word 'slur') or calling someone a racist is off-limits. We can talk about racist ideas and racist actions but not racist individuals."

Other instructors hand out a list of their own ground rules and spend a little of the first class period going over them, asking students for their questions, comments, and additions.[4] In my own classes, I prefer to ask students to make up their own ground rules in small groups with one student in each group assigned to write down the rules as they emerge from discussion. Students feel more invested in rules they create for themselves and begin to deal with conflicting perspectives right away, especially if the cultural backgrounds of the students are quite diverse. For example, some African-American students feel that heated exchange shows that students "care about the issues," while silence or polite generalizations reveal their lack of investment. "When white students hold back and do not voice their opinions, it sparks a dormant suspicion in me that most of them do not even comprehend the issue or simply do not care about their own privilege," writes an African-American student. "Basically, I don't feel like waiting for the day when they are hit over the head with enlightenment." "There is pain in staying the same, and there is pain in change. Pick the one that moves you forward," says the e-mail signature of another one of my African-American students.

Students from other cultural backgrounds may feel quite differently about the best way to approach sensitive issues. For example, international students from West Africa may have more in common with some Asian students who feel that too much clash of opinion is divisive, and that respectful listening is preferable to saying the first thought that comes to mind. Asian American students may feel conflicted about their participation style: on the one hand, their upbringing may have stressed acceptance and harmony and on the other, their experiences with racism may be provoking them to speak out.

"There is a tendency of the Indian people or Eastern people generally to be more quiet," says an Indian American student. "We tend to say, 'Oh well, whatever', or 'Oh yeah, that's probably true.' We're tolerant, I think, and accepting. If something really offends us we'd rather say, 'Let them say whatever they like, I'm going to go study. I'm going to live my life and not bother to explain this to anyone.' But when you hear so many ignorant opinions and all the racism and stereotyping that goes on, you feel you should protest. But then I feel easily intimidated by people with strong opinions or class members who seem to be emotionally invested in an idea that I disagree with."

"Asian Americans may seem happy with the cards we've been dealt because we're quiet," says a biracial Chinese/European American student. "I really hate that. We're constantly left out of discussions on race because we're overpowered by the black people making all the noise. I'm a Chinese woman and I wasn't raised to be so aggressive with my thoughts. I want to shout, to be an activist, to educate people, to tell my story, but I can't always. Everyone in this world—my family, my culture, white people, black people—are telling me not to. I'm limited by stupid stereotypes and expectations." Gender differences among all ethnic groups may also emerge—if not in these discussions about group norms, then later, once the discussion is focused on the course content. Female students may become very annoyed at males (especially white males) who dominate the discussion and who seem to have real difficulty being aware of their tone of voice, their tendency to interrupt when they become engaged, and their readiness to speak longer once they have the floor. On the other hand, males who have learned to be sensitive to gender and racial dynamics may go overboard in the other direction and remain almost completely silent, depriving the class of their opinions and observations. I tell students that whatever comes up in discussion of the ground rules will help them think about their own style and the fact that others may have quite different needs. They don't need to agree on a final version of the rules; simply being aware of differences in communication styles can make the discussion more civil. Once they've written down all the ideas that have emerged, I ask a few students to collect all the ground rules, write them up (culling redundancies), and send them by e-mail to the rest of the class.

Another technique for creating ground rules, developed by psychologist Lorraine Gutierrez for her classes on race and gender, focuses less on students' own style differences and more on empathy with others. Each student thinks of one concern they have about the way class discussion might go and writes it anonymously on a file card. Typical responses are: "We'll just have one of those superficial discussions that never go anywhere." "I'll be forced to speak when I don't want to." "Conservative opinions won't be tolerated." "Certain people will always dominate the discussion." "We'll end up making race a black/white issue, leaving out all the other ethnic groups that have experienced racism." "Some people won't come prepared so their comments, if they have any, will be uninformed." The instructor collects and shuffles the cards, divides the class into groups of four or five, and hands one card to each student. The groups then discuss the concern expressed on each card, trying to come up with a ground rule to address it. The rules generated by all the groups are recorded and e-mailed to the class as in the exercise above. Discussing rules that will make others more comfortable helps students to take responsibility for classroom dynamics along with the instructor. Students have to think, "What *should* we do about students who never contribute to discussion?" "How are we going to include the perspectives of Native American students, since there seem to be none in this class?" "How can we make it easier for someone to decline to speak about things that are too personal?" The animated discussion this exercise engenders is wonderful to hear on the first day of the semester, and the respect for others that it brings out will be important to remember when and if the going gets rough.

Regardless of how much time they have put into creating ground rules, students do tend to forget them when emotions run high. However, once students have made their own rules, instructors can always remind them of what they themselves came up with. A white instructor in Education says:

> I think the first few times things started to erupt in my classes I just stopped and pulled out the ground rules. And I said, 'Wait a minute, we've developed these rules and here's what we agreed on.' So it never was a free for all. I once had a teacher in

training who was really upset that the local schools had stopped celebrating Hallow-een because some religious minorities are against it. She could not entertain the idea that anyone would seriously believe it was devil worship. 'I came to this country to be American!' she told the class. 'We have a culture here and I expect to teach it in the schools!' She and another student went back and forth, disagreeing very forcefully with each other about this. They were both very strong in their tone of voice, but because of the ground rules they had developed, they were very respectful. And they both came away saying, 'Wow, I really learned something about the other side!'

My own students in an advanced course on race and culture came up with some particularly good advice for themselves which I pass on to you below. It must be said, however, that these students, mature and sophisticated as they were, could not live up to their own high expectations for discussion all of the time. When things got uncomfortable, their frustrations and self-righteous anger would sometimes rise up stronger than any rules they could make. But nevertheless, as one of my students said, just talking about the rules and trying to follow them made our classroom "as close to a safe space as can be with a multicultural group."

Assume that everyone wants to learn and understand each other's experiences.

Find out racial/ethnic group names and titles that are the most comfortable for people and use them. Learn why some of these names offend some people.

Speak from the "I" of personal experience, rather than making general statements about people. Say "In my dorm, or neighborhood, or high school, this is what hap-pened, this is what some people did," rather than "This is what happens; this is how people act."

Look out for people who might feel silenced because of their gender, race, back-ground, or personality. Let everyone into the discussion.

Listen to others. Don't talk all the time. Don't always be preparing your rebuttal or next remark. Let a few seconds elapse between exchanges; cultivate patience.

Show you're paying close attention: don't fidget or nod off. Look at the person who is speaking.

Don't "sterilize" the discussion, play it safe, or make certain topics off-limits. Attack the idea, not the person.

Keep these discussions in confidence. Don't belittle people outside class for what they say in class. Talking about incidents, ideas or emotions that arose in class is okay if names aren't used.

Remember, we're human. We don't have to resolve all tension or come to complete understanding. The point is to talk. The process is everything.

# Notes

1. Cliff (1988). In this piece, the biracial Jamaican author writes about how she has been affected by attitudes toward class, color, sexuality, and privilege; its tone is one of increasing outrage and bitterness at the violence of colonialism.

2. A 1994 study of integration trends in U.S. colleges by Sylvia Hurtado and Eric Dey showed that white students are much more likely than students of color to self-segregate. "About 69 percent of Asian American students, 78 percent of Mexican American students and 55 percent of African American students said they frequently dined with members of different ethnic groups, compared with 21 percent of white students" (reported in Jackson, 1999, A1).

3. This is the main conclusion of Michael Reich's (1981) political economic analysis of racial inequality. Researchers using historical data have found evidence that large-scale capitalists profit by keeping racial antagonisms alive. The wages of both their black and white workers will be lower if they succeed. Otherwise, workers produce strong, multiracial unions that can bargain effectively to raise the wages of all workers. Also see Leiman (1993).

4. For an example of ground rules that explicitly address issues of power and privilege, see Cannon (1990). These rules ask students to acknowledge at the outset that racism exists, that "we are all systematically misinformed about our own group and about members of other groups," that we all "agree not to blame ourselves or others for misinformation we have learned," that "we agree not to blame victims for the condition of their lives," and that "we assume that people … always do the best they can." In my own classes, and even in faculty workshops on racism or multiculturalism, I find that these agreements and assumptions are not shared by all members, and that we lose valuable opportunities for discussion and learning by asking everyone to simply accept these precepts as true.

# · 6 ·

# START WITH STUDENTS
# WHERE THEY ARE

## White Student Reactions

When I began to address issues of race and racism more deliberately in my classroom, I found myself getting more and more frustrated with privileged white students who were unaware of their own prejudices and stereotypes. I felt angry and impatient, especially when students were honest. "Why aren't these attitudes changing?" I would ask myself. "How can it be that every semester, these same 'I'm not racist but. …' attitudes keep coming and coming?"

*Teaching Journal, December 15.* I have given my peer tutor class a chapter of Geneva Smitherman's 1977 classic, *Talkin and Testifyin: The Language of Black America,* a marvelous text that is written in both African-American Vernacular English (AAVE) and standard academic language and style. I want them to understand that AAVE is rule governed, with a full grammar, like all language varieties, not just slang, or a sloppy version of Standard English. This, I am hoping, will start them thinking about the role of power in language. Who gets to decide which language variety will be "standard?" Who gets to say who has an accent? What are the implications of this for students who come to the Peer Tutor Center for help with their papers? None of my students—white, black, or Asian American—has thought about these issues before. Most say that they find them "interesting." Gail, a white student, is more honest:

> Let me start off by saying that I am uncomfortable with words like "black" and "white" because using these words creates prejudice and distinguishes people in ways they

should not be distinguished. But for the purpose of this reaction paper I will use them. When I came to college I had no problem making friends with black students. And when you spend a lot of time with them and their friends, anyone would definitely pick up on the fact that they talk with their friends differently, but I just saw that as how I talk differently with my friends also. You let loose, you become comfortable, and don't really pay attention to proper grammar rules all of the time. As for this "comfortable" dialect or whatever anyone wants to call it being a language, I have to disagree. From my point of view, it is simply the laziness of people who don't want to speak proper English all the time. I feel that there should be no excuse why everyone does not grasp and speak the concept of proper English if they are capable of it. Is it maybe that people in the black community feel they need more power in the world? If so, declaring a slang dialect of English a language is not going to be the way to get what they want. Do you think that if forty percent of France's population came in speaking Russian that the whole country would then decide to all speak Russian? In my opinion I think not.

Reading Gail's paper I can feel my muscles tense, my breath come faster. I can hear the voice in my head making incredulous, sarcastic comments: "How can she put her nineteen-year-old opinions on the level of a professional linguist?" "How can someone write and think so poorly, and in the same breath judge someone else's 'bad English' as laziness?" "How can she claim to be colorblind when she is so full of self-righteous anger against 'them'?"

Gail tells me that she comes from one of the richest communities in America where 95% of her high school classmates were white, and where the few African-Americans talked and acted "like everyone else." She has always gotten away with writing "off the top," without any apparent care, or editing, or depth. Her confused thinking comes partly from being passed along in school ("You see," she writes in a confessional journal entry, "when I turn in a paper, teachers have given me better grades than I sometimes think I deserve, due to where I am from and other aspects of my life") and partly because these issues of race are so highly charged. The unfairness of all this really gets to me. But then I read the end of her journal, and I realize that this is harder on her than it is on me. And that in some screwy sense, I agree with her:

> Smitherman's book gave me a headache the whole time, like there was a clamp being tightened on both sides of my head, almost as if the author was trying to pump information into me saying that Ebonics should and has to be a language or else the world will come to an end. Things like this frustrate me, things that promote racism just by the words and conflicts which are presented in the writing. I mean, if you take away what people consider to be their culture, take away people's appearances, and everything that makes a person stand out in sight, and just look at their souls, we are all the same.

\* \* \* \* \* \*

Not all the instructors I interviewed were as concerned about their level of impatience with such students as I have been about mine. Some felt sick about the tension and frustration they were experiencing but thought it couldn't be helped; others felt justified in their anger and seemed to relish arguing with them even when they knew they weren't getting anywhere. But I am convinced that learning how to reach resistant white students is central to our teaching about race. These are the future power brokers of America, the ones who by virtue of their class, their contacts, and their perceived "race" will have a disproportionate share of political and economic clout. If my anger and impatience prevent me from reaching these students, I fear they will retreat even further into their stereotypes and victim-blaming and judgmentalism. Or they will just slip away, relieved it's over, consoling themselves with the thought that their instructor was so biased that nobody could learn anything, anyway. And that will be sad, because I had a chance to reach them and I let it go.

As I looked back at my own reactions in my teaching journal I realized that it was not just the wealthy, underprepared white students that annoyed me. I could also get impatient with the scrappy, articulate working-class whites defending their hard-won turf against "lazy people who use racism as an excuse." Or the progressive white student organizations fighting to save women of color from the oppression of sweatshops but oblivious of the color of their own membership. I cringed at the white liberal Education majors who want to become teachers in order to "help little black kids overcome their terrible families and neighborhoods." Or the multicultural group of students who devoted their spring break to reading to children on an Indian reservation in the naive hope that a week of their presence would somehow inspire them to shake off centuries of broken treaties and imposed poverty.

Some of my students of color annoyed and perplexed me as well. Why did they seem so stuck in their distrust of whites, their proud, angry, isolation, their ignorance of other disenfranchised groups? It pained me to see them deep into their anxieties about their own performance, fearing conferences about their writing, tossing off my feedback, or just giving up way too soon. I worried that such students would never move forward, that they would forever find it easier to blame and complain than to act and achieve. I wanted to prod them, tell them to get over it, tell them we're all stuck on this earth together and we have to figure out how to get along. But in my heart, I knew this was not the message that would move them.

Looking for patience, I spent some time reading and thinking about the values that motivate my teaching and my life and in the process, rediscovered Myles Horton, an inspirational activist and educator I had read about and later met in graduate school when he was in his nineties. Horton was the founder of the Highlander Center, where community leaders and ordinary people have come together since the 1930s to educate themselves and each other on issues of social justice. He had grown up poor in rural Tennessee in the early 1900s, a white youngster in the racially segregated South. From his parents, who were both schoolteachers "in the days before you had to go to college to be a schoolteacher" (1990, p. 1) he learned friendship and respect for people across the racial divide. All his life he was intensely interested in education and sus-picious of teachers—especially good teachers, he says slyly, because then he would have to listen to their ideas instead of developing his own (p. 14). His ideas about teaching and learning grew slowly, through intense reflection on how unschooled adults in the Southern mountains could be led to take charge of their own lives, how segregation might be challenged, and how working people could join together to demand a decent wage. He had learned from his parents that the purpose of education was to do something for others, not just for yourself. Early on, he realized that "it's not important to be good, it's important to be good for something" (Horton and Freire, 1990, p. 35).

Through his reflections as well as his voracious reading, his chance meet-ings and later friendships with Jane Addams and Eleanor Roosevelt, and his visits to Danish folk schools, Horton created the educational model that would later train local people to become activists and encourage community leaders like Rosa Parks to take bold and direct action in the face of injustice. Horton sums up his philosophy this way:

> I think if I had to put a finger on what I consider a good education, a good *radical* education, it wouldn't be anything about methods or techniques. I would be loving people first. ... And that means all people everywhere, not just your family or your own countrymen or your own color. And wanting for them what you want for your-self. And the next is respect for people's abilities to learn and to act and to shape their own lives. You have to have confidence that people can do that. ... The third thing grows out of caring for people and having respect for people's ability to do things, and that is that you value their experiences. You can't *say* you respect people and not respect their experiences. (Horton and Freire, 1990, pp. 177–178)

Finding this quote again made me think about the naive white students in my classes. We need to express our love, confidence, care, and respect—not only for the poor and oppressed, but for "all people everywhere," Horton says.

Though Horton worked mainly with people whose rights were compromised by racial and economic injustice, his words apply equally well to our work with students whose views we abhor: students who are racist, students who are smugly privileged, students who can choose to ignore racism and injustice and use their education to make themselves a lot of money.

Horton doesn't expect people to start in a place where they already feel a warm, sympathetic connection with others and the conviction to act for the good of humanity. Because he grew up on a farm, he says, he knows about growing things. He knows that you have to plant and water and weed and mulch and prune with tender care. "Your job as a gardener or as an educator is to know that the potential is there and that it will unfold," Horton says (1990, p. 133). "You have to posit trust in the learner in spite of the fact that the people you're dealing with may not, on the surface, seem to merit that trust" (p. 131). And in order to do this, you have to start with people where they are without losing sight of where you want them to go. Horton writes:

> When I do education work with a group of people, I try to see with one eye where those people are as they perceive themselves to be. I do this by looking at body language, by imagination, by talking to them, by visiting them, by learning what they enjoy and what troubles them. I try to find out where they are, and if I can get hold of that with one eye, that's where I start. You have to start where people are, because their growth is going to be from there, not from some abstraction or where you are or someone else is. Now my other eye is not such a problem, because I already have in mind a philosophy of where I'd like to see people moving. It's not a clear blueprint for the future but movement toward goals they don't conceive of at that time. I know they're capable of perceiving and moving toward those humane goals because I've see other people like them starting where they are. I know the potential is there. (1990, p. 131)

These words are a talisman for me, an ideal. I know the direction I want my students to go, the humane goals I want them to reach. I want them to develop respect for all people, not just tolerate them. I want them to learn to listen to people whose views and experiences are different from theirs and to see the value, the logic, and the beauty of many different ways of life. I want them to confront the moral contradictions in a society that was conceived in liberty but enslaved and slaughtered millions; a society that believes people advance on their own individual merits but too often judges their abilities and worth on the basis of their ethnic group membership. I want them to understand the effect their beliefs and actions have on themselves and others. And I want them to believe that they, and their society, can change. But how to develop the patience to accept students where they are as they're coming to understand all this? How to nurture them before their growth becomes evident? And how to find the faith that students will grow at all?

A short time after I reread Horton, I came across some theories of racial identity development by psychologists Janet Helms (1990) and W. E. Cross (Cross, Parham, and Helms, 1991) as well as several articles by Beverly Tatum (1992, 1994) that apply these theories to classroom practice. As I read I began to understand, with a great sense of relief and hope, that both whites and people of color go through predictable stages of growth where all the emotions and positions that have so exasperated me are to be expected and are in some sense "normal." Knowing that it is possible for anyone to develop a "positive, healthy racial identity," even in a society that starts almost everyone off in an unhealthy direction, is both comforting and energizing. It helps me accept my students where they are, which in turn, relieves me of moralizing. It helps me make sense of the bitter arguments and scared silence and guilt and despair and outrageous naïveté, for every classroom is full of students in different stages of identity development. It helps me understand faculty when they perpetuate myths and stereotypes and even racism at its most blatant (for stages of racial identity development have nothing to do with age or class or level of education). It helps me understand myself as I progress—and regress—through the stages of my own development.

And learning how whites are analyzed by people of color helps me develop humility. For these stages of racial identity development have been constructed and tested by African-American psychologists and educators who, at long last, are analyzing white people—not in the spirit of tit for tat, in order to label whites as morally and intellectually defective, but in order to help us develop our fullest humanity. And if we resist the idea of being "developed," if we resist having our thoughts and feelings boxed and labeled, we can use this as an opportunity to reflect on "the real question," as black writer W. E. B. Du Bois put it in 1903, the implicit question in the mind of whites in all conversations and interactions with blacks and in fact with all peoples of color at some point in our common history: "How does it feel to be a problem?" (1965, p. 213).

According to Helms (1990), whites in the first stage[1] of racial identity development have had little contact with people of color and have built up a belief system about white cultural, intellectual, and moral superiority based on media stereotypes and family or neighborhood conversations. As I think about the Michigan campus, I can see that our stage one students[2] can be further divided into three groups, each of which expresses its white supremacist notions somewhat differently. First, there are the outright racists who have no qualms about sniggering over a racist joke, yelling racial slurs at students of color out of car windows, writing racial epithets on their doors ("as a joke"), or upholding policies of exclusion in their own student organizations. Since the Civil Rights Movement of the 1950s and 1960s and the dismantling of legal racism there is much less public sanction of such activities, so these folks tend to mute their comments in the presence of white liberals and sometimes (but not always) around people of color. When they are reprimanded they may complain that the "liberal bias" of the campus makes it impossible for them to express their feelings fully or truthfully. Occasionally, but perhaps with increasing frequency, such students join white supremacist organizations via the Internet, and participate in racist activities that are more violent, both physically and psychologically. I would like to think that these students are clinically "abnormal"—that is, their racism is only one facet of a whole range of psychological problems and extremist leanings that have arisen because of violent, soul-destroying experiences in childhood and later exposure to social and religious organizations that are blatantly racist and anti-Semitic. But perhaps this is being overly optimistic.

Another group of whites that I see in this first stage of racial identity development does not participate in blatant, nasty expressions of racism. In fact, they may say they have no trouble making friends or staying friends with people of color. They may have tried to compliment these friends by telling them they are "not like other blacks" or "not really Chinese"—meaning that their friends have successfully adopted European American speech, mannerisms, norms, attitudes, and values and, very importantly, do not appear to notice the racism that surrounds them. These whites, because of their reliance on media and societal stereotypes for information, tend to think of most people of color, especially poor people, as dangerous, deviant, and untrustworthy.

Because whites in this stage have difficulty seeing other cultural styles as "normal," they may find it humorous, for example, to imitate a Korean teacher's accent or turn up their nose at the prospect of tasting Indian food. They may express delight at the "quaint costumes" of Nigerian visitors, or find the physical characteristics of certain ethnic groups exotic or mildly distasteful. They may tap into the internalized racism of their friends and acquaintances of color, believing, for example, that a Korean woman who has an operation on her eyelids to make them rounder is only trying to become more beautiful or that an African-American woman is to be pitied for her "bad hair." These students generally do not see their attitudes or remarks as racist. Racism to them is a violent act, a cross-burning or a law requiring blacks to sit at the back of the bus. They may recognize the racist stereotypes in their parents' or grandparents' conversations—but certainly not in themselves or anyone in their own generation.

Still other whites in this first stage of racial identity development have been raised to be more polite or sophisticated and would not think of making fun of anyone or knowingly treat people of color as "alien." First-year college students from all-white neighborhoods may come to college excited about the opportunity to experience a culturally diverse environment, which they imagine will be friendly and joyful and mutually respectful. When they meet people of color, these students are likely to exhibit a genuine but naive curiosity about them, perhaps asking to touch the hair of an African-American student or making what they believe to be a friendly, sensitive gesture toward an Asian-looking student by asking where she was born. Sometimes these advances are treated with kindness and generosity, other times they are rebuffed, depending on where the students of color are in their own identity development (see Chapter 7). Tentative intercultural friendships will form. But as soon as these white students notice the "politics" on campus, the segregated lunch tables, the separate fraternity and sorority systems, the looks they get from students of color when they walk around campus with their non-white friends, they quickly become cynical and outraged. "The Indian students have their own club! Can you imagine what would happen if the white students decided to form *their* own club?!" "Why do the African American students sit together in class all the time?" "How are we going to make any progress when they won't join 'our' organizations?" Fear and anger emerge as these white students fall back on the stereotypes they learned growing up.

White faculty in the first stage of their racial identity development make campus life painful for students of color—sometimes intentionally, but more often without realizing it. These are the faculty who express annoyance at being asked to give up using the term "Oriental" when referring to their Asian or Asian American graduate students. They are the ones who are openly surprised to receive a superior paper written by an African-American student or see the top grade on an law exam go to a Native American activist. They unwittingly exasperate Chicano students by asking them to give the class "the Hispanic perspective" or look to the only black student in the class to provide "the experience of living in the inner city," believing, perhaps, that all students of an ethnic type live under the same conditions and have similar opinions, experiences, skills, and deficits. Some stage one faculty avoid giving honest feedback to students of color, fearing charges of racism. They may try to derail workshops on multiculturalism or attack other faculty who attempt to revise an ethnocentric curriculum. They may be quite bitter and self-righteous if they lose these battles.

No one, as far as I know, has ventured to guess the percentage of white faculty who are at the earliest stage of racial identity development. But Beverly Tatum, an African-American professor who has taught hundreds of undergraduate students at prestigious Mt. Holyoke College, says, "I would describe the majority of the white men and women I have had in my course [on the psychology of racism] over the last twelve years as being in this [first] stage of development at the start of the semester" (1994, p. 464). This statement was a bit of a shock to me when I first read it, as I imagined that white students who would choose to study the psychology of racism as an elective would have had more contact with people of color and more of an idea of their perspectives and life experiences. But as I began to teach my own course on racism that attracted third and fourth-year white students, many of whom were already activists on other issues, I began to see that these attitudes—especially the naive ethnocentrism and lack of awareness of everyday racism—are quite common.

Some of these folks will never change, of course. Psychological and spiritual growth are not automatic; it takes a certain amount of courage and generosity of spirit to question one's world view. But with new information, open discussion, exploration of their own attitudes and upbringing, and the willingness of people of color to share their experiences, whites in stage one can begin to understand for the first time that they have "privileges" that are so often denied to people of color—that is, respectful or neutral treatment by whites in positions of authority. They begin to see that while modern racism may be muted, compared to the past, it is still a daily reality for many. And they begin to see institutional racism as a spider web of policies, precedents, norms, and practices, ranging from outright racist to unconsciously discriminatory, that make it extremely difficult for people of color to excel and rejoice in being themselves—especially in white environments.

The new awareness that characterizes stage two might begin to dawn on students when they are watching a video on modern racism or reading an article in their coursepack or listening to painful experiences of people of color.[3] It can come to them gradually, in accumulated bits and pieces, or it can come as a sudden shock. A white freshman in one of my composition classes that focused on children in poverty writes in her journal:

As I read Peggy McIntosh's piece on white privilege I realized that my eyes were becoming larger and larger because I was beginning to see that she was talking about *me*. She says, "Whites are carefully taught not to recognize white privilege." I read this statement and found myself slightly confused. I didn't see myself as "privileged." I wasn't racist, or even prejudiced. Or was I? I read on, very fervently, devouring her words and thoughts. Sometimes I even re-read parts just to make sure I really understood it all. "Whites are taught to think of their lives as morally neutral, normative, and average, and also ideal, so that when we work to benefit others, this is seen as work which will allow 'them' to be more like 'us.'" Was this really true? Do I really have this sick, almost pre-programmed agenda? Is my skin really such an asset to myself that I take it all for granted?

Instructors may experience similar insights when they begin collecting accounts of institutional racism for their course packs or read antiracism materials in depth, or as they watch videos about racism with their students. One instructor, asking me for suggestions about how to connect examples of modern racism with the historical material in her course told me that she did not feel confident enough to let students bring their personal experiences into the classroom. "I'm afraid I'm not PC," she said. "I know how I was raised. I might say the wrong thing, not realizing that it would hurt someone. I'm beginning to recognize the amount of racism that still exists today, and I'm appalled. But it's really scary to bring it up."

Fear, guilt, disorientation, questions—all characterize stage two. One of my white students made it a habit to come to my office to talk for an hour before class, telling me how angry she was that historical information about Native Americans had been withheld from her, and how guilty and uncomfortable she felt, remembering the bridge in her town that leads across a river to an Indian reservation. "Nobody goes over there," she said, wide-eyed at her sudden realization. "It's as if all those people don't exist." A white instructor who teaches African history told me about the guilt she felt on the podium, lecturing as an "expert" on the subject of white exploitation of the continent. A white student writing in his journal expressed shame and embarrassment as he thought about the jokes he'd made and the pleasure he'd felt in demeaning people of other races. Another wrote that she was "overcome by guilt, immobilized by the horrors and injustices that my Southern white ancestors have perpetrated."

Stage two is extremely uncomfortable for students because of the psychological dissonance they feel when their beliefs and feelings about themselves and their values are in conflict (Helms, 1990, p. 59). As they come to learn that their perception of themselves as completely free of prejudice is a false one and that the naive remarks they have been making have been causing great pain to others, they may withdraw from classroom discussion, especially discussion of personal issues. Despite their silence, however, white students in stage two often report they are learning more than they ever have in a period of a few weeks. Some have begun to confront their parents on weekends and holidays, making long automobile rides challenging and uncomfortable. Some are educating their younger siblings or putting their boyfriends on the spot. A few are finding the courage to speak up in other classes where views sympathetic to students of color are rare. But because their knowledge is still relatively skimpy they find it difficult to argue effectively, and friends and parents quickly tire of their new radicalism, urging them, sometimes cruelly, to stop being so sensitive or idealistic. Because of the pain and discomfort this stage causes them, white students have good reason to move out of it as quickly as possible. Unfortunately, most don't move toward a positive, nonracist white identity immediately. The pressures from friends and family to disavow their new knowledge are too great; their desire to be accepted and loved as "their old self" is too strong.

Stage three: retrenchment. At this stage, says Tatum, "the dilemma of noticing racism and yet feeling the societal pressure not to notice, or at least not to speak up, is resolved ... [as] whites ... turn to explanations for racism that put the burden of change on those who are the targets of racism" (1994, p. 467). Typically, stage three students say that while they realize that discrimination and racism exist, they are not as ubiquitous as people of color claim, and could certainly not have much to do with the poverty, educational failure, incarceration rate, substance abuse, and other ills that plague so many communities of color. Often stage three students express frustration and self-righteous anger—easier emotions, perhaps, than guilt and anxiety. A white first-year undergraduate writes in response to a question about the extent of racism on campus:

> The fact is that hypersensitive individuals use racial issues as an excuse for either poor performance or as a way to get special attention or treatment. Just because you're not white doesn't mean you deserve me playing the violin for you. You have one life, so live it and stop blaming others for your lack of desire or motivation to do so.
>
> Note: This does not apply to those individuals that truly are discriminated against. However, we are all discriminated against. True discrimination is the lack of control over one's individual actions, always. Discrimination does not apply to those that have their hand raised and are not called on!

Sometimes whites in this stage feel they have "tried and failed" to reach out across the racial divide. When their friendly overtures to people of color are not reciprocated, when they try to involve more blacks or Latin@s in the alumni organization and get no response, when efforts to help in an impoverished neighborhood do not bear fruit, when Peace Corps Volunteers overseas find their suggestions about how to run a small business or teach science are politely ignored, whites often turn (or return) to exasperated put-downs to explain why people of color are not "advancing." "They just won't take initiative," they say. "The culture doesn't value achievement." "Parents don't care about their children's education." "They *want* to be separate."

Because of the social pressure to "ignore racism and accept socially sanctioned stereotypes" (Tatum, 1994, p. 467), white students need extra encouragement and help to move beyond stage three. Above all, says Tatum, they need role models of whites who have moved beyond guilt and victim-blaming and have forged a positive, nonracist white identity. White instructors can help by talking about our own struggles to unlearn harmful stereotypes and assumptions, by providing white speakers who have dedicated their careers to fighting racism and economic injustice, and by drawing on white students' experiences as women, as Jews, as members of Christian minority groups, or as gays or lesbians, all of which may provide a window into the experience of racial oppression.

With continued encouragement and information whites can move into the final three stages where they gradually develop a positive and healthy white identity, one that is not based on superiority, or guilt, or idealism (Tatum, 1994).[4] Gradually they lose their tendency to both blame the victims and to want to help them "be more like us." The idea that people of color should be, as Cornel West says, "'included' and 'integrated' into 'our' society and culture" or that they should be "'well behaved' and 'worthy of acceptance' by 'our' way of life" is replaced by a new view of a multicultural, multiracial America where the "presence and predicaments" of people of color "are neither additions to nor defections from American life, but rather *constitutive elements of that life*" (1994, 6, italics in original).

As whites begin to see specific instances of how they themselves perpetuate racism, they realize that they need to take responsibility for ending it. They begin to see more clearly that their efforts to improve the lives of people of color would be better spent helping other whites confront their fears and prejudices and working to remodel racist institutions. Here are some suggestions about how whites can be allies with people of color on campus that my students wrote in Breaking the Silence, a campus publication they put together to foster conversations about race and racism:

To be an ally, you need to change your entire mindset. You need to start opening your eyes to everything around you. You need to make it a point to take steps, even small ones, every single day and break out of your comfort zone. You need to look conflict in the eye and remember Martin Luther King's words: "There is a type of nonviolent tension ... necessary for growth." It's not about changing the world, making everyone get along; it's about overcoming fearfulness, superficiality and segregation. We need ... to start breaking away from homogeneous circles and tapping into others. [Being an ally] is about BEING there, being real, being able to face that person and talk, listen, and ABSORB on an equal level. It should be a mutual process—no patronizing, no ass-kissing, no competing, no exploiting ... Be natural. Be willing. BE CONFIDENT.

—Stefanie Liang

## How to be an ally on campus?

- Speak up in classes when the dominant paradigms are otherwise unchallenged.
- Write letters to the paper.
- Show up for rallies and demonstrations.
- Inform yourself about issues and people that are unfamiliar to you.
- Recognize the potential of others to be *your* ally.
- Be an example.
- Get involved in campus activism. There are hundreds of groups working on many social and cultural issues in a variety of ways, from theater and music to more traditional forms of activism.

—Josh Meisler

I used to think I had white guilt. I felt guilty for the privileges I had because of my skin color. I felt guilty for what other white people have done to people of color. I felt responsible. Then I realized that I am responsible, but in a different way.
I am responsible because I am a human being that sees other human beings being treated unfairly.
I am responsible as a person that opposes racism and discrimination. I am not responsible for the color of my skin.
I am not responsible for the past. I am responsible for my silence.
I am responsible for my actions. I am responsible for the future.

—Kristie Farrell

Students and teachers who want to read further might check out Crystal Paul's piece: *18 Books Every White Ally Should Read.* http://www.bustle.com/articles/144531-18-books-every-white-ally-should-read "If you really want to support the cause," says Crystal, "it's time check your privilege and get a better idea of where both you and the people you support are coming from, now and historically. Books are only one part of the equation, of course, but they're an important part. So, keep outraged and read on."

## Update

Over the last ten or fifteen years, the racial climate on campus has been changing due to the confluence of several critical events: the entrance of a new generation, the Millennials, into the college scene starting in around 2000, the election of the nation's first black president in 2008 and again in 2012, and the sharp increase in the use of social media to document police abuse of people of color. The resulting shift in social and political dynamics, both in college classrooms and throughout the country, presents interesting challenges and unique opportunities for instructors who teach about race.

Students of the Millennial generation tend to be more politically and socially liberal than their predecessors and at the same time, claim to be more "color-blind" or "raceless," especially if they identify as white. On surveys, at least, they are more inclined to approve of interracial dating and marriage and look forward to coming to a "diverse" campus where they might make friends from backgrounds more varied than in their home neighborhoods. They may join political protests as white allies before they consider their own unwitting complicity in oppression. They may even attempt to lead such protests, or to identify themselves as potential targets of police violence, as if their outrage at inequality makes them indistinguishable from their peers of color. For despite all evidence to the contrary, race, to this generation, is "no big deal." Depending on their age, their learning in other classes, and, above all, their racial identification, many Millennial students truly believe that the majority of people in this country have moved beyond race prejudice. When they are presented with facts about contemporary racism and asked to think about their opinions more carefully, they are likely to say, a bit smugly, that their own generation is different; their grandparents, parents, and even older siblings might be prejudiced—or even racist—but they, themselves, are beyond that. Yet when the subject of race comes up in the classroom, they are just as reluctant to express their ideas and opinions as their predecessors.

This dynamic makes classroom conversations about race more civil, more polite, and less likely to erupt than those of ten years ago. In my own classes, white students are much less likely to become so upset by their classmates' sharp, personal comments that they leave the room in tears. In fact, they rarely hear such direct critique when they make naïve comments about people of color, or question their personal experiences, or even when they make "edgy" racist jokes that demonstrate (so they believe) their sophistication and lack of personal prejudice. While this makes classrooms more calm and friendly, at least on the surface, it can make it more difficult to ensure that white students reflect on their experiences, upbringing, and education, or to look closely at the effects of interpersonal racism on societal institutions. While the stages of white identity development described in this chapter are still valid for the Millennial generation, progress through the stages can be slow since the tendency to deny their generation's racism is so strong.

One way to draw students into conversation and deeper reflection is by using popular culture. These days, students from all backgrounds spend a great deal of time relaxing online, where they can easily come into contact with ideas and opinions about race. They may be fans of ethnic comedy, hip hop, or spoken word. They may be watching YouTube videos posted by young people on interracial dating, stereotypes, cultural appropriation, and other racially charged topics. They may be reading blogs and commenting on them. They are on Twitter and Facebook, where they may be exposed to still more texts and videos posted by their friends. Even though online communities are to some extent segregated, social media have already put students into contact with issues of race. Bringing these resources into the classroom can make students feel more comfortable talking about their reactions and personal experiences, which can lead them into more serious, academic consideration of the ways race and racism are manifested in this "postracial" era. (See Annotated Resources for specific texts, videos and teaching ideas.)

# Notes

1. I will put more emphasis on the early stages of white identity development, as these are the ones that characterize students in most college classrooms today. A fuller account of students in all the stages can be found in Tatum (1992) and Derman-Sparks (1997).
2. I have used the terms "stage one," "stage two," and so on for simplicity, as I find it difficult, myself, to remember the psychological terminology used by Helms: Contact, Disintegration, Reintegration, Pseudoindependence, Immersion/Emersion, Autonomy.
3. Such a moment is captured on the video, *The Color of Fear* (Lee, 1994), when a white male who has been unable to hear the experiences of men of color in an antiracism workshop suddenly catches a glimpse of the world from their point of view. At this quiet, but emotionally intense moment, an African-American participant says, "From here on, I can work with you," and the viewer has a powerful sense that change is possible for just about anyone.
4. Tatum (1994) reminds us that despite the smooth ascent that "stages" imply, racial identity development is not necessarily linear; we may find ourselves in several stages at the same time on different issues, and we may revisit, from different vantage points, stages we thought we had passed through, as if we were pausing on a spiral staircase to view our old—but still curiously present—thinking about race.

# · 7 ·

# MIXING IT UP

## Reactions of Students of Color

Talking about race and racism with white students who come into our classes in so many different stages of identity development is a complex task. As we have seen in Chapter 6, some of our white students don't recognize their own ethnocentric assumptions and find the whole topic of race to be tiresome or irrelevant. Others admit that racism and prejudice exist but believe that people of color are largely to blame for their own problems and are angry at them—and us—for suggesting that white attitudes and practices have anything to do with it. Whites who are more aware of the experiences of students of color may feel guilty and embarrassed by the remarks of the previous two groups but rarely have enough examples or effective arguments to convince them that racism is still a major problem. All these students need more exposure to the perspectives of people who bear the brunt of racism. The most compelling testimony, of course, comes from students of color who are willing to talk about their own personal experiences. And sometimes, giving them the opportunity to do so is just what they need. One of my Latina students reflects back on a class where she sometimes took on the role of educator of white students who "didn't get it":

> The classroom environment was an extremely safe place for me. The experience proved to me that there are places where my opinions and experiences are a

valid source of information. Many times in the past I have disregarded what I felt or thought if it differed from mainstream experience. But by ignoring it, we perpetuate the idea that racism and prejudice do not affect us all and that the little injustices that minorities feel daily are isolated incidents. [Now] when I speak, I try to speak the truth from my heart.

But what if our students of color are not so ready to tell their stories? What if they turn out to be just as unreflective or judgmental as some of our white students? Or—worst case scenario—what if they, too, deny the existence of racism? When I began to do this work I assumed that most college-age students of color knew what racism felt like and could name it when they experienced it. I thought that anyone who had felt the sting of prejudice would want to defend others against false accusations and stereotypes. And I believed that as long as the classroom environment was "safe" most students of color would be willing, even eager, to inform their classmates about their cultures, or tell their immigrant stories, or share their painful experiences with racism and prejudice with whites who were willing to listen. But in fact, as I probably should have guessed, many were not so inclined. A high-achieving Puerto Rican student, for example, might take a strong stance against affirmative action in university admissions, even going so far as to bring in articles for the class to read that disparaged other members of his ethnic group. Or an African-American student from the deep South would claim that never in her life had she been touched by prejudice. Even though I wanted to encourage diversity of opinion among all students, and even though I knew that students of color had vastly different life experiences, seeing them minimize the effects of racism, distance themselves from their cultural traditions, and blame other people of color for not pulling themselves up by their bootstraps was profoundly discouraging.

Of course not all my students of color took such reactionary positions. Many were well aware of the ways racism had affected them and had plenty of stories to tell. But even when they were willing to take on the role of educator they could become frustrated with the wall of resistance from white students—especially those who believed themselves to be liberal nonracists. One of my Asian American students captures the feelings of many of her friends of color in a "raw theater" piece they created to shock students into dialogues in public places on campus:

> The white people in my class are so frustrating. They're so fake and politically correct—all they want to do is "change the world." They think they know what's going on but they really have no clue; they live in a privileged little bubble. They're all in the class so they "can learn about other cultures and hear opinions different

from theirs blah blah blah." I hate how they can't even be real. It's like they need to tiptoe around issues because they are scared of being pinned as racists. They all try so hard to be down and be accepted by people of color. They need to feel good all the time after class to ease their feelings of guilt. Meanwhile, we are the ones being sacrificed—recounting painful memories, spilling tears—for their benefit. And we are the ones who leave class torn up and frustrated. I'm sick of having to teach white people shit. We always have to be the spokespeople and the educators. I'm so sick of rich, suburban white kids talking about racism.

Other students of color would stifle the urge to be sarcastic and judgmental and try to look at the situation from the perspective of their white classmates. Still, this could be difficult and profoundly depressing for them. One of my African-American students reflects:

Towards the middle of the semester I began to feel resentful at the role I was selected to play. I did not enthusiastically embrace the occasion to help broaden the views of my white peers. I was dispirited, tired, and angry at having to discuss race as a reality instead of an imaginary issue. ... Then I reminded myself that because whites were sheltered from the effects of racism, they were unable to view race outside of their privilege. They could easily make the claim that race did not matter, that everyone is equal, and, as an extension to that logic, that everyone is treated equally. I struggled hard trying not to condemn them for their misunderstanding [but] I hated having to explain my point of view. The animosity that I harbor still hinders me from reaching out and aiding others in their understanding.

Some students of color who initially acted as effective educators became overwhelmed with anxiety as they learned more about the extent and virulence of white racism. An African-American student began to withdraw from class discussion about halfway through the semester, scribbling furiously in his journal while the rest of the class listened to outside speakers or debated the issues. One of his entries:

We currently have a speaker from an interfaith group talking about white supremacist groups. He is very educated and intelligent, at least I am speculating. My body is shivering, trying to figure out why individuals deal in hate. I don't understand this. I didn't realize how ignorant I was about some of these groups. I really wish I wouldn't have to come to this class. The conversation is very intimate, but I would love to leave.

Such expressions of fear disturbed me more than any other student reactions. Knowing what students of color face in the world outside, I was determined to make my classroom safe for them. But how was I to do this while still providing my white students with the information they needed to know? And why were my students of color affected in such different ways, some frightened into silence, some disgusted with their white peers, some trying hard to understand the reasons for their classmates' ignorance?

As I expanded my reading about racial identity development to students of color (Cross, Parham, and Helms, 1991; Tatum, 1992), I began to see the behaviors that most puzzled and annoyed me—the collusion with stage one whites, the sarcastic put-downs, the withdrawal from class discussion, the stony refusal to accept tentative gestures of friendship from white students—not as character faults (a stance which probably betrayed my own stage of identity development) but as natural stages in the development of a positive, healthy racial identity.

According to Beverly Tatum, students of color in the first stage have internalized many racist assumptions and stereotypes about their ethnic group including the idea that "White is right" and "Black is wrong" (1992, p. 10).[1] Surprisingly, perhaps, stage one students of color may be among the highest academic achievers. Many of them have grown up in white suburban environments and worked diligently and successfully in mostly white high schools. They may have been singled out by stage one white teachers who told them they were not like other blacks, or different from the typical reservation Indians, or that they speak good English and are therefore superior to the ingrates who speak only Spanish. They have accepted these remarks, sometimes gratefully, sometimes with a sense of discomfort that they do not show and may not fully understand. They have learned to ignore or laugh off racist comments made by white friends and sometimes collude with them in their put-downs of other ethnic groups. They tend to distance themselves both physically and psychologically from people in their own ethnic group who are the most visibly oppressed: those who are poor or whose language or culinary preferences or cultural traits feed white stereotypes.

It can be difficult to find yourself teaching a class where both students of color and white students are in stage one of their identity development. For quite opposite reasons, both groups have a psychological interest in pretending that we live in a colorblind society, that success depends entirely upon individual effort, and that we are all getting along just fine. Both groups also can afford to take strong, emotional positions against "other" students of color who whine about racism or hold loud protest marches that interfere with classroom learning. Both groups may have little sympathy for people of color who suffer economic hardship or who have made "bad choices" in their lives.

For example, in a class where I introduce issues of language and power to upper division English majors, students whose ethnic groups have been mocked for speaking "improper" or "broken" English are often the most vocal in their opposition to the statement put out by the Linguistic Society of America in support of Ebonics, or African-American Vernacular English. When one of my African-American students read that AAVE is "systematic and rule governed like all natural speech varieties: and that characterizations of it as 'slang,' 'mutant,' 'lazy,' 'defective,' 'ungrammatical,' or 'broken English' are incorrect and demeaning" (http://www.lsadc.org/info/lsa-res-ebonics.cfm), she responded hotly that she came from a long line of English teachers, that her mother and grandmother had always insisted that only "proper English" be spoken in their home, and that her goal was to become an English teacher in the black community so she could make sure her students learned to speak correctly. A Japanese American student added that if African-American vernacular was considered good English, then what about the broken English spoken by her immigrant grandfather—was that to be called a language too? The white students sat quietly through this exchange, their opinions conveniently validated by the students of color without their having to say a word.

In such a situation, I now try to separate the idea of learning the dominant language or dialect to gain authority (which I support) from devaluing and demeaning other languages and dialects (which I see as racist and classist). I might ask students to think of examples of dialects that have no racial implications, such as American and British English and ask them to consider which version is "correct." I ask them to think of examples of other languages they know where the dialect of one country or region is considered superior to another—Parisian French over French Canadian French, for example, or Castilian over Mexican Spanish. One instructor uses her own Scottish dialect to illustrate this point, explaining to her students how throughout the history of Scotland, syntax and semantics of different regions were judged as more or less acceptable, depending on the economic and political situation at the time.[2]

If, as sometimes happens, a whole class resists these explanations and examples, I might be tempted to pile on more and more authoritative knowledge that will force my students to question their world view. However, I've learned that this tactic causes stage one students of any ethnicity to resist even more strongly. If instead, I allow them to voice their own opinions, all the while encouraging them to reflect, sometimes in writing, sometimes in small group discussions, on the ways the new information might challenge their positions, sooner or later most will begin to open themselves to new perspec tives—if not publicly, in class discussion—then in response to my questions on their reaction papers and journal entries, and in the privacy of their own minds. Because of the huge shift in world view we are asking stage one students of any ethnicity to make, visible movement toward social justice goals is likely to be slow. As one of my students put it, "Sometimes I think that professors expect us to learn in one semester what it's taken them their whole career to understand." We need to remind ourselves that it takes time and courage to admit that the ways we learned to understand the world are incomplete or flawed, and that this realization is especially painful for stage one students of color, who have so much to lose, at least initially, from allowing themselves to see society's view of them more clearly.

Students of color enter stage two[3] when they begin to encounter blatantly racist attitudes or become involved in painful incidents that jar them out of their more or less benign view of the world. Of course many of our students of color entered this stage long before they came to college, since they were introduced to the realities of racism in early childhood. For those who grew up in impoverished environments the gross disparities between inner city and suburban neighborhoods are painfully apparent. James Baldwin writes about the first time he went downtown with his father, away from their "dark and dirty" neighborhood where junkies and pimps lounged at their doorstep and into the rich, white world of tall buildings and gardens and heroic monuments. "It is clean," Baldwin writes, "because they collect garbage downtown. There are doormen. People walk about as though they owned where they are—and indeed they do. And it's a great shock. It's very hard to relate yourself to this. You don't know what it means. You know—you know instinctively—that none of this is for you. You know this before you are told" (1988, pp. 5–6).

Whether or not they see the blatant socioeconomic divide firsthand, many students of color hear painful stories around the family dinner table about how racism has affected their families. "How did we come north from Texas, where Grandpa grew up?" an African-American teenager might ask in response to a school assignment. "Well," comes the answer, "when Granddad was only a little older than you, he had to jump into an empty boxcar in the middle of the night to escape a Klan lynching." In a Japanese American family, children might hear talk about a relative who went crazy after his experience in an internment camp or how their dad's first business venture was sabotaged by a competitor who hated "gooks." In a Latin@ family, a child who asks why Mom stutters when she speaks Spanish might learn how she was shamed by a first grade teacher for "talking like a dirty Mexican." Or Dad might come home angry, his blood pressure soaring, because he was stopped and questioned—*again*—while taking a peaceful evening drive through their own up-scale neighborhood.

In addition to learning how racism exerts its cruel influence on their families, many children of color have grown up with deliberate instruction from their parents about what racism is, why it happens, and who is responsible for it. This is quite different from the situation in so many liberal white households, where racism, when it is mentioned at all, is described as an unfortunate aspect of past history, or as isolated acts by immoral or deranged white supremacists. While white children are learning how to deny or minimize racism (or, in blatantly racist households, to amuse each other with openly racist jokes and stories) many children of color are being told with frightening clarity how they can expect to be treated by the white world. A Latina psychologist told me that she first became aware of this difference in childrearing practices when her daughter Julia came home from school incredulous that the white children she was working with on a group project had been puzzled by her suggestion that they write about racism. "I don't get it," Julia told her mother. "How can they be ten years old and not know what racism is?" Her mother was just as astounded. "That had never occurred to me," she told me. "As a person of color it never occurred to me that children would grow up not discussing this, not hearing about it, not having people read the newspaper to them, not having people say there's inequality in the world, and people are going to judge you because you're Hispanic or Chinese or Black."

But for the children of color whose families have tried to shield them from racism and who have always played happily with white "best friends" in comfortable neighborhoods, stage two can arrive with tremendous psychological force. An Arab American middle school child, after inviting white classmates over for his birthday party, endures a week of "teasing" about how his house "smells of humus and tabouli and camels," making him ashamed to bring anyone home again. A Filipino American child waiting excitedly for the ceremony that will induct her into a Girl Scout troop is told in a whisper by her well-meaning white friend, "It's okay—because your father is a doctor." An African-American teen who all her life had been welcomed into her white friends' homes is suddenly excluded from sleepovers and finds her phone calls unreturned. The prospect of dating becomes awkward and lonely. Japanese American author David Mura writes:

> [I]t is difficult to underestimate how much as a teenager I wanted to fit in, how deeply I assumed a basically white middle-class identity. When a white friend proclaimed, "I think of you just like a white person," I'd take it as a compliment, a sign I'd made

it. The problem was this: From the onset of my sexuality, I stumbled into experience after experience which pointed to my difference. At some level of consciousness, I was aware of racial differences in standards of beauty, that my sexual desires were crossing racial lines. Yet I had no one to talk with about this, nor any language to describe it, even to myself. Since I was so desperate to deny my racial identity, I never sought to break out of this zone of silence, to become more conscious of how race or ethnicity affected my life and my desires. (1996, p. 83)[4]

Often the effect of such incidents is understood only later, after time, distance, and a broader view of society help the young person make sense of it. A biracial white and African-American student writes:

I had my formal introduction to racism at the start of third grade. I am not sure if it had to do with the school or if it was just that kids at around eight or nine consciously become aware of racial differences that we had been internalizing well before that time. I had my eye on this girl in my class, where as usual, I was the only black person. I thought she was really cute and I mentioned to one of my friends that I kind of liked her. When she found out, she ran up to me and began kicking me over and over and yelling, "If you think I'd ever go with a nigger" and other things to that effect. To be honest, she was only about 4'3" and 65 pounds so her kicking me didn't do much damage, but I don't think I had ever been hurt quite that badly before. It wasn't until I got to college that I really thought about just how deeply that girl had hurt me that day. Looking back on it now I still wonder if it really happened or if it's just an invented memory that I like to torture myself with. I'm pretty sure it did happen though, since that was not the last time I would get to experience racism up close and personal. I was continually reminded in subtle and not so subtle ways that I was different, and different in a bad sort of way.

Such experiences propel students of color into stage three, where they withdraw to their own ethnic groups for safety and comfort and begin to learn more about their own history and culture, information that is so often denied or marginalized or even ridiculed by white society. African-American students at this stage join black fraternities and sororities and participate in all-black cultural activities and political organizations in their high schools or on their college campuses. Indian American students may join together with newly arrived Indian foreign students to put on a gala of ethnic dance and song—attended almost exclusively by Indians. Chinese American students who have grown up in English-speaking households may take their first trips to Taiwan or Hong Kong where they enroll in intensive Chinese language classes set up explicitly for the American born.

This willing separation inevitably causes concern among white students in the early stages of their own identity development. Since most of them have grown up without any meaningful interaction with people of color and have learned to see much of the racism in their families and communities as normal, they have little understanding why this "acceptable level of racism" would be seen as outrageous by students of color, or even leave a reservoir of hurt in their hearts. Some express disappointment that their dreams of a multicultural campus have been spoiled by students of color who "don't want to mix." Those who are more comfortable with open expressions of racism react with anger and sarcasm. A third-year undergraduate who identifies as Hispanic of Chilean descent writes of her experience with these white reactions as she entered stage three of her identity development:

> I grew up in a mostly white, affluent community in the U.S. As an affluent Hispanic with a relatively light complexion (which was still, by far, one of the darkest in my community), I didn't experience any problems as long as I shared in "their" ethnicity. Once I began to grow and explore my own heritage, things drastically changed. In Spanish classes, even though I spoke only a little, I was immediately singled out by the white students as "taking the class for an easy A," or "another wetback taking advantage of the system," or, though I have never been the recipient of federal funds until recently, "a welfare child mooching off the hard 'white work' their parents did." I found solace in friendships with the few other minorities in my high school, but for the most part, I felt alienated from this 99% white community. I have never felt entirely comfortable around whites since high school.

After experiences like these, students of color may quite understandably develop a deep mistrust of whites and the cynical belief that dialogue with white students will ever be anything more than (as one of my African-American students put it) "an exercise in superficial, feel-good political correctness involving liberal whites who will leave the class further convinced of their moral righteousness and ability to save the world, and a few token 'Uncle Tom' students of color who will serve as the whites' 'black best friends.'"

While stage three students of color often reject friendly dialogue with whites, they are also pulling ahead of most of their white peers in their ability to recognize the ways that racism permeates society's institutions. An African-American senior writes in her journal:

> I cannot convey how much I am affected by the usual portrayal of blacks in the media. We are subject to blatant typecasting in Hollywood. The worst is the jokester/professional; even with a stellar educational background the character is not respected. Makes me think of a modern-day, middle-class Sambo. Then there are any number of wanna-be Jezebel, Mammy and Coon characters. Everywhere I look, the media shuts down any truly positive, human portrayal of black people. There are black scholars,

painters, musicians, and philanthropists. Why is it that this information is always out of the reach or interest of Americans?

This ability to see the broader picture can at times make stage three students of color excellent discussion participants and sometimes inadvertent educators of silently listening whites who have gone beyond blaming the victim and are open to a deeper understanding of personal and institutional racism. But when stage three students of color find themselves in a class with white students who have yet to recognize the existence of racism in their own assumptions and behavior, they easily become exasperated at the difficulty of discussing at a sophisticated level what white students are only beginning to comprehend. For while whites in the early stages of their development can easily recognize the "Mammy, Jezebel and Coon" characters on television, they are more likely to accept these stereotypes as "just the way black people are" and feel justified in either laughing at them or turning off the show in disgust.[5]

If you are working with a few stage three students of color in a class of whites in the early stages of their racial identity development (which on many campuses is the norm), you need to support your students of color, often in private conversations during office hours, letting them know you understand what they are up against and explaining as well as you can why white students have difficulty recognizing racism. At the same time, you need to be providing the experiences, texts, videos, and visitors that help your white students move forward, while listening to their frustrations and supporting their growth in private conversations and in your responses to their writing. Unless the students of color agree to act as educators or want the opportunity to vent as Gloria did (Chapter 4), I try to plan classroom interactions that minimize angry confrontation. Videos that offer personal perspectives by people of color (see Annotated Resources) are validating to students of color at this stage and instructive for whites at any stage of their development. However, if careful management of classroom discussion is not your style, or if "race breaks out" anyway, it is important to reassure the whole class that conflict over racial issues is normal, that they are engaged in an honest conversation that most adults in this country are unable to have, and that you have faith in their ability to grow and learn from the course material and from each other.

When the classroom gets hot, conciliatory moves are sometimes made by students of color themselves, even by the very students who are most passionately engaged in the discussion. In one of my classes, a biracial white and African-American student who had grown up in the dual world of a low-income housing project and a progressive private school of the arts was so ready to act as mediator at these times that she insisted that we not leave a difficult class session without standing in a circle, holding hands, murmuring heartfelt slogans of unity. When I brought this suggestion to another class, however, the stage three students of color opposed any comforting mantras or "fake, feel-good tactics," for in their opinion, "the angrier we all leave class the more real and honest we've been." I tend to let students of color set the tone at these times, since it is their hurt and exclusion that are at the heart of any angry exchange about racism. Whatever the group dynamics, talking about my own experiences with race, especially in areas where I'm still learning, can be helpful both to white students, who come to see me as a role model, and students of color, who appreciate the honesty.

As students of color enter stage four they are beginning to feel more secure and positive about their racial identity and are able to reach out in friendship to genuinely respectful whites without losing touch with friends from their own ethnic group. Their stage three retreat to their own ethnic groups has given them a safe space to talk about the daily indignities of racism and explore questions of identity and solidarity among themselves without worrying what white people will think: How should we confront issues of internalized racism? Is it fair for black men to date white women? What about hierarchies of color within black and Latin@ communities? What are some different ways to think about interracial adoption? How can we confront the divisions in our communities along lines of socioeconomic class?[6] After talking about these questions in safe spaces among themselves, students of color are more prepared to learn about the cultures and histories of other stigmatized groups, and to understand the ways that gender, class, sexual orientation, disability, religion, age, and other social identities intersect and complicate experiences of discrimination, ridicule, and hatred. But regardless of their new willingness to reach out to other groups, even mature, self-possessed, high-achieving students of color may need to retreat to spaces where they are most comfortable at various times during their college experience. Regardless of their use to us as educators, these students should not be expected to have endless patience, especially with those white students who resist our own best efforts to reach them.

Racial identity development theory can help us understand the dynamics of our classroom discussions and help us develop patience with students whose ideas we find puzzling or distasteful. But I'll have to admit that linking students' personal beliefs and political positions to a scheme of psychological development can look like an Orwellian nightmare to those who have strong beliefs about individual expression. And they have a point. Can't students of color express conservative opinions about social policy or economics without our pegging them (even in our own minds) as "stage one?" Could a Latin@ student despise illegal immigrants who abuse the welfare system without being thought of as a victim of internalized oppression? Shouldn't it be possible for an African-American student to downplay the issue of racism in her life without our deciding she is "in denial?" Maybe these psychological explanations for students' attitudes are just an easy, condescending way of dismissing opinions we disagree with.

These questions have no easy answers, since it is so hard to distinguish between a person's own, true convictions and the ways their thinking has been shaped by the insidious racism that pervades our society. Although I would often prefer to believe, like many of my liberal colleagues, that all students bring valid opinions to discussions about race and that my role is to let everyone be heard equally, I also realize that some of these opinions, especially those that are the most hurtful to stigmatized groups, have been shaped by strong negative forces that students are completely unaware of.

When I am confronted with questions like these, I reflect back on my own strange relationship with feminism. Raised as a strong individualist by an even stronger single mother, I believed for many years that "life is what you make it" and that the oppression of women of my generation was greatly exaggerated. I knew of course that women didn't develop their talents to the fullest, but wasn't that their own fault—what with their low professional aspirations, their obsessive interest in beauty and diet, their swooning over movie stars, their childish magazines with light, fluffy, easy-read pieces, just like their low-cal desserts? In college I distanced myself from other women students (for it was said that we were only there to find husbands), preferring the company of male classmates who talked about things of intellectual substance, cared little for appearances, and treated me fondly as an honorary male. In the 1970s, with the advent of the women's movement, I avoided consciousness-raising groups; the whole idea seemed so trivial and self-centered. Books promoting feminism made me angry, even after (or maybe especially after) I got myself into a relationship that depended for its survival on my tacit acquiescence to female stereotypes. Looking back at myself, I was as confused about women's oppression as some of my students of color are about racism. I would have been incensed if anyone had suggested I was at "stage one" in the development of a positive feminist consciousness. But it was true.

How did I begin to see things differently? I met more women, that's one thing. Intelligent women. Women who thought deeply and honestly about how they had been taught to see themselves in relation to men. When I went to graduate school I began working with women who were intellectual and moral leaders in their communities, and I could see powerful groups of women beginning to form across nationalities and ethnicities. A growing sense of pride in my own group, the group I had once viewed with condescension and distaste, gave me the strength to see women as more than just individuals who took their luck and made their own—mostly stupid—choices. Now, we were "we," working together to develop a fuller humanity not only for ourselves, but for the world.

Although I have always been my own person: positive, cheerful, and high achieving, for much of my life I also have been naive about power relations between women and men and blind to the ways I have supported my own and other women's oppression. I cannot say that my experience as a woman makes me an expert on all the feelings and thoughts and confusions of my students of color. But it does give me a window on the ways that one can internalize negative ideas about one's own capabilities without realizing it, how easy it is to say, "I'm not like *them*," and how difficult and emotional it is to move into a stage of greater awareness of one's own oppression. And I know that change takes time—much more time than my students have in a one-semester class.

Antiracism teaching is psychologically complex and taxing work. As college educators, most of us have not been trained to deal with our students' emotional needs, nor do we have much knowledge of how to manage uncomfortable group dynamics. We have not been taught ways to see across the great divide between whites and people of color, or even to acknowledge that the divide exists. Nevertheless, we need to develop the capacity to understand and accept all our students, regardless of the biases they have learned and the misinformation they sometimes cling to. We need to recognize the outbursts of emotion, the grim silence, the wounds, scars, and bruises for what they are—the shockingly painful birth pangs of a new society based on true equality. Will it grow up joyful and healthy after all our work and struggle? We will not know in our lifetime. All we can do is to provide, as Myles Horton says, "a climate which nurtures islands of decency, where people can learn in such a way that they continue to grow" (1990, p. 176).

# Update

As I mentioned in the Update to Chapter 6, current students, the Millennial generation, are likely to be more polite, guarded, and "civil" in classroom conversations about race, more willing to seek out interracial friendships, and more liberal on issues of women's empowerment, gay rights, and interracial dating and marriage than students of previous generations. White students, perhaps believing that "seeing color" is tantamount to racism, are more likely to adopt a color-blind attitude, and to deny any racism on the part of their own generation, except perhaps for a few "bad apples." When these students make naïve remarks about race in casual conversation or in class discussion, their peers of color are less likely to react with anger or bitterness than they were in the past. But the tension is still there, beneath the polite veneer.

"When I had to listen to white students defending colonialism and saying that Africa needed more of it, I felt very alienated. Very alone. Very black," wrote an African-American student in an evaluation of a class on international development.

"I felt like leaving the class the day we were discussing what makes a person culturally black," an African-American student told me privately. "I couldn't believe that white people really think those things. But even though I was insulted, I kept my thoughts to myself. I'm not one to reveal my emotions too much."

"When I went to the Native American powwow I overheard some people saying they thought it was just like a carnival but way more entertaining," wrote a black student who had been investigating her own Native American roots. "It reminded me of the way blacks were viewed in the early twentieth century when the only positive images of black people were as jovial dancers, musicians, servants, and entertainers. During the dance competition I heard a lot of mimicking of the chanting and the drumming by both children and adults. I did not see this as a form of flattery, but rather a mockery of tribal cultural practices." Like other Millennials, students of color try their best to "get along." They may take an "observer" role like the student at the powwow, or hold their emotions in check when they are offended in class. But the stress can take its toll, both personally and academically. In such an environment, students of color need support from their teachers, counselors, and mentors, yet the pretense that everyone is getting along just fine can make it difficult to see that the need is there.

For classroom discussion, however, students' reluctance to let "race break out" can be a good thing as long as both white students and students of color have ample opportunity to express their points of view, sometimes in writing, sometimes in small group discussion with like-minded peers, sometimes in debate, and, always, with the support of the instructor. See Annotated Resources for suggestions on how to involve everyone in discussion.

Another difference between Millennial students and those of previous generations is their dissatisfaction with the rigid racial categories we have inherited from the early "race scientists," who used them to justify slavery and colonialism. Some students of African descent are questioning the "one-drop rule" and are becoming more forthright in claiming distant relatives of Native American, Asian, and European ethnic groups such as Norwegian, Polish, or Irish. Biracial and multiracial students, whose numbers have been increasing on college campuses, are choosing among a variety of ways to identify themselves. They might choose one racial identity only, such as Barack Obama did when he declared himself to be "black," despite the white identity of his mother and grandparents who raised him. Or, students might hold multiple racial identities, shifting between them at different times and in different places. "I identify as white most of the time," says a biracial white and Indian American student. "Except when I go to India, or maybe at an Indian wedding or some other get-together in the States." Other students might choose to simply identify as multiracial rather than with any of their specific heritage groups, especially if there are campus organizations that support such a choice. Or they might decide to resist any racial categories, designed as they were by whites to justify oppression. These students' choice of identity might depend on their looks: their color, hair texture, facial features, or body type. Or, it might depend on their cultural or linguistic knowledge: their preference for certain kinds of music, their ability to speak Spanish or Thai, or their expertise with the vocabulary, intonation, and style of Black Vernacular English. Their choice might also be affected by the resistance they encounter from whites who attempt to use their race privilege to categorize them according to their own view of the world ("How can you be Hispanic all of a sudden? You don't even speak Spanish!"), or from people of color who feel more constrained by society to identify with a single race. All this complexity can make it difficult to apply the standard linear models of racial identity development that I have outlined in Chapters 6 and 7 to multiracial students' experiences. When I use those models in the classroom, I ask students who racially identify in nonstandard ways to talk about how the models apply or don't apply to their own experience, and to reflect on the ways they are coming to terms with their heritage in the context of the racism that exists today.

# Notes

1.  Psychologist William Cross developed his model of racial identity development specifi-cally in reference to blacks (Cross, Parham, and Helms, 1991). However, Tatum (1992) extends this schema to other students of color (Asians, Latin@s, and Native Americans), saying "there is evidence to suggest that the process for these oppressed groups is similar to that described for African Americans" (p. 9). Models of biracial and multiracial identity development emphasize the complex web of cultures, identities, loyalties, and community reactions that these individuals must negotiate. Because of the remnants of the "one-drop rule," however, biracial and multiracial students usually identify (and are seen by others) as students of color. See Renn (2008) for a review of the literature; Posten (1990) and Root (1990) for identity development models for these groups.
2.  George Bernard Shaw's *Pygmalion* (1939) also makes this point.
3.  Cross's model of black racial identity development titles the five stages: Preencounter, Encounter, Immersion/Emersion, Internalization, and Internalization-Commitment (Cross, Parham, and Helms, 1991). I am using "stage one," "stage two," and so on for simplicity.
4.  Additional readings that describe intense awakenings to the realities of racism: Dick Greg-ory's autobiography, *Nigger*; James Baldwin', *A Talk to Teachers*; Patricia Raybon's memoir, *My First White Friend*; and Judith Ortiz Cofer's short essay, *American History*.
5.  Excellent videos that show the history of stereotypes in movies and on television are *Ethnic Notions* (Riggs, 1987), *Color Adjustment* (Riggs, 1991), *Heathen Injuns and the Holly-wood Gospel* (KCTS-9 Seattle, 1979), *The Slanted Screen: Asian Men in Film and Television* (Adachi, 2006), and *Reel Bad Arabs: How Hollywood Vilifies a People* (Shaheen, 2007).
6.  All these issues can be of intense interest to whites as well. But since whites are more comfortable seeing people of color as "the problem" than addressing the issue of their own racism and privilege, I try not to dwell on the struggles and divisions among people of color in my mostly white classes. Nevertheless, it is helpful for white instructors, at least, to understand these issues in order to know their students of color better. One means of introduction is through videos: *A Question of Color* (Sandler, 1992) on the origins of the "caste system" of skin tone and hair; *Los Vendidos* (The Sellouts) (Ruiz, 1972) about Latin@ stereotypes, acculturation and class; *My America (... Or Honk If You Love Buddha)* (Tajima-Peña & Thai, 1997) about Asian American lifestyles; *Miss India Georgia* (Grim-berg & Friedman, 1997) about assimilation and identity among Indian Americans; and *Tales from Arab Detroit* (Howell & Mandell, 1995) on the generation gap among Arab American parents and their children.

# · 8 ·

# EXERCISES, ASSIGNMENTS, AND ADVICE

This chapter and the one that follows, "Annotated Resources and More Ideas for Assignments and Discussions," give you texts, videos, exercises, and discussion topics to promote deeper, more intelligent conversations about race in your classrooms. Many are suitable for a wide variety of classroom contexts; others can be modified to suit your class size, subject matter, and time constraints. Some of the advice may seem obvious—until you challenge yourself to put it into practice. As in earlier chapters, I sometimes use the voices of students and instructors to provide a rationale for the approach I advocate. A summary of all my advice can be found at the end of this chapter.

## Setting the Tone

### Model sensitive intercultural interaction

In most of my classes, there are only a few students of my ethnicity. Professors don't seem to know I'm there and students don't bother to say hello to anyone who doesn't look like them. They probably wonder why I'm quiet in class discussion, or why I hang out with my Korean friends after class. I just don't feel particularly welcome. I have come to realize that it is the sense of nobodiness that makes me so sad and frightened sometimes.
—Korean undergraduate

Make everyone feel as welcome in your classroom as you would in your own home. Learn how to pronounce unfamiliar names by asking, with a smile, "Could you tell me your name again? I'd really like to learn how to say it correctly." Recognize any tendency in yourself to confuse two students of an ethnic minority you have little contact with (this has happened to me more often than I care to admit). Express interest, publicly, in each student's home country or community, whether it is an impoverished inner city area, a tiny country you've never heard of, or the very town where you grew up. Talk to students before class or in conference to learn about their interests and goals, and use this knowledge to guide your choice of materials. A news article about a company that has begun to tie promotions to diversity goals will catch the attention of future business people; visits from health professionals of color will cause students headed into medical fields to question their assumptions; an exercise comparing the treatment of slavery in several high school text-books will appeal to future teachers. Your attempts to personalize the curriculum and make warm, friendly connections will provide a model for students of any ethnicity who are unsure about how to approach people who seem different, as well as for those who haven't been taught to care.

On the first day, take time for introductions and other get-to-know-you activities. Students can interview their neighbor for a few minutes around aspects of college life that everyone has in common: "Where's your hometown?" "What's your major?" "What sports or music do you enjoy?" "Where are you staying on campus?" Then ask everyone to introduce their partners to the larger group.

Speak enthusiastically about events on campus put on by ethnic groups other than your own, and urge all students to attend. Go to some of these events yourself and tell your class what you enjoyed about them. Stress the benefits of spending time with people whose language, color, and/or styles of celebration are different from your own. Since I enjoy cultural events so much myself, I have been surprised at the number of students (of any ethnicity) who are reluctant to participate in activities organized by identity groups they are unfamiliar with. Yet when I give an assignment to attend such activities, students are often grateful that I "made them go." "I was amazed to see how many Arab students there are on this campus," one student wrote in her reaction paper. "I don't know why I thought the purpose of this event (an Arab American comedian) would be to inform white people about Arab culture. I guess that's my white privilege—assuming everything's about *me*. I didn't get some of the jokes, but I laughed anyway so I wouldn't stand out. It was uncomfortable, but challenging in a good way."

## Respect students' needs for safety

> Having a person of the same ethnicity sit next to me in class is like having a built-in comfort zone.
>
> —African-American undergraduate

Start out by letting students sit where they are most comfortable, even if that means white students all sit together and smaller groups of African-American or Latin@ or Vietnamese students cluster in various parts of the room. In my own classes, I begin to vary these configurations for small group work after students are comfortable with my teaching style and have some familiarity with the kinds of questions we discuss. The smoothest way to achieve mixed groups without explicitly mentioning it is to have students count off by the number of groups you want to create (e.g., count to four to make four groups). In classes where race is the central topic and where strong needs for safety may come up at various points in the semester, I alternate between letting students choose their own groups ("Get together with students you feel the most comfortable with") and mixing things up ("Get into groups with students who are writing on your topic so you can share resources and help each other with arguments"; "Get into groups with students who are researching different topics so you can explain your topic to a new audience"; or, more explicitly, "Get into a group with people you haven't talked to yet"). You can also ask students to group themselves by the first letter of their last name, the month of their birthday, or some other neutral category.

## Affirm human similarities

I strongly believe that students in the early stages of their racial identity development (that is to say, most white college students) need to hear messages about unity and similarity—that all peoples of the world are a single human family—before they begin delving into the ugly realities of racism, economic power struggles, and the clash of cultural and religious values. Students who have not yet begun to question the outright racist beliefs of their home communities need to hear this message for obvious reasons. But students who truly believe in equality and deplore the "divisiveness" of racial issues need to begin with unifying messages as well. No one likes to hear the worst about themselves or the country that they hold so dear. We can ease these students into more honest personal examination and critique of their society by affirming their idealism at first, "calling them in" to racial justice work rather than "calling them out" on their blind spots. Of course we must not let them rest there comfortably. They need to be pushed, sometimes gently, sometimes more forcefully, into an awareness of what so many people of color find maddeningly obvious: that whites find it "normal" to exclude other perspectives, deny other people's talent and potential, stereotype entire ethnic groups as criminals or deviants, arrange housing and financial services to exclude families on the basis of stereotypes, and so on. I promote friendly, "low-stakes" interaction across ethnic groups by inviting my classes to meet at least once a semester at my house or in other out-of-class settings like a coffee shop, a student co-op, or outside on the lawn when the weather is nice. I do activities and icebreakers that require cooperation among students from different backgrounds and cause them to laugh and cheer for their own multicultural team. I arrange opportunities for students studying a second language to meet with native speakers of that language who want to improve their English—sometimes for course credit. I help organize an annual Intercultural Leadership Seminar that brings students from a great variety of backgrounds together for an intensive three and a half days to share their cultural values, beliefs and perspectives, sometimes far into the night. I act as an advisor to student leaders who want to break down self-segregation on campus and build bridges across ethnic organizations. Sometimes I simply encourage students to develop these projects on their own initiative; students are often the best, most creative organizers, for they know their peers' interests and concerns and how to get them involved.

For a simple first-day exercise that promotes seeing similarities across ethnic groups, ask students to count off into groups of three or four and find at least one thing that they all have in common (a love of classical music? a state they've all visited? an interest in deer hunting?). Rather than suggesting categories, let them talk until they find their own. Then ask them to tell what they've found to the rest of the class. Alternatively, call out areas of student interest and ask students to stand when they hear a category they fit into ("Who is a student athlete? A football fan? Who is thinking about business as a career? Who likes to write poetry?"). Ask athletes to say a few words about their sport, musicians to mention their instrument, and so on.

## Show students of color you can be trusted

As a white teacher, I've come to realize that the best way to make students of color a little more at ease in my classes is to use language that signals my commitment to discussions of race and racism and the ways I actively work to counter racism on campus and in the community. This might simply involve referring to myself as white ("As a white person doing social justice work. ...") and avoiding the ethnocentric mistake of using the word "people" when I mean "white people," or referring to "our communities" when I mean "white communities." I use the term "students of color" to model respectful language to white students (a few of whom still use the term "colored" to refer to African-Americans, or, more commonly, "Mexicans" to refer to any Latin@s, or "Chinese" to refer to anyone who looks East Asian), and to international students, who may not yet understand the racial dynamics in the United States. These small rhetorical moves let students know that race matters in our class—that we can't pretend to be color-blind, either in relation to the course material or to each other. I then mention the sensitive nature of the material I'm going to cover. Instead of issuing vague "trigger warnings" about material that might offend or distress them I address the issue head-on. If, for example, the word "nigger" appears in books on my reading list, I talk about the offensiveness of the term and ask students their opinions about possible approaches to the study of racist literature: Should we avoid reading these novels? Should we excuse the racism of the author because of the time and place the novel was written? How should we consider the present racial context along with the historical context? These serious, scholarly questions not only help students think critically, they show that I take their concerns and emotions seriously.

When the subject of your course focuses on the difficulties experienced by people of color and you are concerned that some of your students will feel singled out or demeaned by the approach you feel you must take, address the issue openly, early on in the semester. A white instructor in the health sciences who presents material on how race and poverty affect health status starts the first class by saying something like this:

> In this class we'll be talking about how some ethnic groups are more affected by poverty and health problems than others. I realize this can be a sensitive issue, since these facts have often been used to stereotype and blame people of color for their own problems. But this is just the opposite of what I want us to do in this class. We need to acknowledge from the start that the history of discrimination in this country has created vast differences in wealth and access to health care. We're going to look at these differences carefully to see how we can work to change the situation.

## Show students that you "expect respect"

Instructors of color report that white students sometimes treat them too casually or even dismissively, especially if they are young, female, or fairly new to the classroom. A black professor who teaches a large, introductory course on American history reports being addressed by his first name by white students on a regular basis. Another black professor who teaches engagingly about hip hop is deeply insulted by white students' casual use of "nigger" in their classroom discussions of rap lyrics. Asian graduate student instructors brace themselves on the first day of the semester for the looks of incomprehension at the sound of their accent, no matter how minimal. An African-American professor of psychology is struck speechless when asked by a white undergraduate for a photograph of herself to adorn the cover of her literary analysis of an African novel.

Senior faculty agree that these frustrating and dehumanizing experiences are all too common, and counsel instructors to approach them with humor, persistence, and firm expectations for students' behavior. Treat rudeness as naïvete: "In high school you may have called your teachers by their first names, but in college, we address faculty as 'Professor,' even in email." "In this class, we will use the term, 'the N-Word,' because the word "nigger" still has great power to insult and demean people—which I know you don't want to do." Instructors who speak English with an accent report that smiling often, remembering students' names, facing their audience rather than the board or screen while speaking, and projecting their voice to the back of the classroom help students who may be worried that their instructor's accent will prevent them from understanding difficult material. As for dealing with the student who wanted to photograph her professor to illustrate a particular body type— one can only laugh, or maybe go out with colleagues after work for a good stiff drink; any real explanation to the student of how it feels to be objectified is likely to be too painful for a one-on-one conversation. Until racial literacy is expected of all students, their capacity to empathize across racial lines will remain underdeveloped.

## Avoid Asking Students of Color to Speak for Their Entire Ethnic Group

When the subject of poverty in Detroit came up in my Sociology class, everyone looked at me for an answer. I had to respond that I have never been poor in

Detroit and I'm searching for answers just like everyone else. I didn't like having
to prove myself to other people; it was uncomfortable.

—African-American Detroiter

Instructors can keep such embarrassing moments from happening by saying
at the outset, "Some of us may know poverty firsthand, some of us may have
lived or worked in impoverished areas, and some of us may have had absolutely no experiences of poverty to draw on. If you want to speak from your
own experiences or those of your friends or relatives, these perspectives are
especially welcome." Then open the discussion to all.

Some students, especially internationals (who may be used to fielding
naïve questions about their country) or students who strongly identify with
a particular religious community, may not mind speculating about what their
entire identity group thinks or how they live. I'll admit that I was puzzled at
first at the touchiness of this issue for U.S. students of color, since when I
travel abroad I am often asked what Americans think, what we eat, or why we
do x, y, or z (which I personally never do). I haven't been offended by these
questions and have tried to answer them as best I can. But upon reflection, I
realized that my position of privilege (which I cannot avoid carrying with me
abroad) insulates me from the racial subtext that people of color sense when
they hear such questions from whites. For example, "What do African Americans think about the drug problem?" can sound like "Why do you blacks have
such a drug problem?" when it's not consciously meant that way. Even when
teachers ask seemingly neutral questions ("What do Asians think about the
Obama presidency?") the assumption that a vast swath of the global community would think alike can still sting. For a more sensitive way to include
students of color in discussion, or simply to gain information, ask, "What do
*you* think about the Obama presidency?" "Here's what I think (or the author
in question thinks) about the drug problem. What's your opinion?" If you're
really curious about what identity groups think, check current survey research.

## Exploring ethnic identities

Multicultural teaching means students will learn about their own culture, too.
Many times white students will say, "Do we, as white students, have ethnicity?"
Learning about your own culture is very important. Once you know about your
culture, you are more able to accept it and also more able to accept other cultures.

—Christina José, Professor of Women's Studies
(quoted in Schoem et al., 1995, p. 282)

**All our ethnicities.** In small groups, ask students to share their ethnic and family backgrounds, some of the influences that have shaped who they are, and/or their concept of "home." Then bring them back into the large group and ask a few to talk about the most interesting things they learned. To help students from European immigrant backgrounds understand why they may know so little of their cultures, I sometimes tell the story about Henry Ford's Americanization classes for the immigrants who worked on his auto assembly lines in the 1920s. At graduation, so the story goes, there would be a huge cardboard soup pot on stage with a door cut in the side. Students would march through the door dressed in the clothing of their home countries and singing folk songs in their mother tongue. Then the door would close and their teachers would pretend to stir the soup with ten-foot ladles. After a few minutes the door would open again and the students would march out dressed in suits and ties, waving little American flags, and singing "The Star Spangled Banner."[1] When my class is small enough, I vary the ethnicity exercise by asking students to all come up to the front of the room together and write, anywhere on the board, the names of all the ethnic groups they know of in their family's history. Soon, we have a whole board full of national, cultural, religious, and ethnic identities to talk about: Who are the Roma, and what countries do they come from? Is "Jewish" an ethnic group, a race, or a religion? Why are the Pennsylvania Dutch called Dutch if they're really German? I wrap up these discussions with positive affirmation of the variety and number of groups that we as a class represent.

## Using online blogs and videos

Explorations of identity written and filmed by young people abound on the internet. They can be thought-provoking, comical, heartfelt or all of these, but they never fail to provoke classroom discussion. I start by assigning links that I find interesting, and later, ask students to find their own examples to share with the class. In a class of twenty, for example, I might ask that each student find a good video or blog on our topic and send it to the whole class list. Everyone watches and reads everything (most videos are only a few minutes long), and comes to class prepared to discuss what they liked, what they questioned, what annoyed or frustrated them, and something new they learned.

For example, in the youtube video, "Being Biracial (The Mixed GirlTag)" https://www.youtube.com/watch?v=Jku7HrVnEzY, a vlogger talks directly and personally to other young people in response to ten questions about parentage and nationality, hair type, interracial marriage, stereotypes, and other issues of racial and national identity. She is so open, so concrete in her descriptions of her experience that students are encouraged to tell their own stories. Her positive attitude about her mixed identity ("I love every part of who I am, and I wouldn't change it for the world.") sets an upbeat tone before we delve into the ugliness of racial stereotypes. Since mixed and/or biracial identity is becoming more and more common these days, with more than nine million Americans identifying as more than one race, students may find the discussion of mixed identity highly relevant to their own experience or to the experience of their friends or the celebrities whose lives they follow on line.

The controversial issue of "white identity" is addressed with light humor in the blog "Stuff White People Like" (https://stuffwhitepeoplelike.com), which claims there are activities, attitudes, foods, styles, music, material possessions, and life choices that are unique to white people, and that people of color (and some whites) find this culture weird or amusing. For example, this blog entry (http://stuffwhitepeoplelike.com/2010/09/08/134-the-ted-conference/) makes fun of the propensity of white people to "create something that will allow them to feel smart but doesn't require a large amount of work, time, or effort"—like a TED Conference. There are countless variations on the "stuff white people like" theme on the internet, all of which can prompt discussion about whether there is, in fact, a "white culture" (or cultures), what it means to be white, what happens to people of color who enjoy the same things that white people (presumably) do, and whether this outcome is similar for all ethnic groups or only some of them.

Other blogs and videos that I have found particularly useful for starting discussions about identity can be found in Annotated Resources.

**Immigrant stories.** White students, especially, will find it instructive to try to find out more about their ancestors' ethnicities by interviewing their parents or grandparents, using Web-based tools for tracing genealogy (www. familysearch. org), and reporting on their findings. A simpler way to approach this is to ask students to write a two or three-page narrative about one of their ancestors who first arrived in America, using any facts they might know about that person and making up the details of the rest (or, if they like, by completely inventing an ancestor) according to what they know or surmise about the time, the culture, the likely economic and social position of their family when they arrived, and how they fared in their new land. I make the point that all of us came to this part of the world somehow, either voluntarily, as ancient migrants or newer arrivals; or involuntarily, through kidnapping and slavery, and that all of these stories are interesting and important to know and share. I have found this exercise to be very useful in classes where students express anti-immigrant sentiments, as it makes the point that today's immigrants have many of the same desires and frustrations as their own ancestors. Most students, including those whose ancestors came involuntarily, enjoy writing these stories and sometimes ask to read them aloud to their classmates. If an African-American or Native American student objects to the underlying idea that "we're all immigrants together" (because it simplifies and glosses over the horror of enslavement and genocide), I support their stance, try to make room for their anger, reiterate the differences between involuntary and voluntary "immigration," and encourage them to write a creative piece about one of the many who resisted—or adapted to survive.

**Identities Exercise.** For groups of about 20 to 150 students. Time: 1–2 hours (larger groups take longer than smaller ones). This exercise, designed by University of Michigan faculty Mark Chesler and Ruby Beale, promotes rich encounters between students of various backgrounds, allowing them to question each other about sensitive issues of race, ethnicity, religion, and other identities. Students appreciate it because, as they say, "it's structured, so we're forced to interact with each other." Large groups need multiple facilitators; I've worked with a multiracial team of seven or eight instructors in a large hall full of students. Prepare the exercise by posting sheets of flip chart paper around the room with the names of identity groups that reflect the approximate makeup of your class. The following categories cover almost any mix: Northern European; Southern European; Asian Pacific Americans (APA); Middle Eastern; African; African-American; Caribbean; Latin@; and Native American. You might also post the names of the major religions: Jewish, Catholic, Protestant, Muslim, Hindu, and Buddhist, which gives students more than one group to choose from and gets them thinking about their multiple identities. Biracial and multiracial students may want to form a "Mixed" category, which is fine, although this may bring up uncomfortable issues between students of color who choose to identify themselves this way and those who object to this category (since it seems to reinforce color and caste hierarchies).[2]

Students choose one of these identity groups (which for some will be a difficult task in itself) and meet with others from the same group for about twenty minutes, talking together about these three questions: (1) What makes this group unique? (i.e., what are the commonalties among students who have chosen this group?) (2) What are some of the differences among people in this group? (3) What do you think other groups think about your group? They then write their answers on the flip chart paper and post it back up on the wall.

Next, students have about fifteen minutes to mill around in silence, reading other groups' responses to these questions and thinking of (and perhaps writing down) questions they want to ask of people in the other groups. Then they have about thirty minutes to question members of other groups, and if there's time, another twenty minutes or so of large group discussion where each group shares the questions they were asked, how they responded, and what they learned from other groups.

The facilitators begin the exercise by talking a little about their own ethnic and religious identities to give students models and put them at ease. The variety of instructors' identities and the complexity of their backgrounds may cause students to question their own stereotypes even before the exercise begins. In our group, an instructor who looks white introduced herself as a mixture of Native American, African-American and European American; another whose ebony skin and French accent seemed to identify her as West African said she grew up in Switzerland and loves to ski; and an instructor identifying as African-American traced some of her ancestors from many Native American tribes as well as "unknown whites." All the instructors talked about the identity category they would choose if they were participating in the exercise and acknowledged that they had created some pretty large and diverse categories (e.g., "Asian Pacific American") and might not have even thought of the category that is most important to some of the participants. We then had to help some students choose: for example, a white student who had never considered that he was anything but "American," and a student who felt strongly that her African-American ethnicity and her Muslim religion could not be separated.

In evaluations of this exercise, students say that talking in their own ethnic or religious groups first helps them feel more comfortable, for they meet students who are in some way like themselves, make new friends, and sometimes learn new things about their own heritage. This gives them confidence for the scarier part, when they question other groups about issues that they may have always wondered about. Black students ask Indian Americans about the meaning of the red dot on some women's foreheads; white students ask Korean students how they feel about being called a "model minority." Native Americans get asked about casinos and pow wows; Jews ask Christians why they try to convert them—and, if you have set up the exercise carefully, all is done in an atmosphere of mutual respect. Giving explicit instructions, allow-ing a specific time period for each part of the exercise, and facilitating discus-sion afterward that validates emotions and feelings all help students who are new to a multicultural environment feel a bit more safe in the minefield of intergroup relations.

**Being an ally.** After students have learned the basics about other ethnic groups and have explored the subject of race and racism in depth (see next section), I promote a deeper, more complex understanding of the experi-ences of different ethnic groups by having students read novels and memoirs (see Annotated Resources) written by and about people from groups differ-ent from their own. Then I ask students to write a five-page letter to the author or a specific character in their own voice and from their heart, show-ing that they have heard and understood the difficulties and frustrations that person has faced and telling them specific actions they might take to become an ally either to that individual or to the group they represent. Brainstorm-ing beforehand about what it means to be an ally to another ethnic group and the specific kinds of actions or activities that this might involve will help students think more positively and realistically about what they might propose. Be sure students think about both the personal and the political. Students come up with ideas like learning more about an ethnic group, com-mitting themselves to using a language they've learned but never practiced in the community, talking with friends about suppressed history, showing a video about the Civil Rights Movement at a family gathering, writing letters to Congress or the student newspaper, or longer term goals such as teach-ing in a resource-deprived school, setting up a medical clinic in a depressed area, or working with their political party to draft legislation that supports targeted groups.

## Promoting Dialogue About Race, Racism, and Privilege

I came into the class with the notion that I held relatively few stereotypes. As I soon found out, I had not even begun to ponder these issues. I had never heard of things such as "white privilege." I had rarely acknowledged that I have been treated differently than students of color. I only knew that I was not a racist, and that I cared a lot about helping minorities in their struggles. I had no terminology, and no comprehension of ways to combat racism. Now, my mind has undergone a huge transformation ...

—white undergraduate

I am embarrassed to say, at the beginning of this semester I really didn't think I had much to learn. In fact, I thought I could teach the class with my experience. I waved the flag of my hometown, Detroit, to prove my commitment against racism, as if claiming that living in a mostly African American city will forever protect me against racist tendencies. I naively used my neighborhood as proof that I was a "good guy." The truth is, this class has taught me more about myself than any class has ...

—white undergraduate

**"What is your race and how do you know it?"**[3] The purpose of this question is to get white students thinking and talking about the ways race is constructed and racial stigma is passed through the generations. To avoid superficial or mocking answers ("by looking in the mirror") from stage one students I model this myself first:

I'm white, as far as I know. But I was never explicitly told I was white, so how do I know it? That's a mystery. I can think of subtle ways that whites in my neighborhood defined themselves and each other as white. There were ways of teasing and insinuating that someone had some black ancestry. It was obvious from the tone of voice that this was something shameful, something to be avoided. People who looked like me talked about other people as "Oriental" or "Negro" or "Mexican" in ways that let me know I wasn't one of "them." "They" were mysterious, different, and somehow dangerous. I knew that some of my Jewish friends were white because they weren't spoken of in such derogatory or frightened tones, even though their skin might be just as brown as those who were "not white." So I think I learned what race I was by understanding what I was not.

When white students are encouraged to question their own learning about race, students of color often feel more comfortable talking about how they learned about themselves. Some will talk about the pride they were taught in their families in stark contrast to the ways they were put down and shamed at school or ostracized in the community.

**"Shouldn't we be colorblind?" and other common attitudes about race.** Early in the semester, when many students are reluctant to speak their minds, I might ask them to think more deeply about some common attitudes about race without tying them to anyone's personal opinion. I might say, for example, "Some people say they are colorblind, or that they don't notice race. Let's try to think of the positive aspects of adopting a colorblind attitude, and also, why that stance might be problematic." I then make two columns on the board and list arguments on each side as students come up with them. Writing down all the possible points for and against helps students to articulate reasons for their beliefs and understand why others might disagree with them. I then ask them to write a couple of paragraphs stating what they believe to be the best argument on each side. We might then come back to a discussion of the issue, this time with students giving their own considered opinions.

Short videos that help students think through the complexity of the issue of "not seeing color" include "Colorblind" (http://www.youtube.com/ watch?v=Xd4X8r2bIdc), a powerful spoken word piece that addresses the stereotyping and exclusion of Asian Americans that make the idea of "colorblindness" a sham. The poignant ballad, "Counting Crows—Colorblind" (http://www. youtube.com/watch?v=y0s7ycdUcHk), expresses how intense attraction can overcome internalized racial barriers. The singer's frequent mention of color while declaring himself free of color prejudice is interesting to ponder.

**"What is race? What is racism?"** Instead of giving students definitions of race, racism, racial hatred, discrimination, prejudice, reverse racism, and ethnocentrism (as in Chapter 3), you might ask them to work in small groups to come up with their own working definitions and examples of each term. I give each group of four students three or four terms, some of which overlap with those I give to other groups (i.e., group one gets race, racism, and racial hatred; group two gets racism, racial hatred and discrimination; and so on). Be sure to tell students that the object is not to get the "right" answer or even come to consensus at all; the process of discussion and critical thinking is more important than the product. Then bring everyone back into a large group and ask each group to give their definitions and examples and mention any issues they disagreed on. Discussion will naturally ensue, since groups will have come up with somewhat different definitions. You can add factual information and historical background, if necessary, to help with accuracy. This exercise can take over an hour. If you don't have this much time, you might ask them instead to survey several of their friends about how they would define these terms and bring the results to class for discussion.

The liveliest conversation—though it brings up the most confusion and disagreement—comes from students' attempts to define racism. At the beginning of the semester, most students think that being racist means acting on the belief that any race is superior to any other race. Because they don't yet understand that racism requires extensive and wide-ranging power to enforce this sense of superiority or that whites as a group are the ones who hold that power, they are confused by the idea that logically, the only people who can be racist are whites. White students who have been bullied or excluded from groups of color may resist this idea very strongly, since they too have been made to feel small and powerless. I acknowledge, with real sympathy, that ostracism, name-calling, ridiculing, and bullying does hurt, no matter who engages in it. But when it's done by whites to people of color it has always had deeper and longer-lasting consequences than when people of color lash out at whites. We can describe racial acts against whites as racial hatred, ethnocentrism, prejudice, stereotyping, racially motivated revenge, or individual acts of meanness, but we need to reserve a potent word—"racism"—to describe organized, pervasive harm by whites to groups they have deemed inferior and/or inconsequential.

Sometimes, a quick-thinking student will counter, "If racism equals prejudice plus power, couldn't whites who live in a predominantly black neighborhood be victims of racism? If, for example, blacks force a white resident to move out of the area just because he's white, wouldn't that be racism? Isn't it obvious that blacks hold the more powerful racial position in their own neighborhood?" The trick is to get such students to see the bigger picture: What long-range effects does black prejudice have on whites, either as individuals or as a group? Could the white resident move to a mostly white area with the same amenities he found in the black neighborhood: the same or better quality jobs, schools, businesses, transportation, housing, and health facilities? Would the hatred and disgust blacks feel for the white resident affect the life chances of whites as a group? Do whites have to be concerned about staying in blacks' good graces? Do most whites even care what blacks think of them? White students who have never thought in these terms may still have trouble with the idea that whites as a group hold the authority in this country, but at least they will be introduced to the idea. Later discussions of white privilege and study of institutional racism will inform them further.

**"How significant is race in your daily life? Why do you think this is so?"** Many white students say that race is not at all significant to them, while students of color will, if they feel comfortable, begin to describe the many ways they are made to feel different, odd, shut out and less than whites. "I wake up in the morning and I'm still black," an African-American student tells her white classmates. "Do you wake up thinking about how the world is going to treat you today?" "In my country, hospitality is a virtue" says an international student from the Middle East. "But here, people treat you as if you have absolutely nothing in common with them." While white students can learn a lot from discussion of this question in mixed groups, students of color may begin to feel frustrated or angry that their experiences are so little known and understood. You might want to ask these questions in a brief, anonymous, in-class writing assignment and then collect the answers and read some of them aloud. A discussion about the gap in perceptions may follow.

These questions can also be used to start a "fishbowl" discussion of the different experiences of whites and people of color. Set up two concentric circles of chairs and ask students identifying as white to sit in the inner circle (the fishbowl) while those who identify as students of color sit in the outer circle. The white students then discuss these questions while students of color listen silently. Then ask the groups to switch places so that students of color are now discussing their experiences among themselves in the inner circle while white students listen. You can then ask the class to write a brief response to the exercise or discuss general reactions in the large group.

In another variation, useful for larger, mixed classes, each corner of the room is designated as a possible response to the question: "How significant is race in your everyday life?"—e.g., "very significant"; "moderately significant"; "somewhat significant"; and "not at all significant." Students move to the corner that matches their own response and talk with the group that forms there about specific instances when race mattered (or didn't matter) and what they make of this. You can add interesting complexity to this exercise by asking students to move to the appropriate corner for gender, sexual orientation, socioeconomic class, and/or religion after they have discussed the significance of race, and to consider how their different identities might intersect, giving them authority, safety, and comfort in one context but not in another. Allow about fifteen to twenty minutes for discussion of each identity category. As students move to different corners they discover similarities and differences across and within racial/ethnic identities. For example, some whites, Asians, and blacks may find that they all grew up in upper-class (or working class) families, or that being female is very significant to them for the same reasons. Discovering similarities in experiences can help promote dialogue later, if issues of race become heated.

If your class is predominantly white, your students may wonder why you are asking about the significance of their race at all. Since whiteness is the unexamined, unnoticed norm, the "water the fish swims in" so to speak, white students may simply answer that race is totally insignificant to them, as it should be for anyone else. Videos and first-person accounts will provide the needed perspectives of people of color. (See "Racism: Contemporary Stories and Examples" in "Annotated Resources")

**"When did you first recognize your place in the racial hierarchy?"** Other ways to ask this question are: "When did you realize that people of different races or ethnicities were treated differently?" Or, more simply, "What did you first learn about people of color? About white people?"

White students are sometimes silent or give superficial answers to these questions since they often feel they have no experiences with race (by which they mean races other than white, a faux pas which should be pointed out to them). On the other hand, they might claim that they have had no negative experiences regarding race since their parents brought them up to treat everyone equally. Underneath these attitudes often lie much tension and fear about revealing deeply internalized racist beliefs. If a white student says she has no stories to tell since she was brought up in a very tolerant household, I ask her gently if she knows that there is a racial hierarchy in this country at all—which of course she does. Then I ask her if she knows where she fits in. She does.

"Now, this is harder," I say, "How do you know that?" When students are stumped for answers, I find that telling my own story helps.

In this very brief, provocative video, "Think Race Doesn't Matter? Then Why the Difference in Adoption Fees based on the Child's Race" (https://www.youtube.com/watch?v=MKHHzaOheHQ) Beth Hall, founder of "Pact, an Adoption Alliance" explains the U.S. racial hierarchy in monetary terms. Even determinedly "colorblind" students will find these statistics challenging—and outrageous.

**"Describe an experience when race seemed particularly important."** Although white students may claim they have no such experiences, this exercise will encourage them to talk about racial incidents that have happened to friends or acquaintances of color, which is helpful in breaking the silence about the racism that permeates the society. The braver students sometimes share incidents where they have been perpetrators or silent bystanders. Some will talk about the racist remarks or harangues of family members. Students of color, if they feel comfortable, will talk about times when they themselves were the victim of racism or prejudice, or they might reveal that they never experienced racism firsthand. Very rarely will students of color bring up prejudices and rivalries between different groups or individuals of color against whites; they know all too well that such discussions give white students more reason to deny or minimize their own responsibility. This exercise is best done in small groups of four or five where each student is under a certain amount of social pressure to contribute experiences to the discussion.

You might use this excellent online video to add to the discussion: "What Would You Do? Shopping While Black" (https://www.youtube.com/watch?v=yAkDHuimJRc). In this ABC Primetime short, actors portray a confrontation between a white sales clerk and an African-American shopper in an upscale New York City boutique while other shoppers comment, sometimes furtively, sometimes in collusion with the clerk, about the motives of the shopper and the store's apparent need for her surveillance. Spencer Patterson, the Mexican American filmmaker, then confronts the shoppers outside the store to ask them why they reacted as they did. The video provokes discussion about people's willingness to act in defense of others who are being unfairly treated, and can encourage students' reflection on their own ability to be allies. Similar confrontations are staged to gauge people's reactions to prejudice against many other groups, for example, Latinos: "What Would You Do? Latino Hate Crime Episode" (https://www.youtube.com/watch?v=ru1F29vu-VKI). Muslims: "What Would You Do? Muslims in America" (https://www.youtube.com/watch?v=7R-QKDCCJM0). And Jews: "Anti-Semitism on the rise? (https://www.youtube.com/watch?v=BRX31HOikws) See Annotated Resources for descriptions.

**"How do you feel about ethnic labels?"** Working individually, students (and instructor) write brief descriptions of their own experiences on flip chart paper in answer to these prompts: (1) the first time you can remember being classified or referred to by your race or ethnicity, (2) the first time someone else referred to you by your race or ethnicity, and (3) the first time you referred to yourself by your race or ethnicity. As they finish, students post their flip chart paper on the walls around the room in a "gallery" format. Everyone walks around in silence and reads everyone's experiences. All sit down again and the instructor simply asks: "First impressions?" "Questions?"

Follow up activities might include watching and discussing short videos such as "Latinos and Identity: Why Labels Don't Fit." (https://www.youtube.com/watch?v=tRsIf9ZY5u8) Here, Mark Hugo Lopez of the Pew Hispanic Center discusses the results of their yearly survey of Hispanic Americans. One finding is that the most common identifying label people use to describe themselves is country of origin rather than the all-purpose category of Latino or Hispanic that was created by the Nixon Administration. This can bring up the issue of "American" identification. You might ask, for example, what it means when a U.S. citizen defines herself as 'Peruvian' or 'Cuban' or 'Chicano.' Shouldn't she define herself as American, or at least, Peruvian American? Why would she want to do otherwise? Are some self-identifying labels divisive or worrisome? Or are they empowering? Why do you think so?

In "Stop Labeling Me: All American Muslim" https://www.youtube.com/watch?v=KGQb2cMUk08), interviewees discuss the individual choices they have made in how they label themselves: Muslim, Muslim American, American, or by country of origin. Their conclusion: nation and religion are equally important to them.

In the poignant music video "Labels: The Asian/American Divide" (http://www.youtube.com/watch?v=72rUJLN2Bxw) young men act out the ways that Asian American and Asian immigrant students often label each other and what it takes to "undo the damage."

**"What is it to be American? What was it to your parents?"** These deceptively innocuous questions can sometimes bring out the essence of the problem of race in U.S. society. Whether white students take a positive or negative tack on this (mentioning either patriotism, freedom, and pride, on the one hand, or consumerism, imperialism and environmental destruction on the other) they rarely explicitly bring up race. However, when I ask them to close their eyes and think of a typical American, they often picture a white male. Students of color, especially those at later stages of their racial identity development, may talk frankly and with evident frustration about being made perpetual outsiders. First and second-generation immigrants will have different takes on these questions, depending on how much racism and anti-immigrant feeling they or their family have experienced. A discussion of these questions could lead into an assignment to read a memoir or novel written by an immigrant author and/or to read the suppressed history of the publicly condoned racism against Native Americans, Asian Americans, and other ethnic groups in our nation's past. (Loewen, 1995; Takaki, 1998). The discussion at the beginning of the excellent video, *Color of Fear* (Lee, 1994), also deals with identifying as American; the participants all have somewhat different perspectives, many of which are startling to white students.

**"Where did you learn what you know about race and ethnicity?"** This exercise was created by one of my students as she was reflecting on her own assumptions and stereotypes of various ethnic and religious groups. Make a list of everything you know about several ethnic or national groups you are unfamiliar with (e.g., Muslims, Jews, "Gypsies" (Roma), Egyptians, Mexicans, etc.). Now write where you learned each thing (e.g. the movie, *Aladdin*, grandparents, playground rhymes, a project about pyramids in 4th grade, etc.). Talk about your list with a partner.

Along with this activity, you might use the short, online video, "Racial Stereotypes in Children's Entertainment" (https://www.youtube.com/watch?v=fS3e-n8Mj7I), that shows clips of Hollywood's portrayal of Mexicans, African-Americans, Thais, Chinese, and other identity groups in popular films. The stereotypical accents, dress, behavioral characteristics, talents, and food choices of the characters were likely considered "cute," "inoffensive," or "just for fun" by students when they were children, and many will not have reconsidered these notions. This video easily leads to a discussion of how children learn stereotypes (even of their own identity group), and how filmmakers could be convinced to be more socially responsible.

**"In what ways are you (or are whites) privileged at this university/in this town/in this organization?"** Peggy McIntosh's (1992) article on white privilege is important background reading for this conversation, as she lists many ways her white skin buys her "an invisible package of unearned assets." After discussing their reactions to the article in depth, ask students to form groups to list the privileges that whites have in their college community—perhaps in their dormitory, their classes, or their social or political organizations. Model this by mentioning a few of your own privileges. I might say that as a white instructor I can bring up the subject of race in my department without being thought of as a complainer; I can benefit from affirmative action without being accused of incompetence (white females have been the major beneficiaries of affirmative action); I can take a drive in the country and stop for gas in a small town without fear of violence (there is Klan and other hate group activity in some areas of rural Michigan); and I could break into my own house in mid-afternoon, if I forgot my key, without passers-by calling the police.

In doing this exercise, my students have discovered white privileges that include: not having to prove to their classmates that they are qualified to attend a top school; not having to discuss the pathological aspects of their race in sociology or psychology class; being able to choose from a wide variety of courses that discuss the contributions of whites while minimizing or ignoring contributions of people of color; knowing that the adults they see in the halls are more likely to be professors than janitors; being able to find familiar food in the cafeteria; being able to show up late for class without having their entire race judged as irresponsible; being able to buy necessary cosmetics and hair care products at the school store; being able to get a good haircut near campus; not being questioned about their choice of headwear or clothing; not being expected to laugh at jokes about their race; not having to worry about police closely monitoring their weekend parties; not having to show their ID to get into a university function, and so on.

For some quick historical background on the invention of the "white" category, see this ten-minute video clip of a talk by antiracist activist Tim Wise called "the creation of whiteness" (https://www.youtube.com/ watch?v=J3Xe1kX7Wsc).

**"How does it feel to be a victim? A perpetrator? A silent bystander? An intervener?"** This exercise could follow the viewing and discussion of a short online video on the theme of "What would you do?" For example, see "Shopping While Black: Social Experiment" (https://www.youtube.com/ watch?v=yAkDHuimJRc). In small groups, ask students to discuss some or all of the following prompts: "Talk about a time you felt different from the people around you. How did you feel about it?" "Talk about a time when you were the victim of harassment, discrimination, stereotyping, or racism. How did you feel about it?" "Describe an incident where you were perceived as being prejudiced or racist. How did you feel about that? What was your response to the person who told you about it?" In the large group, ask students: "How did you feel when answering these questions?" "Which questions were the most interesting?" "What did you learn about yourself?" (adapted from Meyers and Zúñiga in Schoem et al., 1995, p. 318).

You can do a variation of this as a "four corners" exercise. Designate each corner of the room as a place where students talk about (1) a time when they have been oppressed or put down by others; (2) a time when they have oppressed someone else; (3) a time when they have stood by and watched someone oppress another; and (4) a time when they have intervened in an act of oppression. Students move from one corner to another at the instructor's signal (the time allowed depends on the size of the group). Both exercises are good levelers of differences; they allow white students to see that they do not have to automatically assume the role of oppressor and that they can be allies with people of color and others by standing up to oppression. Talking about the issue from all sides also helps students of color acknowledge their own prejudices and see their fight against racism as part of a larger enterprise of human rights which they can engage in with whites as well. If students get into arguments about which kind of oppression is worse or argue that one kind of oppression doesn't count, Audre Lorde's short piece, "There Is No Hierarchy of Oppressions" (1993) is a sobering, heartfelt reminder of some of the larger issues in the struggle.

You can also do these exercises as writing assignments, either in class or as homework. Ask for volunteers to read aloud from their writing or have students read aloud to each other in small groups as prompts for further discussion. This writing exercise works best as an ungraded assignment; students shouldn't feel pressured to invent good stories that never happened.

**Privilege Walk** This exercise helps students understand how socioeconomic class, gender, and other identities interact with race. It can be particularly insightful for students who are (or believe they are) "blind" to race and class. Ask students to form a line shoulder to shoulder down the middle of the room and to listen carefully to the following statements,

- If you are a white male, take one step forward.
- If your ancestors did not come to this country by choice, take one step back.
- If one or both of your parents has a college degree, take one step forward.
- If you were raised in a neighborhood where there was prostitution or drug activity, take one step back.
- If your parents are paying for your college education, take one step forward.
- If you have ever been afraid of violence because of your gender, ethnicity, or sexual orientation, take one step back.
- If people of color worked in your household as servants or gardeners, take one step forward.
- If you ever tried to change your appearance, mannerisms, speech, or behavior to avoid being judged or ridiculed, take one step back.
- If you studied the history and culture of your ancestors in elementary school, take one step forward.
- If there have been times in your life when there was no food in the house, take one step back.
- If you took an SAT prep course before you took the SAT, take one step forward.
- If your family ever had to move because they couldn't afford the rent or your home was repossessed, take one step back.
- If you feel good about the way your ethnic group or culture is portrayed in the media, take one step forward.
- If you were raised by a single parent, take one step back.
- If there were more than fifty books in the house where you grew up, take one step forward.
- If you or your parents come from a rural area take one step back.
- If you attended private school or summer camp, take one step forward.
- If you have visible or invisible disabilities, take one step back.

- If the majority of the faculty who teach your classes are of your race or ethnicity, take one step forward.
- If you or your ancestors have ever been led to believe that because of your race, skin color, or ethnicity, you are ugly or inferior, take one step back.
- If your family had health insurance when you were growing up, take one step forward.
- If you were ever stopped or questioned by the police for being in the "wrong neighborhood" or other bogus offenses take one step back.
- If you were given a car by your family, take one step forward.
- If you have trouble finding familiar hair products or a good haircut in your college community, take one step back.
- If you were told by your parents you were beautiful, smart, and capable of achieving your dreams, take two steps forward.

Students should now take a look around and see where they are standing in relation to their classmates. Then, everyone returns to their seats and discusses what they learned from the exercise. You can vary the statements, depending on your particular student group, your region of the country, or the issues you'd like to bring up. **Note:** While this exercise is often eye-opening for students in dominant identity categories, it can be annoying and even humiliating for students who end up at the back of the room, especially if they have had to participate in the exercise in multiple venues. You might ask your class if anyone has done the privilege walk before, and if so, if they think it would be helpful for the class to do at this point in the semester. If they say they're tired of it or show signs of discomfort, be prepared to substitute another activity.

**Using Popular Culture.** Although students may be reluctant to deal with the topic of race in a classroom setting, they are already talking, laughing, rapping, singing, and even writing comments about race online. You can use this generation's ease with electronic media to bring popular portrayals of race into the classroom. For example, ethnic humor can be intelligent, bold, and seriously funny; for example, see Chris Rock's message on the eve of the 2012 election for "undecided voters of the Caucasian variety." (https://www.you-tube.com/watch?v=EDxOSjgl5Z4). Both the content of the comedian's performance and the medium of ethnic humor itself present analytical questions for discussion: "Is there any truth to the idea of Obama as a 'white candidate'?" "What does it mean for blacks to 'act white'?" "In your opinion, is there more than one way to be authentically black or authentically white?" "What about Chris Rock himself—is he also a 'white guy,' according to his own definition?"

"What is it, exactly, that makes this piece funny?" "Who might not find it so amusing, and why not?" "What do you make of the online comments on the video that call Chris Rock a racist?" "Where, in your opinion, does ethnic humor cross the line?" Small groups of students can find many examples of ethnic or racial humor to share with the class along with questions they have prepared for discussion.

## When discussion is silent or superficial

**Using videos.** If students are still reluctant to address personal experiences and attitudes about race directly, or when the class is all or almost all white, watching a video together can make it easier, since discussion centers on the individuals on screen, rather than on students' personal experiences. After showing the video, ask students to reflect quietly, then write for a few minutes to capture their feelings, thoughts and questions. Open the discussion by asking students to share their feelings (everyone says one word describing their feelings at this moment), then their thoughts and questions. Ask: "What struck you as interesting or important?" "What reminded you of something in your experience?" "What surprised you?" "What do you disagree with or question?" Excellent full-length videos that prompt these discussions can be found in the Annotated Resources section.

Numerous short videos that highlight personal feelings and experiences about race can be found on YouTube. See, for example, "Rant on Indian/ South Asian Stereotypes" (https://www.youtube.com/watch?v=8TwVj0Ix-dik); I am not Spanish (https://www.youtube.com/watch?v=lGVcztH96ZY) Latino or Hispanic? (https://www.youtube.com/watch?v=KBDGwB50YBY), "A Girl Like Me" (http://www.understandingrace.org/lived/video/index. html); and especially, "What Would You Do? Shopping While Black" (https:// www.youtube.com/watch?v=yAkDHuimJRc) (See Annotated Resources for descriptions and more examples.)

**"Why is race so hard to talk about?"** If discussion continues to be guarded, try this question. Well-meaning white students often respond, "Because we don't want to offend anyone." I then continue to probe: "Why are we (including myself is very important) so afraid of offending each other?" "Does anyone have a story or incident that they would be willing to share about a time they offended someone inadvertently?" If there is still no answer, I might remove the personal element by telling a very general story about what unnamed others have experienced: "Sometimes students have told me that they inadvertently referred to someone as black when that person wanted to be called African-American—or vice versa—and this led to some tension and anger. Has anyone heard of something like that happening?" On multicultural campuses, almost everyone has. Their stories can lead you to ask another question to your mostly white classes: "Why do you think people of color are sensitive about race?" There is always at least one white student who will venture, "Because they have had bad experiences?"

This discussion can often go further in this direction if you ask, "What kinds of prejudice do people of color suffer?—do you know of any incidents or have you read about any?—think about Asians, Latinos and Latinas, Native Americans, Arab Americans as well as African Americans." This takes it out of the personal arena for a while, which is helpful when people are wary about revealing themselves. Students may then bring up (or you can suggest) indignities such as police harassment, anti-immigrant legislation, media stereotyping, lower expectations in education, ridicule (of an accent, of physical characteristics), fear and avoidance, questioning of abilities, and so on. If students bring up incidents in which whites have been harassed by people of color, acknowledge these experiences (I might give a sympathetic nod and perhaps a brief comment: "That must have been painful") and then move the discussion back to the original question.

"One thing I've been reluctant to say." When dialogue falters, or when you or some class members see the need for more depth and feeling in students' responses, pass out file cards and ask students to write anonymously one thing they have wanted to say in previous class discussions but have been afraid or reluctant to reveal. Collect the cards, shuffle them, and read some of them aloud as prompts for discussion.

"What makes it difficult to have meaningful relationships across the racial divide?" Posing the question this way makes it harder for white students to claim that everything is fine since they have black friends or since they went to a school with people from different backgrounds. Starting from the premise that trust and depth of friendship are difficult, students are prompted to think about what might be lacking in their relationships with friends of other ethnicities. Students of color may say, if they feel safe enough, that the reason for the difficulty is that most whites don't recognize the everyday racism that is so much a part of the lives of people of color. If the conversation gets deeper, they may also reveal that they talk about race and racism all the time with their friends of color when their white friends and acquaintances aren't around. This, more than any other comment, will make the white students reflect, perhaps silently, on the ways they do not know their friends of color. Other whites, who know they don't have meaningful friendships across the racial divide, may advance all kinds of reasons why this is the fault of people of color: they don't respond to their offers of friendship or collaboration, they accuse whites, implicitly or explicitly, of being racist, and so on. You might then ask why they think this is true, and perhaps give some reasons from your own experience why trust is so difficult. I like Gloria Yamato's (1992) reminder to well-meaning whites that we should not fool ourselves into thinking that if we have a few good conversations with a friend of color or a successful collaboration on a project that we now have "the people of color seal of approval" (p. 70). We need to stay open to continued personal introspection and show ourselves to be trustworthy again and again.

## Promoting Discussion of Texts

### Using Reading Journals

> In the beginning of the semester it was hard for me to write even a few lines because I really didn't know what I was feeling; I had thought about these issues for a long time throughout my life but never critically analyzed my thoughts.
> —white undergraduate

> This journal has provided me with an opportunity to express my thoughts without being criticized or looked down on for my views.
> —Vietnamese American undergraduate

Most conversations about race are short on facts; students of all ethnicities typically don't know enough about the histories, definitions, arguments, laws, and perspectives of other groups to dialogue or argue effectively. I begin with texts that define terms (such as "race"), give specific examples of racism, reveal privilege and prejudice in a personal way, and discuss suppressed histories of people of color in the United States. I introduce institutional racism much later, after students are convinced that interpersonal racism does exist in the United States today and that it affects every one of us intimately. (See Annotated Resources for the best texts I have found on the following topics: Genetics and Human Origins; Social Construction of Race; Histories, Cultures and Contemporary Realities of People of Color in the United States; Identity; "Whiteness" and White Privilege; Racial Socialization; Racism: Contemporary Stories and Examples; Psychology of Racism; History of Racism; and many aspects of Institutional Racism: Government, Criminal Justice, Health, Urban Neighborhoods, Education, Language, and the Media; as well as texts on Activism and Teaching Issues.) In a mostly white class, I start with texts whose tone is moderate or even soothing to white hypersensibilities. I find that using strident texts early on puts many white students off and discourages the kind of personal questioning and tentative exploration they need to do at first.

To help students dig into the material, I ask them to record their thoughts, feelings, reactions to discussion and reactions to reading in a journal that I collect and comment on every couple of weeks. If I want them to interact more with the texts I've assigned, I ask them to respond to four or five quotes of their choice from each article they read. They can ask themselves questions and attempt to answer them, they can question or argue with the author, they can bring in their own personal experiences, and they can refer to other pieces they've read. Sometimes I give them specific questions (or a choice of questions) to write about. Sometimes I ask them to write three questions for class discussion that they won't answer in writing at all; just thinking of topics they'd really like the class to consider helps them reflect more deeply (See Student-generated Questions for Class Discussion, below). To push for greater clarity and depth I grade these entries ++ for excellent work, + for acceptable work, and RW (rewrite) for comments that need more depth of reflection and/ or attention to clarity of ideas. At times, I have given students nearly endless opportunities to rewrite these entries until their thoughts come clear. This system makes it clear that personal engagement and critical analysis are my expectations of every student in the class.

## Video journals, vlogs, and blogs

Since facility with electronic media has become a standard component of literacy, both for communication among peers and in the workplace, you can help students gain valuable skills by having them produce their own videos and blogs. They might video-record their feelings and ideas about questions that have come up for them in the reading assignments, either to share with class members or for your eyes alone. Or, they might pair up to produce video interviews of other members of their community on questions the class has found intriguing: "How would you define white privilege?" "How would you describe the racial climate on this campus?" "Why do you think students tend to self-segregate at this school?" "Some say that with the election of a black

president, our country has become 'post-racial' or colorblind. Do you agree?"
The resulting videos can be shown and discussed in class or at an event that
includes the larger school community.

Blogs use a unique communication style that combines graphics, photos, video clips and commentary. While some might argue that the style and
language of blogs are so informal that they are inappropriate for teaching
college-level writing, I find that designing and writing blogs requires students
to think about their audience in ways that writing a standard college paper
does not. Blogs tend to go straight to the point; they avoid abstract, vague, or
pretentious words that students often use as "filler" for college papers. Unlike
writers of many school assignments, bloggers are invested in their subject matter; with a potential audience of thousands, young people are conscious of their
image. Of course, like all writing, blogs vary in quality. If you want to be sure
your students approach their topic intellectually and in depth you can give
them a model of a high quality blog, for example, "The Negress: Black Feminist
Thought Meets American Culture" (https://negress.wordpress.com/?s=mas-
culinity). This excellent post, "Charles Ramsey: Black Masculinity and the
Narrative of Villainy," comments on media ridicule of the African-American
man who initiated the May 2013 rescue of three young women held captive in
a Cleveland neighborhood for a decade.

Students might also try vlogs, or video blogs, where they comment in
person on a topic as if they had the floor for four or five minutes in class discussion. Like written blogs, this genre requires students to use skills that are
essential to good writing: brevity, focus, awareness of audience and purpose,
appropriate tone and vocabulary, and meaningful commentary. At times, students will write their comments first, then unobtrusively read them on camera, a tactic that nicely fits two academic purposes at once. Students who need
advice on how to be a vlogger can find some helpful tips here: http://www.
wikihow.com/Be-a-Vlogger.

## Student-generated questions for class discussion

To make sure my students engage fully with the reading and the films that I
assign for homework, I often require them to write several questions for class
discussion. I tell them that their questions should be clear and specific; they
should include any context their peers need to understand their meaning;
they should refer to page numbers in a reading or a specific part of an online
video; they shouldn't be too speculative (e.g., "What would race relations

look like today if Barack Obama had never been elected?"), rhetorical (e.g., "Can't we all get along?"), or have easy answers (e.g., "Don't you think that more courses on race and racism should be available to students?"); and most importantly, they should be interesting to the students themselves. After this explanation, and perhaps after sharing a model question of my own, I ask them to write three questions on a specific reading or online video. In class, I have students work in pairs to edit each other's questions, reminding them they're looking for clarity, discussability, necessary context, and so on. Once students are satisfied with the edited version of their questions, I ask them to choose several of them to discuss in small groups, and finally, to bring the most interesting of these questions to the large group for general discussion.

**Allowing anonymous reactions.** When students have read a text on a particularly contentious subject (white privilege, affirmative action, immigration, terrorism), ask them at the beginning of the class period to jot down a few words describing their feelings as they read or thought about the material. Collect these, then ask them to write down whatever thoughts and questions came to them. Read aloud both piles of anonymous reactions, first the feelings, then the thoughts and questions. Or, read the feelings, then shuffle the thoughts and questions, pass them back to students, and ask them to read them aloud. Discussion will follow.

**Using quotes as prompts for discussion.** As a fun variation on the standard discussion format, I sometimes ask students to pick out the quote from the reading for the day that most impressed them, write it down, walk around and compare quotes with other students, and finally, gravitate to small groups for discussion. Ask groups to address questions such as the following: "What does the quote mean to you?" "How does it apply to the subject of race or racism?" "How does it pertain to your life?" "What are your reservations or questions about the quote?" After twenty minutes or so of discussion, ask each small group to share with the larger group the most interesting points that came up.

**Talk Circle.** This exercise allows space for quieter students to voice their ideas and can produce remarkable results. Ask students to write for five minutes on the topic or article to be discussed in order to collect their thoughts. Each student then has exactly one minute (timed by you) to express his or her ideas about the topic without interruption. Students are not obliged to speak, but if someone chooses to remain silent, the whole circle of students must also keep silent until that person's minute has expired. If the class is larger than about fifteen students, you might want to split it into several groups and have student volunteers time the contributions of students in the other groups.

**Coins Exercise.** Here is another equalizer that many students find both fun and instructive. Have students sit in a circle, and place a wastebasket or a baseball cap in the center. Ask students to take out two pennies and a silver coin. (I bring extra pennies and encourage sharing, telling the class they will get their coins back at the end of the exercise.) Tell students: "The pennies represent statements and the silver coin represents a question—not an information question, but a question that turns the discussion in some new direction. When someone wants to speak, s/he throws a coin into the center. That person then has the floor and no one can interrupt. When s/he is finished speaking, someone else can throw in a coin. When you use up your coins, you can't speak any more and you must stay silent; no begging, buying, or stealing of other people's coins! You don't have to use up all your coins, but I encourage you to do so. I also will have three coins and follow the same rules."

This exercise is fascinating to many students since the big talkers use up their coins quickly, leaving space for the quieter ones to discuss their perspectives, sometimes for the first time. I end the exercise when the group has been completely silent for about two minutes. In a group of fifteen to twenty students, this takes about an hour. Be sure the text and/or topic you choose is rich enough to sustain the discussion, and that everyone has done the reading. You might want to give students five or ten minutes to skim over the text first.

**Student-led discussions.** Ask for pairs of student volunteers to lead discussions of specific readings. The pair should meet together before class to plan specific questions to ask and to prepare to give their own take on the questions if discussion falters. Pairs from different ethnic backgrounds sometimes find their own meeting and discussion time extremely instructive. If you have been using a variety of formats for discussion, students may follow your lead and try some of these.

## Discussion of key concepts

Although my aim is to encourage independent learning, responsible reading and intelligent discussion among peers, at times, I take the lead in large group discussion, especially when I want to be sure everyone grasps the most important concepts of the course. Instead of lecturing (which I find a waste of class time, since students can read a prepared lecture on their own) I might start by asking students to consider a quote from the reading or to say how the author defines a concept or argues a particular point. I then might ask students' reactions, opinions, examples, and so on, that help them analyze and evaluate the concepts. I fill the board with students' ideas, reminding them of points from the texts, and asking questions that make sure they delve deeply into the material and come to their own carefully drawn conclusions. When differences of opinion arise, I praise students for considering different points of view, and encourage them to say why they think the way they do. If too many similar opinions are expressed, I play devil's advocate, offering opposing views that an "intelligent, reasonable person" might have on the topic. Depending on the focus of the course, key concepts might include the meaning of a "postracial" society, current scientific explanations of "race," the definition of race privilege, the history of affirmative action, the long-term effects of scientific racism, psychological studies of implicit bias, and so on.

Our discussions of key concepts are necessarily more "teacher-centered" than those that arise from the dozens of other topics, questions, and issues that students bring up each day. These student contributions might range from perceptive comments in response to a video we see in class together (such as how the African-American hair industry as detailed in Chris Rock's humorous video, "Good Hair" pertains to someone's personal observation in a community barbershop), to political or social questions that arise naturally from general discussion (such as why some citizens of color in this country are reluctant to identify themselves as "American"). For questions of this nature I try to stay out of the way of the student conversation as much as possible. Even if an unmoderated discussion becomes a bit circular, repetitive, or shallow, I trust that students will benefit from being able to air their views, ideas, and concerns, and that they will continue to think about the issues more deeply after class.

My goals for this kind of free-flowing discussion are always to encourage as many voices as possible in each conversation. In a class of upper-division students, especially, I am not so concerned whether these interactions are emotional or coolly rational, just so long as students talk about race. It doesn't even matter to me whether students come to like each other. They must be civil, of course, but they don't always have to "be nice." If a student laughs at a naïve comment, or shouts, "No way!" at an opinion they think is ridiculous, or shakes their head in frustration but refuses to explain, I don't express disapproval, though I might remind them in a friendly way that we all make naïve comments from time to time when we're learning something new, or that "No way!" needs to be followed by some kind of explanation. I consider my goals for discussion achieved when students linger after class to argue with each other, or carry the discussion out into the hall, or arrive early to discuss an issue raised in the reading before class officially begins.

By the last weeks of the semester, I hope that all students' perspectives will have changed markedly through interaction with each other and the course material and that these broader and more informed views will be reflected in the class dynamics. Questions and comments will be more perceptive and meaningful; interactions with each other will be deeper; and students will know they all have a stake in this thing called "race" together. If students have become friends, especially across racial lines, if they laugh with each other as well as occasionally at each other, if they choose to sit together at campus events that I've assigned for extra credit, if they friend each other on Facebook, or express disappointment that the course has ended all too soon, all this is icing on the cake. It can happen, but it doesn't need to happen for the course to be meaningful and even life-changing for many students.

## Students calling on students

Unless I am moderating a discussion about key concepts, I often ask students to call on someone whose hand is raised after they have spoken. In other words, Jason says his piece in response to a passage in the reading or a moment in a film we have watched together and then looks around the circle to see whose hand is raised and chooses Emily or Rashid or Kim to respond next. If Kim's style is to dominate the conversation, Jason can bring in other voices by choosing Rashid or Emily. On the other hand, he might choose Kim because he finds her comments perceptive, or funny, or for any other reason. After Kim speaks, she might call on Tony, who is tentatively raising his hand, just because we seldom hear from him, or she might choose Rashid, who is looking agitated because he has something urgent to add to the discussion. Ideas are now starting to flow from student to student, rather than bouncing back and forth to the instructor. If the discussion lags and no one is raising their hand, I might ask a follow-up question for the class to consider, or ask someone to find a new quote in the reading or comment on another passage in the film. In these kinds of discussion sessions, I raise my hand along with the others when I have something that I believe will add depth to the discussion. First year students tend to defer to me with a laugh, but upper division students treat me as a regular class member. I only intervene in the sequence if I need to add point of information or to remind a student to call on the next person. Students take to this technique easily and quickly. Once the routine is fully established, a real dialogue between students ensues. Students are looking at each other, rather than at me (although with a class of first year students I might need to look down at my notes to prevent them from seeking my tacit approval); they are remembering each other's names; they are calling on people who they truly want to hear from. The discussion has momentum, energy, and vibrancy. Students are leaning toward the center of the circle, showing their involvement through their body language. Comments lead to new questions that appeal to those who have not spoken previously. While these discussions can be repetitive at times (with students simply expressing the same opinions in different words) and can be superficial if energy is low (in a morning class during midterms, for example), at its best, the method can help classmates develop real, intellectual relationships that continue after the class is over.

## Simulations

Exercises that simulate "real world" events give students practice in talking about race and racism to a variety of audiences and making recommendations based on their own research. Here are two examples of simulations I've used in my classes.

**The President's Advisory Commission on Hate Crimes.** Two groups of four or five students will act as advisors to the current presidential administration on the problem of hate crimes. First, they find information about the extent and types of hate groups and hate crimes in the United States by searching the website of the Southern Poverty Law Center (www.splcenter. org). One group then develops a ten-minute presentation that informs the administration officials about the problem, while the other group decides what steps the administration should take in response, and the reasons for their recommendations. As each group presents, the rest of the class acts the part of the administration officials, asking questions and giving their opinions on the feasibility of the recommendations.

**Consultants on children's books.** Near the end of the semester, when students have enough background on racism, white privilege, and suppressed histories, I choose four or five children's picture books for them to analyze and recommend—or not—to teachers in a neighborhood school. I choose books that, intentionally or not, bring up issues of class, race, cultural difference, poverty, colonialism, occupation and slavery: Hans Christian Andersen's *The Little Match Girl* (1996), Marcia Brown's *Shadow* (1986) (about an African village); Ina Friedman's *How My Parents Learned to Eat* (1984) (about how an American soldier and his Japanese fiancée adapt to each other's cultures); Alice Dalgliesh's *The Thanksgiving Story* (1954) (which presents the classic view of the first encounter between whites and Native Americans); Carolivia Herron's *Nappy Hair* (1997) (a book that raised a furor among African-American parents when an inexperienced white teacher read it to her third grade class); and Faith Ringgold's *Tar Beach* (1991) and *Aunt Harriet's Underground Railroad in the Sky* (1992), which portray responses to slavery and racism from the perspective of young African-Americans.

I give one of these books to each small group of students and ask them to read the story together and discuss the effect they think it would have on a first or second grade class of children from different ethnic backgrounds, what objections their parents might have, what facts or perspectives are absent or skewed, and whether or not they would recommend the book to teachers. Each group then presents their recommendations to the rest of the class, who play the part of parents, teachers, and other community members. I encourage vigorous (even raucous) commentary from audience members, who can act as bigoted, angry, conciliatory, or clueless as befits their roles. Because identity is important in these audience reactions, I tell students to mention their chosen ethnicity and perhaps gender and role in the community during their comments, which sometimes jolts students' sense of the racial order. I join the audience to model this. Once, when I raised my hand and said in an aggrieved tone, "Excuse me—as an African American parent, I have to object to your recommendation," a black student interrupted with glee, "You black now, Helen!" Multiracial groups have fun with this exercise since it allows them to express points of view rarely heard in class and to counter those viewpoints with abandon.

## Helping students recognize racism

**Use videos and texts** that tell personal stories and give detailed examples about everyday racism in the lives of people of color. (See Racism: Contemporary Stories and Examples in "Annotated Resources.") Students of color frequently say that it's not their job to educate white students—or even their white friends—about race and racism. Their friends can feel bewildered by this, as they don't recognize at first how painful, frustrating, and humiliating it can be for many people of color to go on at length about the ways their group has been demeaned, disbelieved, shut out, ignored, stereotyped, profiled, belittled, and discouraged from achievement. Fortunately, there are ample texts and videos created by youth and adults of color who don't mind educating others about race or even take it as their life's mission. Their work is a tremendous help to educators.

## Teach students media analysis

Students enjoy learning to critically analyze the media that present them with subtly racist and ethnocentric images, texts, and reporting styles. By looking closely at television, feature films, children's books, history textbooks, advertisements, video games, and news articles, students can begin to notice what and who is absent, whose perspectives are ignored, who is ridiculed ("in fun"), who participates in self-ridicule or self-stereotyping and why, and what information presented as fact is just plain wrong.

**Movies and television.** Show the videos *Ethnic Notions* (Riggs, 1987) and *Color Adjustment* (Riggs, 1991) (or clips from them) that document the racist depictions of blacks in cartoons, film, "blackface" and minstrel shows from pre-Civil War days through the television shows of the 1980s. After discussion of these films, ask students to choose a movie, a television series or several news broadcasts to document the stereotyping of blacks that remains today. If you want your students to learn how to do a more detailed and sophisticated media analysis, see Barbra Morris's excellent (1999) article, "Toward Creating a TV Research Community in Your Classroom," which explains how to teach students to formulate research questions, develop hypotheses, design coding charts, categorize and analyze data, and evaluate results.

**Newspapers, online articles, and media blogs.** Hand out a *New York Times* or *Wall Street Journal* article or find a news post online that is not "obviously" reactionary or racist, but that you find somewhat ethnocentric or racially biased. The article might leave out certain perspectives, or use "code words" to refer negatively to certain ethnic groups, or adopt a condescending tone towards working class people or people of color. Articles detailing problems in "third world" countries are good candidates for this exercise, as they may be even more likely than pieces on U.S. minorities to engage in such stereotyping. Ask the class to read the article and, in small groups, make a list of whatever biases they find. Students share these with the large group and discuss why "objective" media can be biased, and whether they think this bias is intentional or reasonable from the point of view of the writer.

**Magazines and websites.** Have students compare the ways a particular group of color is portrayed in "mainstream" magazines or websites to the ways they are shown in texts designed by and for that group. How often and in what ways are the members of the group portrayed? What idea does this give readers about the ethnic group as a whole? For example, you might compare women of color in a mainstream fashion magazine such as *Glam* (www.glam.com) to those in *Essence* (www.essence.com) or the way Native American issues are portrayed in mainstream publications such as *Old West New West* (http://old-westnewwest.com/index.php) as compared to those in *Indian Country Today* (www.indiancountrytoday.com) or on *NativeWiki* (www.nativewiki.org).

## Developing antiracist arguments

> I like that you stress knowing facts. No one can fight you when you know better than they do. I've noticed a difference in my ability to communicate more concisely and convincingly. I feel like I've got a few missiles in my arsenal.
>
> —Latina undergraduate

Students need more help than we usually give them in learning to refute arguments, especially on a topic as emotional as race. You can use the following discussion formats to help students discuss race among themselves, or use them to help more advanced students develop both the confidence and the facts to confront bigoted arguments in their communities.

**Fishbowl.** Place four chairs in a square, facing each other, in the center of the room. Have students help move the rest of the chairs to a circle around these center chairs. Explain that four volunteers will take the seats in the center and start off the discussion on the topic of the day. They can give their own arguments and opinions or take on the role of someone whose opinion they disagree with (or don't really know whether they agree or disagree with). Students sitting in the outside chairs must remain silent. However, at any time, a student from the outside circle may tap the shoulder of any student in the center and change places with them.

This technique almost always produces lively debate and a fun, competitive atmosphere as students jump in and argue with each other. If your purpose is to let all students in on the discussion, you can add an additional rule that students may tap someone only once (or twice). I sometimes also participate (I can't help myself), but I find I need to encourage students to tap me out of the inner circle. The fishbowl also works well without any instructor participation at all.

**Role play argument.** This technique helps students explore ideas they are unsure about or to anticipate and answer arguments from their friends and families. I ask students to stand in a circle, and tell them I will start an argument with a volunteer who agrees to come into the center of the circle with me. As in the fishbowl exercise, students in the outer circle must stay silent; if they want to get into the argument they can tap either one of us on the shoulder while we're talking, and we'll change places with them.

The difference between this and the fishbowl is that this exercise is strictly play-acting; students can argue a opinion they disagree with as if it were their own. I make this very plain when starting off the exercise by choosing a role and/or expressing opinions that students know I don't hold. I might play a doubting parent, for example:

> "Mike, I know you're really involved in this course on racism you're taking, but can't you lighten up a little bit when you come home? After all, racism is a thing of the past by now. A black man is President, for heaven's sake! We sent you to an integrated high school, you've always had friends of other races, why are you making such a big deal about it all of a sudden?"

Or I might play a student who argues hotly against affirmative action:

> "I can't believe you went to that affirmative action rally, Sherri. Don't you remember in high school when those black kids got into the Ivy Leagues and we didn't? They weren't even in the advanced placement classes! It's not fair! We worked our butts off and they got a free ride!"

The identities of the combatants can be tricky because the perspectives they take will have different meanings and/or be perceived differently depending on what they look like (try imagining the above roles played by a Latin@ or an Asian American). Since I want my students to explore all perspectives as freely as possible I tell them that they can take on the identity of someone from another ethnic group if they want and argue from that position—but they should let us know through their dialogue that's what they are doing. Then I model this, maybe taking the part of some identity group that's missing in our class:

> "As a black man I really take offense to your argument that racism is a thing of the past. Every time I walk down the street at night, I see white people crossing to the other side to avoid me. Do you realize how painful that is?"

Usually we can keep a dialogue going for about twenty minutes; it tends to range over many topics and jump around rapidly, but it does give students both the arguments and the experience to put their ideas into action and is quite instructive even for those who choose not to enter the fray themselves.

I sometimes use this assignment as a prelude to a paper where I ask students to write a dialogue between themselves and another character, using realistic conversational language and tone, about a racial issue they have discussed in class or encountered in their family or neighborhood. The object is to show they can listen fairly to their imaginary character, no matter how obnoxious s/he is, and keep that person listening while they help move the conversation toward a more accurate and compassionate understanding of the racial situation. This is more difficult than students first imagine. They tend to let one character lecture the other, rather than letting both sides of the argument come out. They may resort to emotional language or exasperated put downs rather than reasoned argument or jump from one issue to another without exploring any of them fully. Often, first drafts of these dialogues end in a stalemate, with both characters angry at each other. Sometimes their own unintended biases come out, as when a Korean American student tries to convince her father that blacks are naturally athletic and Asians are naturally good at math or when a white student lets her imaginary character get away with arguing that Latin@s who live in poor neighborhoods are all quite dangerous. Peer review of these papers (reading the dialogues aloud to a group of three or four other students and asking them for feedback) helps writers learn more about the experiences of others and the points of view of their opponents, as well as thinking about the best ways to reach the stubborn character they have created. They can learn more about this with practice in the LARA Method (see below).

**Arguing both sides.** Set up nine chairs in a circle, seven of them facing inward and two of them, the "debate chairs," facing each other. Ask for nine volunteers to fill the chairs while the rest of the class looks on. Whoever sits in the two chairs that face each other will take opposing sides in a debate about a contentious issue the class is studying (police brutality, immigration policy, reparations for slavery, racial profiling, etc.). About five minutes into the debate, at the instructor's signal, everyone stands and moves one place around the circle so that the two "debate chairs" are now occupied by one new participant and one former participant—who now must argue the other side of the issue. The debate continues for another five minutes, and so on. Continue until everyone in the circle has had a chance to argue on both sides of the question. Some of the class can be observers; listening to others argue helps the weaker or more reticent students develop their own arguments.

**Debate Teams.** After students have read an article or watched a video on a controversial topic, and after some initial discussion of the issue, I might divide students randomly into two debate teams. Each team must argue the side they are assigned, regardless of their real opinions or feelings about the issue. To prepare for the debate, the teams have about twenty minutes to plan their strategy and develop their arguments together. Depending on the level of the class and the complexity of the issue, I might listen in for a few minutes to each team's preparation, suggesting arguments they have missed, and reminding them to think of the points the other team might make and to decide how to counter them. I let them know I expect everyone in the group to contribute at least one point, so they should prepare accordingly. Then we arrange the chairs in two rows facing each other and the team members take their places. I usually set up the debate informally, allowing each side two minutes to either advance an argument or reply to the other side, or both. I am often impressed by the number and variety of the arguments each side comes up with, and their agility in answering points made by the opposing side. Occasionally, I have jumped in on one side or the other if they are faced with arguments they cannot answer. The point is to keep the debate going, to get students thinking creatively and logically, and to give them practice anticipating common objections, all of which will help them have more productive conversations about race outside the classroom and to write better argumentative papers. When the debate starts running out of steam, I end the session and congratulate both teams. Then, I let students express their real positions on the issue, which is often a relief to those who had to argue a side they opposed. Alternatively, I might have students indicate their real opinions by moving to the side of the room that I designate pro or con. Students sometimes spread themselves across the room according to the strength of their opinions rather than clustering at each end. Once they have moved to the spot that represents their opinion, I ask several students to explain why they feel the way they do. This sometimes leads into the best discussion of the day, as students are now much more informed, and many realize that the issue is more complicated and interesting than they originally thought.

**LARA Method.** This deceptively simple method of dialogue on emotionally charged issues was developed by Bonnie Tinker of "Love Makes a Family" using nonviolence techniques she had been trained to use in the Civil Rights Movement. It involves four steps: Listen, Affirm, Respond, and Add. The idea is to listen deeply "until you hear the moral principle that [your opponent] is speaking from or a feeling or experience you share." Then affirm by "express[ing] the connection you found when you listened," letting the person know that you agree or feel for them on a deep level. Third, respond to the issue the person raised fully and honestly, and finally, add new information that will correct mistaken ideas and give a more factual basis for discussion. The point is not to "win" the argument but to reach a deeper understanding and connect on a human level, despite differences.

I have students practice LARA in class by handing out written scenarios that are familiar to them: a person who thinks minorities are unfairly advantaged by affirmative action; someone who thinks immigrants are coming to this country to "take our jobs"; another who argues that Native Americans lost the war and shouldn't be hollering about land claims. I have also used recent political cartoons from local news sources that depict Arabs as evil predators or that stereotype white police officers as ignorant, lower-class jerks. I ask one student to argue that these depictions are dangerously racist and/or classist and the other to argue that everyone is too sensitive these days.

The LARA Method can be difficult, especially the first two steps, which are the least familiar to students. Model it by choosing an argument they are familiar with, say the Native American land claims issue. Pull up a chair and sit next to a student volunteer. Ask the student to take the opposing side and start arguing about the unfairness of these claims, the advantage that Indians get just for being Indian, etc. Listen closely for something, sometimes unstated, that you can sympathize with. Then affirm: "I agree that fairness is important. Life isn't easy for a lot of white people, either, these days. Lots of us are struggling to own our own homes or to have a bit of land to call our own." Then respond to the student's point of view and add information that s/he hasn't mentioned: that treaties guaranteeing land to Native Americans were repeatedly broken; that tribes lost most of their land and some whites grew rich from what they appropriated as their own. That it isn't fair for whites who didn't personally benefit from broken treaties to have to pay for the mistakes of the past, but neither is it fair for Native Americans to have lived for generations without the land and resources guaranteed them, growing poorer because of it. Continue the process of listening and affirming as the student continues her side of the argument. After this demonstration, ask students to get into small groups and practice. Two students can role play while two others observe and give feedback. Then switch positions and perspectives.

## Counseling frustrated, angry, or resistant students

As students learn more about racism and privilege they can become emotionally overloaded with frustration, anger, or guilt. I encourage them to express these feelings in their journals and to come and talk to me privately in conference. Sometimes all they need is a sympathetic ear, a little encouragement, and some assurance that the process will ultimately be productive. Occasionally, though, students are so overwhelmed by their emotions that they are ready to give up on the whole enterprise. Here's how I modify the LARA Method (Listen, Affirm, Respond, Add) to reassure such students in conference:

1. **Listen** to students' frustrations and points of view. Let them spill. Just having someone listen can relieve tension and make students more open and willing to question their own views.

2. **Affirm** the student's feelings and experiences: Commiserate, if necessary, with their position, even if you feel it's inappropriate or immature:

   I can see you're angry. This stuff is really difficult, really emotional for everybody. I'm sorry you felt so threatened when you were in high school. Nobody should have to feel unsafe in their own neighborhood.

   It must be frustrating to be a white male in discussions like this. Everyone is looking at you, thinking you're the enemy. And you're thinking, "They don't know me! I'm not like that!"

   Find a way to agree and support something in their thinking—some sentiment, some value, some fear. Sincerity is very important here:

   Of course you didn't intend to offend anyone. I can see you're a sensitive person who cares about others.

   Yes, it would be wonderful if we could all accept each other as individuals without regard to color. That's the kind of society we're working towards.

   I can see you worked extremely hard to get into this university and that you want to uphold its high standards. I admire that.

3. **Respond** to the argument the student raises without engaging in direct confrontation. Let the student know where you stand without insisting that s/he hold your views:

Let me tell you how my experience working with students has led me to support affirmative action policies.

There's been some interesting work done on why students from some ethnic groups are resistant to the kinds of teaching and subject matter taught in most high schools. Let me tell you about it and then you can decide for yourself what you think.

You know, I used to think that everyone had an equal chance to succeed until I spent some time working in an economically depressed community. Here's what I saw.

4. **Add** information that clears up students' confusions:

Clarify the purpose of the course or the discussions that trouble them. This simple strategy can have unexpected results. An Asian American professor told me the story of a resistant white student in one of his multicultural literature classes who went through an entire course very defensive and upset, thinking that everything about multiculturalism must be bashing him. His papers were confused because he was trying to argue a point of view he clearly didn't believe in, and as a result, he didn't do very well in the class. "And then," the professor continued, "for some perverse reason, he signed up for another course with me, and I thought, boy, this is going to be a waste! He's sitting in the back of the class, all sullen, and one day I happened to remark, 'I hope you all understand that we're not talking about racial superiority here, if we're talking about African Americans or Asian Americans, or Native Americans, or Latinos. We're talking about looking at things equally.' And that must have made a difference to him because suddenly I could see, in the back of the room, a spotlight going on for him. And he came up after class and said, 'You know, I think I misunderstood everything for a semester and a half! I thought you were talking about all these different cultures because you thought they were superior to whites!' I said, 'What? No way!' And he said, 'Wow, everything is different now!'"

Reassure students that their opinions and political perspectives won't affect their grade as long as they can show that they thoroughly understand the points of view of those who disagree with them.

## Working with large classes

**Group students into "quads" for discussion.** In large Sociology lectures at the University of Michigan, instructor Terry McGinn assigns students to "quads" of four that will sit together the entire semester. Two students plus the two in the row directly behind them make up a "quad." After a film clip or a section of the lecture, the instructor projects a question on the screen and asks students to discuss it with members of their quad. Terry says, "After they have had a few minutes to do that, I ask for quads to volunteer interesting things that came up in their conversation. Responses usually come quite quickly. After a few of these reported comments, I find I can pose follow-on questions to the entire class and students will respond quite well individually. Over the course of time, students become more comfortable responding individually to questions that I pose to the entire class, so that it is not always necessary to start with a quad discussion." Quad discussions can serve several purposes: "I might check whether or not they are grasping the material: 'What question would you like to ask about the material I just presented?' or solicit their reaction/opinion: 'What did you think of the author's position on this point?' or ask for input on something related to the administration of the class: 'How can I help you prepare for the quiz?'"

**Find humorous ways to encourage students to ask questions.** Even in the largest classes, instructors can get students to loosen up and take an active role in the learning process by interacting with them in amusing, unexpected ways. A biology professor (Klionsky, 1999) shares his tactics: "When I was a teaching assistant, the instructor told the class to hiss if they did not understand. It worked. The students found it easy to hiss because they did not have to specifically identify themselves. It is also hard to ignore a group of students who are hissing at you. I opt for a slightly different approach and ask students [who don't understand a point] to yell 'stop.' ... Amusingly, I have on numerous occasions heard a student yell "stop" only to look up and see him or her pointing at someone else whose raised hand I had missed." http://www.mcdb.lsa.umich.edu/labs/klionsky/TP.pdf

**Ask for a show of hands.** As Klionsky (1999) explains, questions that call for specific answers from one or two individuals can be intimidating to students in a large lecture hall but asking for a show of hands gets many involved. Questions of fact can be used to check students' knowledge and/or arouse interest in the subject matter, e.g., "Raise your hand if you think the number of active hate groups in the U.S. is greater than fifty? Greater than 100? Greater than 500?" Survey-type questions can help provide evidence for a point made in the lecture. For example, before a discussion of school and neighborhood segregation, you might ask: "How many of you grew up in a community where most people looked like you?" "How many of you went to an all-white or nearly all-white high school?" Questions that solicit students' opinions and ideas can work well in moderate-sized classes (50–100) when you've made sure your questions are clear, that they ask for relatively brief answers, and that they are not a "pop quiz" in disguise. For example, you might say, "As we've seen, affirmative action has increased ethnic diversity on campus, though this practice has now been blocked by voters in a ballot initiative. What might be some other ways of achieving the same goal that don't explicitly use race as a factor in admissions?" "What do you think of these strategies?" Students can be given a few minutes to jot down their thoughts or talk with a partner (or see "Quads" section above) before you call on them.

**Use clickers.** Students purchase wireless, hand-held transmitters which they bring to each lecture. The instructor can use the technology to take instant surveys of students' prior knowledge, or to give quick, anonymous quizzes to assess students' understanding of new material. They can also be used to generate discussion on controversial or emotionally charged topics by having students click on their choice of several "common sense" responses projected on the lecture hall screen (Zhu, 2007). A majority of students report that clickers make lectures more interesting and that they appreciate being able to check their understanding of key concepts and think more deeply about the material. For more on student attitudes, types of questions and activities to use with clickers, see The Center of Research on Teaching and Learning (http://www.crlt.umich.edu/inst/responsesystem)

**Show of hands.** Keep students focused and interested by asking them questions throughout your presentation. "How many of you come from mostly white communities?" "How many of you think that racial integration in housing has increased since the 1970s?" You can then present facts that show that a common belief is, in fact, incorrect without embarrassing any particular student who holds that view. You might also ask questions that give you an idea of how clear and thorough you have been in your lecture: "How many are convinced by Jones's argument that the idea of whiteness is tied to economics?" "How many feel you could now explain her argument to a friend or roommate? You can then ask your teaching assistants to bring up this topic in section, where students can say more freely what convinces them or causes them to doubt.

**Questions from the floor.** Some lecturers conduct their class as they would a conference presentation, allowing time at the end for questions. Since asking questions in front of a large audience can be intimidating, even to the best of students, the instructor might pass around file cards for student input, and then, with the help of an assistant, collect and choose two or three of the most interesting questions to comment on at the end of the class period.

**Questions posted before class.** Asking students to post questions about the reading online (and giving them credit for doing so) can give you a good idea of how students are interacting with the material, where they misinterpret a concept, where they are not reading carefully, and so on. Finding out what students want to know helps you prepare your lecture in a way that directly addresses their concerns and makes sure they understand the key concepts. As students compose their questions, especially on a complex topic, they may find that they have already discovered the answer ("What exactly does Rattansi mean when he says that 'ethnic identities are constantly subject to contextual negotiation'? Oh, he explains that right here!") Requiring them to quote from the text and ask specific, rather than overly general questions ("I don't get how Rattansi defines racism") will improve students' ability to read carefully and give them confidence that they can decipher complex material.

## Community Projects

In some of my classes, I build in community action to encourage students to become allies in antiracism work. Small groups of students choose their own projects and meet outside of class to plan, organize, and implement their ideas. My only stipulation is that their purpose should be to educate and change the dominant culture, rather than do research, or provide service or support to disenfranchised populations. While the latter are worthy goals, they generally do not address the lack of information and unwitting complicity of whites in contemporary racism. This is the work that most urgently needs to be done.

My classes are excited about doing projects together and come up with all sorts of good ideas. About a third of the way through the semester, I get them started by asking them to brainstorm all possible projects they can think of, regardless if they're committed to them or not. I write all their ideas on the board and then ask them to vote, first for two projects (thus eliminating many of the ideas on the board), then for one, which they still don't have to commit to personally. This usually narrows the ideas down to four or five, which a class of twenty can easily take on. Students choose their project (making sure that every project has at least three students), then meet briefly in class to set a date for their first out-of-class meeting and to choose a "point person" who will manage communication among members, facilitate the group discussions, and contact me for advice and support when necessary. Several times during the ensuing weeks I ask each group to give a brief update on their planning process in class, both to make sure students are on track and to generate excitement for each other's projects. All students (and myself) are expected to attend each other's events and presentations.

Over the years, my students have created public art that raises awareness about white privilege. (One such installation involved a large mirror, surrounded by questions and quotes from our readings, and several large sheets of flipchart paper where passers-by could record their reactions.) They have videotaped interviews with students and faculty about the racial climate at the university. They have written dialogues between believable characters on contemporary racial issues and performed them at public gatherings, sometimes enlisting their friends as actors. They have put on a film series of the videos we watched in class (see Annotated Resources) and held discussions after each one. They have interviewed professors and students about their views on race-related topics and produced a high-quality magazine, complete with artwork, that they distributed free on campus. They have experimented with Augusto Boal's "Theater of the Oppressed" (1993), staging racialized incidents that pull in unwitting passers-by for discussion and debate. And they have replicated and enlarged classroom dialogues by inviting friends, instructors, staff, and other members of their community for evening conversations about race that they facilitated with icebreakers, carefully chosen questions, and of course, plenty of snacks. The experience of actively educating their peers is almost always positive and energizing. As students move from the position of learner to facilitator, as they begin to ask the questions and anticipate reactions, set up the exercises, and analyze the outcomes, they gain courage and self-confidence. As one of my students said, delightedly, after a community discussion, "We love doing this. We get to be you!"

## Now What?

To plan your own ways of integrating more successful conversations about race into your classes, here are some suggestions and a summary of my advice so far. Even if you've never tried having such discussions before, even if you are not blessed with small classes like mine, even if your subject matter is only tangentially about race (but race breaks out anyway) I suggest you try out a technique or discussion topic with one of your classes, modifying it for your particular audience. Then, solicit feedback from your students, both by observing their reactions and by asking some of them in conference what they thought about the discussion. Then choose another technique to try so that you gradually discover the teaching style and resources you're most comfortable with. You might try keeping a teaching journal for a semester to record the activities or readings you used in each class, the issues students brought up, who was silent and why, what were the points of tension, and so on. Start a support group, even if it's only you and one other instructor over coffee once a month, where you talk about the discussions you've attempted in your classes, the readings you've assigned, the reactions of your students, and the questions and feelings you're left with. Then spread the idea throughout your department or school. Start conversations among the faculty about ways to include race-related topics in the curriculum or how to teach such issues more knowledgeably. You also might want to refer to the following summary of the advice I have given, sometimes implicitly, throughout this book.

## Summary of Advice

Think about the goal/s you want your students to achieve. Any of the following goals are worthy, in my view. But it's important to articulate, at least to yourself, what you want to accomplish. Then let your goals guide your selection of texts, videos and formats for discussion.

- Do you want an exchange of all points of view where everyone's opinion, however wrong-headed, is given equal respect and worth?
- Do you want the experiences and views of people of color to be given more space and understanding?
- Is your primary objective to make white students more conscious of their own racially biased assumptions and privileges?
- Is it important that your students develop skills in argument or debate?
- Do you want to concentrate on facts: suppressed histories, present-day oppressive practices, and specific examples of how racism is institutionalized?
- Do you want to promote "raw, honest dialogue" where students argue passionately and often feel uncomfortable?
- Or do you want to stress creating safe spaces for the exchange of feelings and experiences?

Think about the amount of class time you can devote to issues of race and racism. If time is limited, try to find ways to integrate discussion and/or background reading into the other topics you must cover. Use the Annotated Resources for ideas.

Think about the teaching style you are most comfortable with. If you want to let students argue openly and passionately with each other, be sure they are starting with facts—good, accessible texts and videos—and from experiences—both their own and those of outside speakers who might be called in to present viewpoints and backgrounds that are underrepresented in your class. If you want to have a certain amount of control over the discussion, use ground rules developed by students themselves, discussion formats that allow controlled expression of many points of view (coins, fishbowl, debate, small group, etc.). If you want to completely control the discussion or must do so because of the large size of the class, use lecture, film, texts and other formal instruction that present various points of view, allowing students to grapple with the material through short reaction papers and large-class discussion techniques.

Start with students where they are. You can gauge something about your students' racial identity development from their written responses to class discussion, the arguments and source material they use in their papers, their comments, questions, tone of voice, silences, and body language in class and in conference. Remember that identity development is not linear: anyone can revisit stages they previously passed through and even be in several stages at once—perhaps on different issues. Adjust your goals, readings, videos, visitors, discussion formats, and responses to your students' comments (especially their writing) accordingly. Students in classes that deal exclusively with the subject of racism appreciate reading Beverly Tatum's (1992) article on racial identity development and determining for themselves where they are at the beginning and the end of the semester. Tatum alerts readers to common reactions (feelings of guilt, shame, avoidance, or burnout) that students sometimes prefer to know about in advance.

Consider where you are in your own racial identity development. No matter how many friends of color white instructors have, or how much reading we've done or classes we've taught, we'll never finish learning—and unlearning—about race. Develop patience and openness for feedback from students and colleagues of color about the ways you're not quite as sensitive as you'd like to be. Learn more about ethnic groups you don't know enough about and show your enthusiasm for diversity and multiculturalism. Actively promote cultural events on campus, go to them yourself, make friends with colleagues of different ethnicities, let them know what you're trying to achieve, seek their guidance and perspectives.

Since most of your students, especially your white students, will be in the first stages of their identity development, start slowly, with positive, safe, egalitarian sharing about identities and cultures. Give students good reasons to want to get to know people from different identity groups. They need to see each other as human beings with similar interests, goals, abilities, and interests before exploring differences in cultural and class backgrounds and experiences around race. After some trust has been established, help students set ground rules for discussion and introduce them to present-day inequalities through videos, novels, history, and the personal experiences of willing class members and visitors. Choose readings that move students gradually into the emotions and conflicts; if you start with angry, accusatory pieces by people of color or sarcastic antiracist pieces by whites, stage one white students will fume silently, or follow their example by taking on a tone of bitterness or ridicule, or worse—turn off entirely. Passionate readings are more valuable after students have learned some facts, definitions, and histories, and are more attuned to present-day realities.

Challenge all students—but especially white students—to deepen their understanding of racial inequalities after your class is over. Since whites are in the majority and since there is great pressure in society to ignore racism and blame people of color themselves for any difficulties they might experience, whites need to be prodded, gently but firmly, to acknowledge that the world they know is not the world as seen through the eyes of many people of color.

Show understanding and encouragement for angry, exasperated or frightened students in various stages of their identity development. Learning about racism in greater detail inevitably arouses emotion in both whites and people of color. Reassure students that emotion and conflict over these issues are normal. Talk with students of color about why white students don't recognize racism and the power of whiteness in our society, using stories from your own experience. Help white students deal with feelings of guilt or anxiety by reassuring them that it is normal to have racist thoughts and assumptions when you grow up in a society so permeated by unacknowledged racism and implicit bias. Encourage them to move beyond guilt by taking action against racism when they see or hear it.

Model sensitive cross-race/cross-cultural interactions both with your students and in role plays with colleagues of different ethnicities. Show how tone of voice, argumentative stance, generalizations, and assumptions can irritate and insult people of color, while respectful questioning and listening for understanding can further the dialogue. Stress the importance of educating one's self on the issues as well as asking respectful questions of people of color—who get these questions all the time.

Remember that international students, even students from Canada, may be unaware of many of the racial issues in the United States and/or may experience race and racism differently in their home countries.

In teaching about present and past injustices, include stories of whites who have fought against injustice and have successfully forged deep friendships across racial lines. Help students see how they too can get involved in reducing prejudice and working for social justice on campus, and later, in their professional lives. Invite student activists who have started multicultural organizations on campus, crossed boundaries, and educated others. Talk about what it means to be an ally and have students generate their own plans for antiracist action.

When confronted with very difficult conflicts or negativity in the classroom, ask the advice of colleagues, bring in colleagues of color to present their perspectives, and allow plenty of opportunity for students to express frustrations privately, in journals, to you in your office, or to an understanding colleague or counselor. If students or administrators try to undermine your promotion of frank talk about race in the classroom, think of the words of James Baldwin (1988) [1963] in "A Talk to Teachers":

> [Y]ou must understand that in the attempt to correct so many generations of bad faith and cruelty, when it is operating not only in the classroom but in society, you will meet the most fantastic, the most brutal, and the most determined resistance. There is no point in pretending this won't happen. … The obligation of anyone who thinks of himself as responsible is to examine society and try to change it and to fight it—at no matter what risk. This is the only hope society has. This is the only way societies change. (pp. 3–4)

# Notes

1. Recounted in Anne Fadiman's book about the cultural clash between Hmong immigrants and their Euro-American doctors (1997, pp. 182–183).
2. See Sandler (1992), *A question of color* (video).
3. This exercise is described by T. Alexander Aleinikoff, who has used it in his law classes, in Schoem et al. (1995, pp. 81–82).
4. It's very important to let students decide which group to join, and not to question—or even appear to be questioning—their choices. Some may be thinking about their racial identity for the first time, and/or may be deeply conflicted about it, especially biracial students, students whose families identify by ethnicity rather than race (e.g., "Mexican" for Mexican Americans who speak Spanish and maintain strong cross-border ties), or international students whose "race" in their home country is different from the one tacitly assigned in the United States (e.g., a Nicaraguan student identifying as *blanco* or white in their home country yet seen as "Latin@" or "brown" in the United States).

# BIBLIOGRAPHY

ABC News. (1996). *America in Black and White: #2 How much is white skin worth?* Distributor: ABC News.

ABC Primetime Live. (1991). *True colors.* Video. Distributor: Journal Graphics. Adachi, J. (2006). *The slanted screen: Asian men in film and television.* Video. AAMM Productions.

Allen, P. G. (1988). Who is your mother? Red roots of white feminism. In R. Simonson & S. Walker (Eds.), *Graywolf annual five: Multi-cultural literacy.* St. Paul, MN: Graywolf Press.

American-Arab Anti-Discrimination Committee Research Institute. (2007). *Report on hate crimes and discrimination against Arab Americans 2003–2007.* http://www.adc.org/PDF/hcr07.pdf

Andersen, H. C. (1996). *The little match girl.* New York: The Putnam & Grosset Group.

Anzaldúa, G. (1987). *Borderlands/La frontera.* San Francisco: Aunt Lute Books.

Applied Research Center. (2009, May 18). *Race and recession: How inequity rigged the economy and how to change the rules.* http://arc.org/downloads/2009_race_recession- pdf

Appling, C. (1998, Summer). Passing patriots: The four multiracial U.S. presidents. *Interrace,* 8(42), 20.

Arboleda, T. (1998). *In the shadow of race: Growing up as a multiethnic, multicultural, and "multiracial" American.* Mahwah, NJ: Lawrence Erlbaum Associates.

Baldwin, J. (1988) [1963]. A talk to teachers. In R. Simonson & S. Walker (Eds.), *Graywolf annual five: Multicultural literacy.* St. Paul, MN: Graywolf Press.

BBC. (1985). *Are you a racist?* Distributor: Films, Incorporated.

Bhopal, R., & Donaldson, L. (1998, September). White, European, Western, Caucasian, or what? Inappropriate labeling in research on race, ethnicity, and health. *American Journal of Public Health*, 88(9), 1303–1307.

Boal, A. (1993). *Theatre of the oppressed.* New York: Theatre Communications Group.

Brown, M. (1986). *Shadow.* New York: Simon & Schuster.

Browne, K. (2008). *Traces of the trade: A story from the Deep North.* Ebb Pod Productions.

Bulosan, C. (1996) [1946]. *America is in the heart.* Seattle: University of Washington Press.

California Newsreel. (2008). *Unnatural causes: Is inequality making us sick?* Video series.

Cannon, L. W. (1990, Spring–Summer). Fostering positive race, class, and gender dynamics in the classroom. *Women's Studies Quarterly (18)*, 126–134.

Carracedo, A., & Bahar, R. (2007). *Made in Los Angeles (Hecho in Los Angeles).* Video. Distributor: California Newsreel.

Center for Research on Learning and Teaching. (2009). *Teaching with clickers: Students' attitudes.* www.crlt.umich.edu/inst/clickerattitudes.php

CEPR. (2006). Decline in auto industry undermines well-paid jobs for African Americans. http://www.cepr.net/index.php/press-releases/press-releases/decline-in-auto-industry-undermines-well-paid-jobs-for-african-americans/

Cleaver, E. (1968). *Soul on ice.* New York: McGraw-Hill.

Cliff, M. (1988). If I could write this in fire, I would write this in fire. In R. Simonson & S. Walker (Eds.), *Graywolf annual five: Multi-cultural literacy.* St. Paul,: MN: Graywolf Press.

CNNPolitics.com. (2009, February 19). Holder: U.S. a "nation of cowards" on race relations. http://www.cnn.com/2009/POLITICS/02/18/holder.race.relations/index.html

CNNPolitics.com. (2009, June 25). Blacks in survey say race relations no better with Obama. http://www.cnn.com/2009/POLITICS/06/25/obama.poll/index.html

Cofer, J. O. (1997). American history. In H. Augenbraum & M. F. Olmos (Eds.), *The Latino reader.* New York: Houghton Mifflin.

Conrad, J. [1897] (1976).*The nigger of the "Narcissus."* In J. Conrad, *The Nigger of the "Narcissus"/Typhoon/and other stories.* New York: Penguin.

Coon, C. (1965). *The living races of man.* New York: Knopf.

Cotton, S. (1998). *Silent terror: A journey into contemporary African slavery.* New York: Harlem River Press.

Cross, W. E. Jr., Parham, T. A., & Helms, J. E. (1991). The stages of black identity development: Nigrescence models. In R. Jones (Ed.), *Black psychology* (Third Edition). San Francisco: Cobb and Henry.

Crow Dog, M. (1990). *Lakota woman.* New York: HarperPerennial. Dalgliesh, A. (1954). *The Thanksgiving story.* New York: Simon & Schuster.

Dalton, H. L. (1995). *Racial healing: Confronting the fear between Blacks and Whites.* New York: Doubleday.

Democracy Now. (2005, September 5). Kayne West: "Bush doesn't care about black people." http://www.democracynow.org/2005/9/5/kanye_west_bush_doesnt_care_about

DeMott, B. (1995, September). Put on a happy face: Masking the differences between blacks and whites. *Harper's Magazine*, 31–38.

Derman-Sparks, L. (1997). *Teaching/learning anti-racism*. New York: Teachers College Press.

Dobrin, S. I. (1997). Race and the public intellectual: A conversation with Michael Eric Dyson. *JAC: A Journal of Composition Theory, 17*(2), 143–181.

Du Bois, W. E. B. (1965)[1903]. *Souls of Black folk*. In *Three Negro Classics*. New York: Avon Books.

Dubose, H. (2005). *The vanishing Black male*. Video. Distributor: Seven Generations Productions.

Ellis, D., & Mueller, D. (2004). *You can't be neutral on a moving train*. Video. Distributor: First Run Features.

Fadiman, A. (1997). *The spirit catches you and you fall down*. New York: Farrar, Straus, and Giroux.

Finnegan, W. (1998). *Cold new world: Growing up in a harder country*. New York: Random House.

Fish, J. M. (1995, November/December). Mixed blood. *Psychology Today, 28*, 55–58. Fletcher, M. A., & Cohen, J. (2009, January 19). Far fewer consider racism big problem; Little change, however, at local level. *Washington Post*, p. A06.

Fox, H. (2012). *Their highest vocation: Social justice and the Millennial generation*. New York: Peter Lang.

Friedman, I. R. (1984). *How my parents learned to eat*. Boston: Houghton Mifflin. Gaertner, S. L., & Dovidio, J. F. (1986). The aversive form of racism. In J. F. Dovidio & S. L. Gaertner (Eds.), *Prejudice, discrimination and racism: Theory and research*. Orlando, FL: Academic Press.

Gates, H. L., & West, C. (1997). *The future of the race*. New York: Vintage Books. Gillespie, A. (2009, Autumn). Postracial? Really? Emory Magazine. http://www.emory.edu/EMORY_ MAGAZINE/2009/autumn/coda.html

Gomez-Peña, G. (1993). Califas. In G. Gómez-Peña, *Warrior for Gringostroika*. St. Paul, MN: Graywolf Press.

Gorlick, A. (2009, March 2). Stanford Report. Backing Obama gives some voters license to favor whites over blacks, study shows. http://news.stanford.edu/news/2009/march4/ obama-moral-credentials-favor-whites-030409.html

Gregory, D. (1964). *Nigger: An autobiography*. New York: Dutton.

Grimberg, S., & Friedman, D. (1997). *Miss India Georgia*. Video. Distributor: Urban Life Productions.

Grossman, R. (2005). *Homeland: Four portraits of Native activism*. Video. Katahdin Productions.

Helms, J. E. (1990). Toward a model of White racial identity development. In J. E. Helms (Ed.), *Black and White racial identity: Theory, research, and practice*. Westport, CT: Greenwood.

Herbst, P. (1997). *The color of words: An encyclopaedic dictionary of ethnic bias in the United States*. Yarmouth, ME: Intercultural Press.

Herron, C. (1997). *Nappy hair*. New York: Alfred A. Knopf.

Hoerl, K. (2012, April). Selective amnesia and racial transcendence in news coverage of President Obama's inauguration. *Quarterly Journal of Speech 98*(2), 178–202.

Horton, M. (1990). *The long haul: An autobiography*. New York: Doubleday.

Horton, M., & Freire, P. (1990). *We make the road by walking: Conversations on education and social change*. Philadelphia: Temple University Press.

Howe, N. & Strauss, W. (2000). *Millennials rising: The next great generation*. New York: Vintage Books. Howell, S., & Mandell, J. (1995). *Tales from Arab Detroit*. Video. Distributor: New Day Films.

Jackson, I. L. (1999, April 18). U-M, EMU students segregate themselves. *Ann Arbor News*, A1.

Joseph, B. (2007, November 16). The 9 most racist Disney characters. *Cracked.com*. www.cracked.com/article_15677_9-most-racist-disney-characters.html

Kaiser Family Foundation. (2009). *Key health and health care indicators by race/ethnicity and state*. http://www.kff.org/minorityhealth/upload/7633-02.pdf

Kaufman, S. B. (2009, February 24). Obama is president so racism is over. Right? *Psychology Today Blogs*. http://www.psychologytoday.com/blog/beautiful- minds/200902/obama-is-president-so-racism-is-over-right

KCTS-9 Seattle and United Indians of All Tribes Foundation. (1979). *Images of Indians Series Part 4: Heathen injuns and the Hollywood gospel*. Video. Distributor: Great Plains National.

Kivel, P. (1996). *Uprooting racism: How white people can work for racial justice*. Philadelphia: New Society Publishers.

Klionsky, P. J. (1999). Tips for using questions in large classes. *The Teaching Professor, 13*, 1–3.

Kochar, R., Fry, R., & Taylor, P. (2011, July 26). Wealth gaps rise to record highs between Whites, Blacks, Hispanics. http://www.pewsocialtrends.org/2011/07/26/wealth-gaps-rise-to-record-highs-between-whites-blacks-hispanics/

Kochman, T. (1981). *Black and white styles in conflict*. Chicago: University of Chicago Press.

Leahy, P. (2008, November 5). A revolutionary celebration. *The Michigan Daily*. http://www.michigandaily.com/content/2008-11-06/blue-revolution

Lee, M. W. (1994). *The color of fear*. Video. Distributor: Stir-Fry Productions.

Lee, M. W. (2002). *Last chance for Eden, Part One*. Distributor: California Newsreel.

Lee, M. W. & Jang, L. (1998). *Stolen ground*. Stir-Fry Productions.

Leiman, M. M. (1993). *The political economy of racism: A history*. Boulder, CO: Pluto Press.

Loewen, J. W. (1995). *Lies my teacher told me: Everything your American history textbook got wrong*. New York: Simon & Schuster.

Lorde, A. (1993). There is no hierarchy of oppressions. In P. Myers & R. Cleaver (Eds.), *A certain terror: Heterosexism, militarism, violence, and change*. Chicago: Great Lakes Regional Office of the American Friends Service Committee.

Mahan, L., & Lipman, M. (1996). *Holding ground: The rebirth of Dudley Street*. Video. Distributor: New Day Films.

Martinez, E. (1997, Spring). "Unite and overcome!" In *Teaching Tolerance*. Montgomery, AL: Southern Poverty Law Center.

McIntosh, P. (1992) [1988]. White privilege and male privilege: A personal account of coming to see correspondences through work in Women's Studies. In M. L. Andersen & P. H. Collins (Eds.), *Race, class, and gender*. Belmont, CA: Wadsworth.

McKinley, J., & Wollan, M. (2009, June 26). New border fear: Militia violence. *New York Times*. http://www.nytimes.com/2009/06/27/us/27arizona.html?_r=1&scp=1&sq=minutemen&st=cse

Michigan Daily. (2008, November 4). Liveblogging the Obama victory celebrations in Ann Arbor. http://www.michigandaily.com/content/2008-11-04/live-ann-arborelection-day

Michigan Student Study. (1994). Office of Minority Affairs in collaboration with the Center for the Study of Higher Education and the Department of Psychology, University of Michigan, Ann Arbor.

Miller, J. P. (1998). Suburban college town blues (make me wanna holler). In C. Smith, R. Edelman, S. Munro, & S. Eaton (Eds.), *Breaking the silence*. Ann Arbor: University of Michigan.

Monastersky, R. (1992, October 3). The warped world of mental maps. *Science News, 142,* 222–223.

Morris, B. S. (1999). Toward creating a TV research community in your classroom. In *Trends & issues in secondary English*. Urbana, IL: National Council of Teachers of English.

MSNBC. (2007, September 27). *More blacks, Latinos in jail than in college dorms*. http://www.msnbc.msn.com/id/21001543/

Mura, D. (1996). *Where the body meets memory*. New York: Doubleday.

National Commission on Fair Housing. (2008, December). *The future of fair housing*. http://www.nationalfairhousing.org/Portals/33/reports/Future_of_Fair_Housing. pdf

Ogbu, J. (1989). *Cultural models and educational strategies of non-dominant peoples*. The 1989 Catherine Molony Memorial Lecture. New York: City College School of Education, The Workshop Center.

Ogbu, J., & Simmons, H. D. (1998, June). Voluntary and involuntary minorities: A cultural-ecological theory of school performance with some implications for education. *Anthropology & Education Quarterly, 29*(2), 155–188.

Oyserman, D., & Sakamoto, I. (1997, December). Being Asian American: Identity, cultural constructs, and stereotype perception. *Journal of Applied Behavioral Science, 33*(4), 435–453.

Palmer, P. J. (1998). *The courage to teach*. San Francisco: Jossey-Bass. PBS American Experience. (2009). *We shall remain*. Video series.

Posten, W. S. C. (1990). The biracial identity development model: A needed addition. *Journal of Counseling and Development, 69,* 152–155.

Poten, C., & Roberts, P. (2007). *Contrary warriors: A film of the Crow tribe*. Video. Distributor: Direct Cinema Limited.

Potok, M. (1997, Fall). Roots of racism: An interview with an expert on racism. *Intelligence Report, 88,* 11–13.

Potok, M. (2009, Summer). Resurgence on the right. *Intelligence Report*. http://www.splcenter.org/intel/intelreport/article.jsp?aid=1052

Raju, S. (2008). *Divided we fall: Americans in the aftermath*. Video: New Moon Productions.

Raybon, P. (1996). *My first White friend*. New York: Viking.

Reagan, G. (2009, June 29). In the battle between Facebook and MySpace, a digital 'White flight.' New York Observer. http://observer.com/2009/06/in-the-battle-between-facebook-and-myspace-a-digital-white-flight/

Real Clear Politics (2010, January 27). MSNBC's Matthews on Obama: "I forgot he was black tonight." http://www.realclearpolitics.com/video/2010/01/27/msnbcs_matthews_on_obama_i_forgot_he_was_black_tonight.html

Reich, M. (1981). *Racial inequality: A political-economic analysis*. Princeton, NJ: Princeton University Press.

Reid, F. (1995). *Skin Deep: College Students Confront Racism*. Distributor: California Newsreel.

Renn, K. A. (2008, Fall). Research on biracial and multiracial identity development: Overview and synthesis. *New Directions for Student Services*, 123. https://www.msu.edu/~renn/Renn-NewDirectionsMR2008.pdf

Remnick, D. (2008, November 17). The Joshua generation: Race and the campaign of Barack Obama. *The New Yorker*. http://www.newyorker.com/reporting/2008/11/17/081117fa_fact_remnick?currentPage=1

Renn, K. A. (2004). Mixed race students in college: The ecology of race, identity, and community. Albany, NY: SUNY Press.

Riggs, M. (1987). *Ethnic notions*. Video. Distributor: California Newsreel. Riggs, M. (1991). *Color adjustment*. Video. Distributor: California Newsreel.

Remnick, D. (2008, November 17). The Joshua generation: Race and the campaign of Barack Obama. *The New Yorker*. http://www.newyorker.com/reporting/2008/11/17/081117fa_fact_remnick?currentPage=1

Ringgold, F. (1991). *Tar beach*. New York: Crown.

Ringgold, F. (1992). *Aunt Harriet's underground railroad in the sky*. New York: Crown.

Root, M. P. P. (1990). Resolving the "other" status: Identity development of biracial individuals. *Women and Therapy*, 9, 185–205.

Rosenstein, J. (1997). *In whose honor? American mascots in sports*. Distributor: New Day Films.

Ruiz, J. L. (1972). *Los vendidos*. Video. Distributor: El Teatro Campesino. Sandler, K. (1992). *A question of color*. Video. Distributor: California Newsreel.

Schoem, D., Frankel, L., Zúñiga, X., & Lewis, E. A. (Eds.). (1995). *Multicultural teaching in the university*. Westport, CT: Praeger.

Shaheen, J. (2007). *Reel bad Arabs: How Hollywood vilifies a people*. Video. Distributor: Media Education Foundation.

Shaw, G. B. (1939). *Pygmalion*. New York: Dodd, Mead & Co.

Smith, A. D. (2000). *Twilight in Los Angeles*. Video. Distributor: PBS Home Video. Smith, C., Edelman, R., Munro, S., & Eaton, S. (Eds.). (1998). *Breaking the silence*. Ann Arbor: University of Michigan Press.

Smitherman, G. (1977). *Talkin and testifyin: The language of Black America*. Boston: Houghton Mifflin.

Stavans, I. (1995). *The Hispanic condition*. New York: HarperCollins.

Steele, S. (2008, November 5). Obama's post-racial promise. Los Angeles Times. http://www.latimes.com/news/opinion/opinionla/la-oe-steele5-2008nov05,0,6049031.story

Sugrue, T. J. (2009). *Not even past: Barack Obama and the burden of race*. Princeton, NJ: Princeton University Press,

Tajima-Peña, R., & Thai, Q. (1997). *My America (… Or honk if you love Buddha)*. Video. Distributor: SAI Communications.

Takaki, R. (1998) [1989]. *Strangers from a different shore: A history of Asian Americans*. Boston: Little, Brown.

Tatum, B. D. (1992, Spring). Talking about race, learning about racism: The application of racial identity development theory in the classroom. *Harvard Educational Review*, 62(1), 1–24.

Tatum, B. D. (1994, Summer). Teaching white students about racism: The search for allies and the restoration of hope. *Teachers College Record*, 95(4), 462–476.

Taylor, J. M. (2009). *New Muslim cool*. Video: POV Documentary.

Telles, R., & Tejada-Flores, R. (2005). *Race is the place*. Video. Paradigm Productions. WGBH Boston, for PBS. (1994).

West, C. (1994). *Race matters*. New York: Vintage Books.

WGBH Boston, for PBS (1994). *Toxic Racism*. Distributor: Films for the Humanities. Winik, L. W. (1999, July 18). There's a new generation with a different attitude. *Parade Magazine*, *Ann Arbor News*, 6+.

Wise, T. (2008). *Tim Wise: On white privilege*. Media Education Foundation.

Wise, T. (2010). *Colorblind: The rise of post-racial politics and the retreat from racial equity*. San Francisco, CA: City Lights Publishers.

Yamato, G. (1992). Something about the subject makes it hard to name. In M. L. Andersen & P. H. Collins (Eds.), *Race, class, and gender*. Belmont, CA: Wadsworth. Zhu, E. (2007). *Teaching with clickers*. Occasional Paper No. 22. Center for Research on Learning and Teaching. University of Michigan, Ann Arbor. www.crlt.umich.edu/publinks/CRLT_n022.pdf

# ANNOTATED RESOURCES AND MORE IDEAS FOR ASSIGNMENTS

*This section contains resources that are especially recommended for classroom use. V indicates full-length video or DVD; SV indicates a short, online video usually found on YouTube.*

## Genetics and Human Origins

**V** BBC (2008). *In the blood: Episode #4, Divided we stand*. Video, 49 minutes. Distributor: Films for the Humanities & Sciences. A thought-provoking introduction to the history of racial essentialism—the idea that "race" is biological, fixed, and immutable. Popularized during the nineteenth century by European and North American scientists to establish the superiority of "whiteness," the idea has more recently been taken up by several black academics to claim the even greater superiority of blackness. The film gently corrects the latter view by showing how new work on the human genome reveals the astonishing similarity of the human family—only six out of sixty thousand genes control skin color, for example. This film can lead into a discussion of more common essentialist ideas such as the "natural athletic superiority" of black basketball players, the "natural mathematical superiority" of Asians, or the "genetic connection" of Native Americans to the environment.

**V** PBS (2002). *The journey of man: A genetic odyssey*. Video, 120 minutes. Geneticist Spencer Wells relates how scientists discovered, through DNA research, that all modern humans can be traced back to a single female ancestor, "Eve," who lived in Africa around 150,000 years ago, and "Adam," who (surprisingly) lived 60,000 years ago. More details of how and why humans migrated out of Africa to populate the earth, and how we came to look different though remaining genetically almost identical, are explored in a book by the same title, published by Random House (2002).

**V** PBS (2003). *Race, the power of an illusion: #1. The difference between us.* Video, 58 minutes. California Newsreel. Students from a variety of ethnic backgrounds analyze and compare their own DNA, discovering some surprising similarities and differences. As the young people relate their expectations before and after the tests, viewers may begin to question their own family backgrounds and their assumptions about the nature of race. The film explores how human differences emerged and how talents that we may think are tied to race—athletic and musical ability, for example—evolved long before modern humans left Africa. The PBS website has links to background readings, a fascinating "Ask the Experts" page, and hundreds of other resources on race. http://www.pbs.org/race/000_General/000_00-Home.htm

**V** TEDMED (2015, November). *The problem with race-based medicine.* https://www.ted.com/talks/dorothy_roberts_the_problem_with_race_based_medicine?language=en In this excellent TED talk, sociologist Dorothy Roberts explains how unscientific assumptions about race and biology run deeply through all medical practice, from genetic testing, to diagnosis of disease, to the development of new, "race-specific" drugs and treatments. Even though sociologists have long understood race as a social construct that changes over time and varies from country to country, medical researchers and practitioners continue to rely on assumptions about race that add no important biological information and can send dangerous messages about social groups. These racialized assumptions may not only be incorrect, they also can be harmful to patients. For example, blacks and Latin@s are twice as likely as whites to receive no pain medication for the same painful long-bone fractures based on the false notion that black and brown people feel less pain, exaggerate their level of pain, and are predisposed to drug addiction. Roberts argues that medical practitioners should abandon the "backward legacy" of race and instead, turn their attention to the social and economic factors that plague poor communities of color: lack of access to high quality medical care, lack of healthy food choices, high rates of incarceration, and the stress of everyday racism. Roberts is an excellent speaker: clear, passionate, straightforward, and highly knowledgeable.

Bonham, V. L., Callier, S. L. & Royal, C. D. (2016, May 26). Will precision medicine move us beyond race? *New England Journal of Medicine.* Students headed into the medical professions will be interested in this controversy about the newest forms of diagnosis and treatment: "race-based medicine" vs. "precision medicine." As this article explains, prescribing certain medications based on the socially constructed and biologically imprecise concept of race has its pitfalls; for example, a treatment for heart failure that is marketed to self-identified black patients will inevitably miss some individuals of other races, and may not help some who identify as black. "Precision medicine," which takes into account an individual's unique history, genetics, social and environmental factors, family background, and so on, can be more accurate, as its name suggests, but is not yet cost-effective and may remain unaffordable for many, even those who are insured.

Byrd, W. C. & Hughey, M. W. (2015, September). Race, racial inequality, and biological determinism in the genetic and genomic era. *Annals of the American Academy of Political and Social Science*. http://ann.sagepub.com/content/661/1.toc The entire edition of this journal is a treasure trove of academic articles that explore how the idea of race continues to be misused in science and public policy. Articles detail the history of biological determinism; the reemergence of the now-discredited "race science" in the guise of a genetic conception of race; the ways racial essentialism can appear objective to public policy makers; how media construct racial differences in athletics; and a dystopian view of the future if biological concepts of race continue to influence public and scientific policy. An excellent resource for student papers and class presentations.

Frayer, D. (2013, May 2). Who're You Calling a Neanderthal? *New York Times*, Op Ed. Fascinating new research suggests that modern humans, perhaps in Europe, perhaps in the Middle East, mated with Neanderthals to the extent that up to 4% of European DNA is of Neanderthal origin. Africans, on the other hand, had no direct contact with the Neanderthal population so they carry no (or very little) Neanderthal DNA. This short, engaging piece describes some of what we now know about Neanderthal capabilities, culture, and even language. Since popular depictions of Neanderthals have so often portrayed our nonhuman cousins as "stumbling, bumbling, mumbling fools who aimlessly wandered the landscape eking out a miserable, forlorn existence," students are shocked to discover that they may carry Neanderthal DNA. Does this mean we should extend our concept of diversity across species as well as ethnic or racial lines?

Hughey, M. W. (2015, August 20). The risk of turning races into genes. *Huffington Post* http://www.huffingtonpost.com/matthew-w-hughey/the-risks-of-turning-race_b_8010956.html In this short piece sociologist Matthew W. Hughey takes issue with a central, problematic argument about race and genetics: that race must have a biological basis since scientists have been able to map clusters of genes that correspond to specific areas of the world. But these genetic clusters are not actual "races," argues Hughey; rather, they are simply "collectives that analysts construct using computer programs." In other words, even scientists see what they are predisposed to see. "If we believe there are five racial groups, we can then find five clusters of genetic material to match up with those five racial groups. However, if we believe there to be fifty racial groups, we can also then discover fifty clusters of genetic patterns that seemingly validate the fifty-race assumption." This piece pairs well with articles on the history of racial classification, which has changed dramatically (and sometimes amusingly) over time.

Ingraham, C. (2014, December 22). A lot of Southern whites are a little bit black. *Washington Post*. https://www.washingtonpost.com/news/wonk/wp/2014/12/22/a-lot-of-southern-whites-are-a-little-bit-black/ Students may be surprised to learn that according to a recent study, six million Americans who describe themselves as white turn out to have some African ancestry. Many of these individuals are concentrated in the South, especially Louisiana and South Carolina, but whites with black ancestry can also be found in Nevada, Vermont, Michigan, North Dakota and in fact, most states in the Union. Whether or not they know the details of their ethnic heritage, people with 15% or less of African ancestry generally don't describe themselves as African-American, while those with 50% or more do. These figures, presented briefly and without much commentary in the Washington Post's *Wonkblog* provide an opportunity for students to discuss why whites (and blacks) might not know the ethnic heritage of their relatives, why "race" is an imprecise biological concept, and whether finding out about how "mixed" we are as Americans could help break down our self-imposed racial divisions.

Yudell, M., Roberts, D., DeSalle, R., &Tishkoff, S. (2016, February 5). Taking race out of human genetics. *Science.* http://science.sciencemag.org/content/351/6273/564 Scientists "draw wildly different conclusions on the utility of the race concept in biological research," say the authors of this short essay. Some find race the "best proxy we have for examining human genetic diversity"; others find it irrelevant and inaccurate in scientific research; while still others say that since "racial" groups are really quite heterogeneous, race-based predications are questionable at best. The authors take the latter view, adding that popular misinterpretations of the use of race in genetics continue to fuel racist beliefs about the presumed genetic basis of social differences between races. They propose that scientific journals encourage the use of the terms "ancestry" or "population," which more accurately describe human groups, and to require authors to define how they are using these variables. "Language matters," the authors argue, "and the scientific language of race has a considerable influence on how the public (which includes scientists) understands human diversity." An excellent piece for students heading into the biological or medical sciences.

Wade, N. (2000, February 1). What we all spoke when the world was young. *New York Times*, Science Times, D1. "In the beginning there was one people, perhaps no more than 2,000 strong, who had acquired an amazing gift, the faculty for complex language. ... [Their] epic explorations began some 50,000 years ago and by the time the whole world was occupied, the one people had become many. ... Differing in creed, culture, and even appearance, because their hair and skin had adapted to the world's many climates in which they now lived, they no longer recognized one another as the children of one family. Speaking 5,000 languages, they had long forgotten the ancient mother tongue that had both united and yet dispersed this little band of cousins to the four corners of the earth." Dr. Joseph H. Greenberg's appealing theory, which traces words and concepts from modern languages back to a possible common origin, has attracted the attention of geneticists and anthropologists but is eyed skeptically by linguists. Interesting controversy for science and nonscience student alike, and a positive, "safe" way to begin to approach the subject of race.

# Social Construction of Race

American Anthropological Association. www.aaanet.org. The AAA project, "Teaching Race and Unlearning Racism" maintains an interactive website www.understandingrace.org that looks at race through the lenses of history, human variation, and lived experience. An especially interesting quiz explores many of the common beliefs about the "natural" abilities of athletes from various racial and ethnic backgrounds. The site also features a "game of life experience," that shows how race influences where we live, work, and go to school, and how we are perceived and treated by others. Another quiz (which reassures viewers that it has no right or wrong answers) asks their opinion about which nationalities are considered "white." The site also has a "For Kids" section useful for middle schoolers.

Brodkin, K. (1998). *How Jews became white folks and what that says about race in America*. New Brunswick, NJ: Rutgers University Press. This personal, highly readable account of working class Jews in Brooklyn shows how class, gender, anti-Semitism, and "not-quite white" racial assignment shaped Jewish identity over three generations. Contains little-known general history as well; for example, the GI Bill of Rights, "arguably the most massive affirmative action program in American history," extended "financial support during the job search, small loans for starting up businesses, and ... low-interest home loans and educational benefits, which included tuition and living expenses," to 16 million people, mostly white males. For a film made about this same community that focuses on the tumultuous events of 1940 to 1960, see Broadman (2005), *Brownsville: Black and White* (in "Institutional Racism: Urban Neighborhoods").

Coates, T. (2013, May 15). What we mean when we say "race is a social construct." *The Atlantic*. http://www.theatlantic.com/national/archive/2013/05/what-we-mean-when-we-say-race-is-a-social-construct/275872/ The photo that heads this article says it all: a teenage graduation picture of Walter White, leader of the NAACP for over twenty years, who looks, by anyone's reckoning, 100% white. Coates's comment: "Black dude." How is it that someone who looks white not only identifies as black but is celebrated as a black leader within the black community? Coates goes on to explain that race is not an obvious fact of life needing no careful definition, since "no coherent, fixed definition of race actually exists." Historical examples abound. One of the most interesting is that at the time of the Civil War, Southern whites "not only thought of themselves as a race separate from blacks, but as a race apart from Northern whites."

Ignatiev, N. (1995). *How the Irish became white*. New York: Routledge. The caste oppression and extreme poverty that Irish Catholic immigrants had suffered in Ireland made them sympathetic, initially, to the condition of U.S. blacks. But they soon discovered the economic and social rewards of adopting anti-black racism, for "[t]o enter the white race was a strategy to secure an advantage in a competitive society." A vivid, extended example of how race is socially constructed.

Jones, B. (2015, June 25). The social construction of race. *Jacobin*. https://www. jacobinmag.com/2015/06/racecraft-racism-social-origins-reparations/ Written in language and tone that appeals to high school students, this history-packed article is an excellent primer on how and why race was invented, why skin tone is darker or lighter in different parts of the world, the reasons for indentured servitude and slavery in the United States, several of the most famous legal challenges to racial privilege, and some of the ways people have rebelled against the unjust and pernicious idea of race, both historically and today.

Kendzior, S. (2013, April 21). The wrong kind of Caucasian. *Aljazeera*. http://www. aljazeera.com/indepth/opinion/2013/04/2013421145859380504.html. Media reports of the bombings at the Boston Marathon "were quick to demonize an entire ethnicity" when the two young suspects, Dzokhar and Tamerlan Tsarnaev—who had never lived in Chechnya—were accused of terrorism. Although people from the North Caucasus had long been considered "white" (or "Caucasian") in the United States, the group's status fell when the media began portraying the lives of the suspects "through a Chechen lens, [and] political strife in the North Caucasus, ignored by the press for years, [became] the default rationale for a domestic crime." This piece can add to a discussion of the mutability of racial categories, the idea of "white" as more than just skin color, and the targeting of ethnic groups when several of their members commit horrific crimes.

Macedo, D., & Gounari, P. (eds.) (2005). *The globalization of racism*. Herndon, VA: Paradigm Publishers. The contributors to this volume comment on the ways racism is enacted in a variety of countries and contexts. Macedo and Gounari point out in the Introduction, for example, that there is no "generic racism" produced by inevitable historical forces, human biology, or nature; it is always historically specific to particular locations and contexts, and it continually creates new global forms. In France, anti-Muslim racism is reaching new heights, while Germany has experienced the resurgence of neo-Nazism, and in the United States, mass slavery has been replaced by mass incarceration. Greece has seen the racist exclusion of the "white" Albanian minority by the "white" Greek majority, and in Palestine, the racism of the Zionist project is linked more closely with nationalism than with notions of biological difference. In many locations, racism and xenophobia are exacerbated by neoliberal policies that cause rural people to relocate in massive numbers to cities and flow across national borders from poor to rich countries. It's worth wading through the dense prose and the (possibly) unfamiliar Marxist premises to get at the provocative observations of these authors.

Mills, C. (1999). *The racial contract*. Ithaca, NY: Cornell University Press. European philosophers of the seventeenth century proposed the idea of a "social contract" whereby men transcended their "state of nature" by coming together as equals to establish formal mechanisms to regulate civilized life. But as Mills points out, most of humanity at the time were considered "the other"—dark, savage, and uncivilized, and thus, beyond the protection of any state. This unspoken "racial contract," or common knowledge of who were to be considered "men" and who were not, justified "white" exploitation of "non-white" bodies, lands, and resources. But the idea of the social contract continues to be discussed by contemporary philosophers without mentioning this central contradiction, and this, according to Mills, amounts to mass self-deception among white scholars, a "consensual hallucination." This pithy, raw exposé of how white supremacy continues to shape scholarship, politics, and economic relations, is accessible to undergraduates, and affords them a view of a distinguished scholar of color they will seldom come across in the rest of their studies.

Wade, L. (2015, October 2). The US Census and the social construction of race. *Sociological Images*. https://thesocietypages.org/socimages/2015/10/02/the-census-and-the-social-construction-of-race/ In this short, easy-to-read article, sociologist Lisa Wade demystifies the racial categories defined over the years by the US Census. Students can easily see how categories have changed drastically, both in name and in quantity, over time. In 1870, for example, respondents were supposed to fit into one of four categories: White, Black, Mulatto, and Indian. By 1890, when "the US government was obsessed with race-mixing" the categories were White, Black, Mulatto, Quadroons, Octoroons, Indian, Chinese, and Japanese. Students can look up other census forms over the years, bring their findings to class, and discuss what these changing categories might tell us about the significance of race.

# Histories, Cultures, and Contemporary Realities of People of Color in the United States

## African-Americans

V Banks, J. (2001). *One drop*. Video, 45 minutes. Distributor: California Newsreel. An exploration of color and class discrimination within the black community. Interview clips reveal a variety of opinions on questions such as: "Who gets to be called black—or black enough?" "What is it like to be seen as racially ambiguous?" "Who and what defines black culture?" "How are blacks treated by other blacks if they date or marry outside their race?" "How do whites employers and customers react to blacks of different skin tones?" "How do the media aggravate color prejudice?" In mostly white classes, students should already have an clear understanding of white privilege before viewing this film, as it is all too easy for whites to analyze "black problems" without seeing their own complicity in the racial order.

V Blackside Productions. (1987). *Eyes on the prize: America's civil rights years*. Distributor: PBS Video. Six videos, 57 minutes each. A documentary history of the Civil Rights Movement from 1954 to 1965 shown through interviews and historical footage. *Awakening* covers the murder of fourteen-year-old Emmett Till and the Montgomery bus boycott; *Fighting back* focuses on the integration of Little Rock's Central

High School and the University of Mississippi; *Ain't scared of your jails* depicts the lunch counter sit-ins and the Freedom Rides of 1961; *No easy walk*, probably the most exciting and inspirational of the series, chronicles the young blacks who confronted Bull Connor's fire hoses; *Mississippi: Is this America?* covers the struggle of blacks to vote; and *Bridge to freedom* details the evolving strategy of nonviolent protest ten years after the Movement started.

**V** Discovery Productions. (1995). *Promised land*. Distributor: Discovery Channel. Series of three 90-minute videos. This three-part documentary traces the "greatest peacetime migration in American history": the black migration from the South to the urban centers of the North in the 1930s, 1940s, and 1950s. Based on Nicholas Lemann's book of the same name, Part I portrays both beautiful and appalling footage from the days of sharecropping: the blues harmonica music that grew up around the railroad, the punishing work of picking cotton, the terrifying inevitability of white power, and the unspeakable living conditions that finally led to the vast migration into a postwar economy where any black man from Mississippi could walk into the Chicago stockyards and be hired on the spot. Part II features the Pullman porters and their prominence in union organizing, the rise of the great, black-owned newspaper, *The Chicago Defender*, and the experience of coming into the great, glittering city on a train that "took you to heaven." Part III shows blacks' disillusionment with the present-day conditions in Chicago, "the most racially segregated city in America." Students of all ethnicities should have the opportunity to see this lively history of the people who worked so hard and built so much during the thirty years in which opportunity was open to them.

**V** Sandler, K. (1993). *A question of color*. Video, 56 minutes. Distributor: California Newsreel. A light-skinned African-American filmmaker spends eight years researching the ways that slavery, apartheid, and institutional racism have affected how blacks feel about color and class. Blacks speak graciously and honestly about their attitudes and understandings about this painful topic. Archival photos of slave families, speeches by Malcolm X, and footage of the "Black Is Beautiful" movement of the 1960s provide historical context. This film can provoke reflective discussion among black and white classmates who have established a measure of trust, and can help everyone understand how internalized oppression works, and how it can be combated.

Alexander, M. (2010). *The new Jim Crow: Mass incarceration in the age of colorblindness*. In this provocative, engrossing book, civil rights lawyer and legal scholar Michelle Alexander shows how the American criminal justice system has recreated the system of racial exclusion of the post-Civil War South through racist laws and practices implemented swiftly and nearly invisibly in the Reagan era and beyond. "Today it is perfectly legal to discriminate against criminals in nearly all the ways that it was once legal to discriminate against African Americans," Alexander writes. From barriers to employment, housing, educational opportunities, and public benefits to the denial of the right to vote and serve on a jury, people who are labeled "felons"—whether in prison or out—have "scarcely more rights, and arguably less respect" than blacks living in Alabama at the height of Jim Crow. "We have not ended racial caste in America;" she says, "we have merely redesigned it." A must-read for students interested in law, crime and justice.

Amsden, D. (2015, February 26). Building the first slavery museum in America. *New York Times*. http://www.nytimes.com/2015/03/01/magazine/building-the-first-slave-museum-in-america.html?_r=0 Whitney Plantation, an on-site memorial to the sufferings and heroism of enslaved people living near New Orleans before the Civil War, was constructed by an improbable benefactor, a 77 year old white Southerner who "spent the last 15 years and more than $8 million of his personal fortune on a museum that he had no obvious qualifications to assemble." Why did he take on such a project? "I've been asked all the questions," says John Cummings. "About white guilt this and that. About the honky trying to profit off of slavery. But here's the thing: Don't *you* think the story of slavery is important?" It was his own ignorance of the period, he says, that led to the decision to turn his real estate purchase into the first museum that would chronicle the lives of the enslaved people who lived and died there. "If 'guilt' is the best word to use, then yes, I feel guilt," Cummings said. "I mean, you start understanding that the wealth of this part of the world—wealth that has benefited me—was created by some half a million black people who just passed us by. How is it that we don't acknowledge this?"

Anderson, C. (2003). *Eyes off the prize: The United Nations and the African American struggle for human rights, 1944–1955*. New York: Cambridge University Press. This scholarly book details the little-known history of how post-World War II blacks contended with white racism, Cold War politics, and their own quarrels with each other in their efforts to gain full human rights. "For far too long, civil rights has been heralded as the 'prize' for black equality. Yet, those rights, no matter how bitterly fought for, could only speak to the overt political and legal discrimination that African Americans faced. Human rights … had the language and the philosophical power to address … the education, health care, housing, and employment needs that haunted the black community." Yet even a successful Civil Rights Movement left blacks far short of this goal.

Baptist, E. E. (2014). *The half has never been told: Slavery and the making of American capitalism*. N.Y.: Basic Books. In this impressive work, historian Edward Baptist shows how slavery made it possible for the United States to achieve a monopoly on the cotton trade at the height of the industrial revolution, becoming a modern, industrial and capitalist economy. This is the half that had never been told: "Stories about industrialization emphasize white immigrants and clever inventors, but they leave out cotton fields and slave labor." This omission implies that slavery had little influence on the rise of the U.S. to a world power in the nineteenth century, and that the slave system was fundamentally at odds with the more liberal political and economic system of the North. Not so, says Baptist. "If slavery … was a drag and not a rocket booster to American economic growth, then slavery was not implicated in

U.S. growth, success, power, and wealth. Therefore none of the massive quantities of wealth and treasure piled by that economic growth is owed to African Americans." A fascinating, passionate rewriting of American history.

Coates, T. (2015). *Between the world and me*. N.Y.: Random House. In this book-length letter to his fifteen-year-old son, Ta-Nehisi Coates recalls a question put to him by an intelligent, thoughtful talk-show host who asked why he felt that America's progress [or rather "the progress of those Americans who believe they are white," adds Coates] was built on looting and violence. "Hearing this," Coates writes, "I felt an old and indistinct sadness well up in me. The answer to this question is the record of the believers themselves. The answer is American history." This book, which has become a "must read" among liberal, white Americans, speaks to a well-meaning white audience, a black audience that shares Coates's sadness, and the young, black generation who knows little of their parents' history. "I propose," continues Coates, "to take our countrymen's claims of American exceptionalism seriously, which is to say I propose subjecting our country to an exceptional moral standard. This is difficult because there exists, all around us, an apparatus urging us to accept American innocence at face value and not to inquire too much. And it is so easy to look away, to live with the fruits of our history and to ignore the great evil done in all of our names." You can see from the elegant writing why the book has become so popular, despite its very difficult message.

Fast, H. (1944). *Freedom road*. Armonk, NY: M. E. Sharpe. A remarkable historical novel of the Reconstruction era, written from an African-American/white ally point of view. Reconstruction has often been depicted as a time when undeserving blacks occupied positions of power which they quickly lost through incompetence. This more accurate version emphasizes the achievements of ex-slaves during that period, when, despite their lack of formal education, they taught themselves and each other to be strategic thinkers and effective leaders.

Google Cultural Institute. Black History and Culture. https://www.google.com/culturalinstitute/u/0/collections?projectId=black-history-and-culture This searchable database features items from museums and exhibits of African-American history and culture from all over the country. Students can view historic photos, artifacts, handwritten documents, posters, art works, comic books, and music videos from such venerable institutions as the U.S. National Archives, the Smithsonian, the Schomburg Center for Research in Black Culture, and many more.

Kelley, R. D. G. & Lewis, E. (Eds.). (2000). *To make our world anew: A history of African Americans*. New York: Oxford University Press. An accessible volume that depicts Africans as active agents in American and world history. Black labor, black resistance, black creativity, and black visions of freedom are detailed here, beginning in 1502 with the advent of the slave trade and ending in the 1990s with some of the challenges to blacks today: police brutality, interethnic conflict, and continuing economic disadvantage. Archival photos of ordinary and extraordinary people, historical documents, and art add dignity and meaning to the struggle.

Love, D. (2016, February 19). President Obama will dedicate the National Museum of African American History and Culture in September. *Atlanta Black Star.* http:// atlantablackstar.com/2016/02/19/president-obama-will-dedicate-national-museum-african-american-history-culture-september/. Finally! A great museum on the National Mall that celebrates black history and culture in all its pain, aspiration, creativity, and achievement. Visitors can see the glass-covered coffin of Emmett Till, the 14-year-old black boy from Chicago who was murdered in 1955 by the Mississippi Klan; the original Emancipation Proclamation and Thirteenth Amendment signed by Abraham Lincoln; a segregated railroad car; an exhibit dedicated to Black incarceration; Nat Turner's bible, items from the Black Lives Matter movement, and many other artifacts. A video "fly-through" of the new building is included in the article.

Obama, B. (2008, March 18). A more perfect union. *Huffington Post.* http://www.huffingtonpost.com/2008/03/18/obama-race-speech-read-th_n_92077.html. Students can read or watch the video of President Obama's speech on race on this and many other online sites. Deeply patriotic, yet honest about "the nation's original sin of slavery," soon-to-be President Barack Obama tells the story of how the experience of growing up in a multicultural, multiracial family convinced him that Americans can solve our problems by working together across racial lines. Reminding us that he won some of his most impressive campaign victories in states with "some of the whitest populations in the country," Obama distances himself from Reverend Jeremiah Wright, the controversial pastor of the black church that he frequented in Chicago. Yet, Obama says, he can no more disown someone who makes offensive remarks about whites than he can disown his white grandmother who confessed her fear of black men and sometimes "uttered racial or ethnic stereotypes that made me cringe."

Robinson, R. (2000). *The debt: What America owes to blacks.* New York: Penguin. In this passionate, hard-hitting argument for reparations, lawyer Randall Robinson describes how slavery and the Jim Crow era continue to disadvantage many blacks today, and how America's silence about that history confuses and alienates black youth. Students of all ethnicities are fascinated with this book, even when they disagree with the author's conclusions.

Wilkerson, I. (2010). *The warmth of other suns: The epic story of America's great migration.* N.Y.: Random House. In this popular novel, Pulitzer prize winter Isabelle Wilkerson tells the story of three African-Americans who participated in "the Great Migration," the exodus of six million blacks from the U.S. South over the 55 year period between 1915 to 1970. "Over time, this mass relocation would come to dwarf the California Gold Rush of the 1850s with its one hundred thousand participants and the Dust Bowl migration of some three hundred thousand people from Oklahoma and Arkansas to California in the 1930s. But more remarkably, it was the first mass act of independence by a people who were in bondage in this country for far longer than they have been free." The story of this dramatic internal migration has never been appreciated, or even known, by most Americans. Wilkerson's story-telling ability and impeccable research has begun to change that.

## Arabs, Arab Americans, Middle Easterners, and Muslims

V Abu-Assad, H. (2005). *Paradise now*. Video, 91 minutes. Distributor: Warner Independent Pictures. This feature-length film tells the story of two Palestinians who, for different reasons, allow themselves to be recruited as suicide bombers. When things do not go as planned, each man makes his own decision about how, whether, and why to proceed. The film highlights the humanity of people who carry out inhumane political acts; it brings alive the insupportable conditions of the Israeli occupation; and it encourages students to think about the various reasons people choose to die— and kill—for a cause.

V Kasbo, A. (2015). *A thousand and one journeys: The Arab Americans*. http://arabamericandoc.com This full-length film counters negative stereotypes about Arab Americans through interviews with both ordinary people and well-known public figures with Middle Eastern heritage. The interviewees stress all the values that America holds dear: patriotism, love of family and community, military service, and a bootstraps mentality. Despite the indignity of being profiled and searched at airports, depicted as terrorists in the media, and being told by random strangers that they don't belong here, these Arab Americans are unfailingly positive about the immigrant journeys of their ancestors over the last 200 years. "I believe the American Dream because I've lived it" seems to be a common sentiment. A good choice for students who have no idea about the diversity and success of Arab Americans, or who express anti-Arab fears and stereotypes.

V Majidi, M. (1998). *Children of heaven*. Video, 89 minutes. Distributor: Miramax Films. This quiet gem about young siblings who conspire to share a pair of shoes so they can both go to school is a reminder of the humanity of ordinary Iranians. Filmed in rich and poor neighborhoods in Teheran, the story gives us a glimpse of Iranian family life, a schoolroom, a mosque, a sports competition, and a humorous, though ill-fated bicycle trip undertaken by father and son. Appropriate for all ages.

V Shaheen, J. (2007). *Reel bad Arabs: How Hollywood vilifies a people*. Video, 50 minutes. Media Education Foundation. From the days of silent film to the present, Hollywood has portrayed Arabs as uncivilized, bumbling fools, compliant sex objects, and inherently violent "others." These degrading images make it easier to deny the humanity of real Arabs and Arab Americans, especially when one has little contact with them in daily life. Excellent for class discussion; students are shocked to discover that even their favorite films are rife with stereotypes. You might show the film after a brief exercise: "Quickly make a list of all the characteristics of Arabs that you've heard about, whether you believe them or not, and where you heard each one. Talk about your lists with a partner."

V Winterbottom, M. & Whitecross, M. (2006). *Road to Guantánamo.* Video, 95 minutes. Riveting true story of how three young British Muslims, traveling in Afghanistan soon after the September 11th attacks, were erroneously declared enemy combatants and shipped off to Guantánamo. The conditions of their two-year confinement, their interrogations, their responses to torture, and their will to survive are graphically illustrated in this reenactment. The film brings realism and personal involvement to theoretical discussions about how the United States should treat its captives and to what lengths we should go to protect ourselves from terrorists.

Bakalian, A. & Bozorgmehr, M. (2009). *Backlash 9/11: Middle Eastern and Muslim Americans respond.* Berkeley, CA: University of California Press. Scapegoating of people who appeared to be Muslim or "Arab" began immediately after the September 11th attacks. Hate crimes and bias incidents spiked, and government-instituted policies targeting ordinary Middle Easterners and Muslims legitimized the backlash in the eyes of the general public. Responding to the crisis in their communities, activist groups began to fight back in "typical American fashion—through activism and legal challenges." This book examines how fear and hatred of "foreigners" (both citizens and noncitizens) has had similar consequences throughout history, and identifies unique characteristics of the post-9/11 case. Sixty interviews with heads of Middle Eastern and Muslim advocacy organizations identify who the victims of the backlash are, how they vary, how they reacted to the "double threat" of 9/11 (both the threat of terrorism that all Americans experienced and the threat of retaliation by their "fellow Americans"), and how their organizations responded to these threats. This book is of special interest to students studying social movements and grassroots organizations, yet individual chapters (for example, Chapter 5, "Hate Crimes and Bias Incidents") can be instructive reading for any students who are unaware of the extent, variety, and frightening nature of these attacks.

Bayoumi, M. (2008). *How does it feel to be a problem? Being young and Arab in America.* N.Y.: Penguin Books. This delightful book, based on interviews and informal conversations with a wealth of Arab Americans of all ages in Brooklyn, portrays the lives and experiences of seven young people, whose "very American stories about race, religion, and civil rights [show] how the pressures of domestic life and foreign policy push on individual lives." Readers meet Rasha, a typical New York teenager until her family was jailed for a minor visa infraction after 911; Sami, who signed up for the Marine Corps "in a moment of insanity" in May, 2001 and was alarmed to discover he would be part of the invasion of Iraq; Yasmin, who fought like a tiger to retain her elected membership in the leadership council of her high school when her religious practices clashed with the requirements of the office, and other life-like characters. This book reads like a series of short stories, with humor, suspense, and detailed descriptions of the lives of these attractive young people. A great read for students who have not had the opportunity to make friends with Arab Americans—which is to say, most students.

Cole, J. (2016, March 23). How not to talk about Muslims after a fringe terrorist group attacks. http://www.juancole.com/2016/03/how-not-to-talk-about-muslims-after-a-fringe-terrorist-group-attacks.html "Stop calling Daesh 'the Islamic State,' says Middle East historian Juan Cole. "They are manipulating you. They aren't a state and they aren't Islamic. If some fringe cult took over some villages in Mexico and called itself 'The Vatican,' then committed terrorism, would journalists blithely say on air 'Today, the Vatican killed 39 and injured 200 with a bomb belt'? People in the Middle East hate this small desert fringe, and they term it 'Daesh,' not 'Islamic.' They should know." Seven more pithy pieces of advice follow. It's worth the read. Also see Faisal Irshaid's BBC News piece, "Isis, Isil, IS or Daesh? One group, many names." http://www.bbc.com/news/world-middle-east-27994277.

Hirsch, S. (2004, May 10). "Torture at Abu Ghraib." *The New Yorker.* www.newyorker.com. Seymour Hirsch details the abuse of Iraqis by the U.S. military in Abu Ghraib prison in 2003, questioning which authorities knew what, when and who should ultimately be held responsible. Since first-year students were children when this scandal unfolded, they typically don't know what happened or why the abuse and torture have been swept under the rug. I ask them to find an online site that has photos of the detainees taken by their U.S. captors, to look at as many of them as they can stomach, and then read Hirsch's article.

Hughes, A. W. (2016, February 19). No, it isn't all one thing: The variety of religious experience in Islam. http://www.juancole.com/2016/02/no-it-isnt-all-one-thing-the-variety-of-religious-experience-in-islam.html In this short, information-packed blog post, Aaron Hughes explains the historical roots of ISIS by charting the striking regional variation in Islamic practice. Culture, tradition, political context, legal schools of thought and their interpretations, even the presence of other religions all contribute to the ways one and a half billion Muslims learn and practice their faith around the world. But despite this diversity, many Muslims and non-Muslims refer to Islam and Sharia as if they were stable entities. This creates confusion about where the so-called Islamic state comes from. Is it simply a misinterpretation of some original doctrine, or simply a fanatic offshoot of the ultraconservative elements of Islam? This author suggests it is the latter.

Jamal, A. & Naber, N., eds. (2008). *Race and Arab Americans before and after 9/11: From invisible citizens to visible subjects.* Syracuse, NY: Syracuse University Press. This thought provoking collection examines such themes as the "white but not quite" status of Arab Americans before the September 11th attacks and their transformation into a more defined, non-white "other" in the aftermath; the ways that becoming "visible" targets of hate crimes has obscured the historical effects of colonialism and the "present-day structural inequalities that produce hatred and racism," and many other topics. Individual chapters appeal to students at various stages of their understanding of race. For example, Chapter 2 "Thinking outside the box" (Cainkar) adds depth to classroom discussions of racial identity through interview quotes that express the frustration of being categorized in ways that deny the diversity and complexity of nationality, religion, culture, history, and international relationships. Chapter 8, "The prime-time plight of the Arab Muslim American after 9/11" (Alsultany) describes the fascinating shift in U.S. media depictions of Arabs from villains and terrorists to misunderstood victims of hate crimes. Yet "ambivalence about racism" in the liberal media has the effect of "reworking US sovereignty" over Arab and Muslim peoples. The use of popular media to illustrate this interesting concept draws students in and encourages them to look more critically at the programs they watch.

Satrapi, M. (2004). *Persepolis: The story of a childhood*. New York: Pantheon. Students love this graphic novel of Marjane Satrapi's coming of age in Iran during the Islamic Revolution. The humanity of the characters, the humor, the family relationships, the heroism of the resistance, and the young girl's growing activism help create an affinity between readers and ordinary Iranians. Each frame, like a poem, is full of emotion and connection.

Shora, N. (2009). *The Arab-American handbook: A guide to the Arab, Arab American & Muslim worlds*. Seattle, WA: Cune Press. This introduction to the beliefs and practices of people in the Arab world is informative and fun, especially for students who have little contact with Arab Americans. The author's light humorous touch, his knowledge of history and politics, and his ability to dispel readers' stereotypes quickly and painlessly make this book ideal for first-year students. The second half of the book is a collection of memoirs, short political pieces from a variety of perspectives, and comments on history and religion in the Arab world.

# Asian Pacific Americans (APA)

V Adachi, J. (2006). *The slanted screen: Asian men in film and television*. Video, 60 minutes. AAMM Productions. Asian American actors discuss the roles available to Asian men during 100 years of American cinema. Viewers will be surprised to discover that in the early silent films, the Japanese actor, Sessue Hayakawa, played the romantic lead with white women, and was even seen as a heartthrob by white female fans. Later, however, roles for Asian actors became more and more stereotypical and at times, blatantly racist. The film challenges the common idea that racism diminishes over time as people become more educated and knowledgeable, and prompts students to consider why this might be so.

V Adolfson, N. (1998). *Passing through*. Video, 37 minutes. Distributor: Center for Asian American Media. A bittersweet film made by a Korean adoptee just out of college who travels to Korea to study and eventually finds the courage to meet his Korean siblings. The filmmaker's warmth and gentle humor, his subdued sadness, his difficulty connecting with both his "real" family in Minnesota and his relatives in Korea is touching and compelling. Questions of identity, intercultural communication and adoption can be explored with the help of this film. I would use it with care if I had a student in my class who had been adopted from another country. Talking with the student about the film beforehand or asking the student to view the film and give you an opinion about it before showing it publicly is one way to approach this sensitive topic.

V Ina, S. (1999). *Children of the camps.* Video, 57 minutes. Distributor: National Asian American Telecommunications Association. A psychotherapist helps adult survivors of the Japanese internment during World War II revisit the pain and confusion of their childhoods. This intimate look at the suppressed emotions and "seeds of self-hatred" that successful adults still carry with them from the internment experience helps students understand the ways racism and exclusion deeply affect the personality.

V Lee, M. W. & Jang, L. (1993). *Stolen ground.* Stir-Fry Productions. Video, 43 minutes. Distributor: National Asian American Telecommunications Association. Six Asian American men gather for dinner and conversation about the racism they face in their daily lives. An insightful look at where the stereotype of "overachiever and model citizen" comes from and the toll it takes on Asian Americans. The film is divided into convenient segments for class discussion, dealing with such topics as the costs of assimilation, the risks of confrontation, the effects on parents and children, and responses to racism.

V Okazaki, S. (1990). *Days of waiting.* Video, 28 minutes. Distributor: National Asian American Telecommunications Association. The experience of the Japanese internment camps is shown through the eyes of Estelle Ishigo, one of the few whites to be interned along with Japanese Americans. When she and her husband were released at the end of the war, Ms. Ishigo saved the scraps of paper on which she had recorded and sketched her experiences. Nearly thirty years later, former internees found her living alone in poverty and resolved to make her story known.

V Puhipau & Lander, J. (1993). *Act of war: The overthrow of the Hawaiian nation.* Video, 58 minutes. Distributor: National Asian American Telecommunications Association. A detailed but accessible history of the conquest, overthrow, and annexation of the Hawaiian Islands from a Native Hawaiian point of view. Excerpts from journals of missionaries, politicians, planters, and Hawaiian royalty; archival photos and film clips, and racist cartoons of the day are woven together by two Native Hawaiian historians.

V Raju, S. (2008). *Divided we fall: Americans in the aftermath.* Video, 90 minutes. New Moon Productions. Almost the moment the twin towers fell on September 11th, Sikh Americans were targeted as "terrorists" and "Arabs," despite the fact that their ancestors came from India, their religion has no relation to Islam, and Sikhs had nothing to do with the terrorist attacks. Produced by a Sikh American college student, the film chronicles her journey around the United States interviewing other

Sikh Americans whose family members were victims of violence. The film is a plea for unity and understanding of people from all ethnic and religious traditions.

V Tanaka, J. D. (2002). *When you're smiling: The deadly legacy of internment*. Video, 60 minutes. University of California Extension Center for Media and Independent Learning. How racism, economic and social exclusion, and the stress of internment were passed down through the generations in many West Coast Japanese families, resulting in a hidden epidemic of drugs, gangs, and suicide in a formerly middle-class Japanese American community. This thoughtful film can enrich discussions about identity, the "model minority" stereotype, the place of Asians in American society, and the need for openness about painful episodes in our history. The film can also provide much insight to discussions of David Mura's (1996) memoir, *Where the body meets memory*.

Bulosan, C. (1973) [1946]. *America is in the heart*. Seattle: University of Washington Press. Classic memoir of a Filipino immigrant-poet who worked the fields and harvests throughout the American West in the 1930s and 1940s. Bulosan's warm, personal voice, his honesty about the racism he faced, and his talent for capturing personalities and conversations make the period come alive.

Cheney-Rice, Z. (2015, May 29). The real story of Asians in America that hardly anyone is talking about. http://mic.com/articles/119672/the-real-story-of-asians-in-america-that-hardly-anyone-is-talking-about#.NYCTLWdn8, "People tend to think that if you're Asian-American, you're doing just fine. But that negates the experiences of the people who are struggling," says Karthick Ramakrishnan, public policy and political science professor at the University of California, Riverside. The reality in Asian American communities is far more complex than the "model minority" or "spelling bee champion" stereotype. Health disparities, struggles with persistent poverty, and immigration problems (many Asians in the United States are undocumented) are underreported and therefore unknown to many Americans. "So much of the Asian-American experience gets defined through the success of groups like Chinese-Americans and Indian-Americans, who average some of the highest income and education rates of any group in the country."

Fadiman, A. (1997). *The spirit catches you and you fall down: A Hmong child, her American doctors, and the collision of two cultures*. New York: Farrar, Straus and Giroux. The true story of the efforts of a Hmong family to get emergency help for their young daughter who was afflicted with *qaug dab peg*, a condition caused by the escape of the soul from the body. American medical providers, who called her affliction *epilepsy*, treated her with multiple medications and scientific precision—to the endless distress of the family. Students in the health sciences are engaged by this beautifully written account and learn much about Hmong history and culture as well as the interplay of medical world views.

Lui, M., Robles, B., Leondar-Wright, B., Brewer, R., & Adamson, R. (Eds.). (2006). *The color of wealth*. Ch. 5: The perils of being yellow: Asian Americans as perpetual foreigners. New York: The New Press. This chapter begins with a brief history of Asians in America, the government's exclusionary policies and attitudes, and the "creation of the 'yellow' race" by whites in order to restrict land ownership and citizen status. Explains how the economic growth of Asian American communities was intentionally curtailed and the repercussions of this long after the restrictive laws were overturned. I ask students to vote for the most ridiculous law they can find in this chapter (my favorite: San Francisco's Anti-Ironing Ordinance, which targeted Chinese nighttime laundries in the 1890s). Helps dispel stereotypes of Asian Americans as wealthy professionals who have been immune to racism.

Takaki, R. (1998). *Strangers from a different shore: A history of Asian Americans*. New York: Little, Brown. A very readable blend of narrative history, personal memoir, and interviews. Covers immigration stories of Japanese, Chinese, Korean, Filipino, Indian, Vietnamese, Cambodian, Hmong, Mien, and Laotian Americans. Short sections of this book make good background reading for videos on the Asian American experience.

Wise, T. (2002, October 7). "Con-Fusion Ethic: How whites use Asians to further anti-black racism." *ZNet Commentary*. www.zmag.org/znet. Tim Wise explains how admiring Asians for their success in the United States, especially compared to African-Americans, is neither accurate nor innocent.

Wu, F. H. (2002). *Yellow: Race in America beyond black and white*. New York: Basic Books. This wide-ranging, informal, yet deeply instructive book covers topics such as affirmative action from an Asian perspective, intermarriage, common stereotypes and misconceptions, the model minority myth, and the power of coalitions between identity groups. I often assign Chapter 3, "The Perpetual Foreigner," which describes in great detail how Asian Americans continue to be marginalized, ignored, and "othered" by whites.

Wu, F. (2007). *Born in the U.S.A: The landmark legal case of Wong Kim Ark and how Asian-Pacific Americans won the right to be Americans*. http://www.imdiversity.com/villages/asian/history_heritage/wu_kimwongark_ asiancitizenship.asp. Law professor Frank Wu describes how "contrary to images of a submissive subculture isolated from the mainstream, Chinese communities in the early twentieth century engaged in civil disobedience in the best traditions of American liberty" to win the right to citizenship. A short, succinct, overview.

## Latin@

V Carracedo, A., & Bahar, R. (2007). *Made in Los Angeles (Hecho in Los Angeles)*. Video, 70 minutes. Distributor: California Newsreel. A touching, intimate portrait of Mexican American women who organized to change their intolerable working conditions in the Los Angeles garment industry. The lives of several of the women are detailed: we follow them into their homes and neighborhoods; become involved in their relationships with their families; cheer them as they tentatively join their first boycott, and feel their growing confidence as they develop into leaders. Helps dispel the common, yet incongruous assumption that people of color must be rescued from their oppression by whites.

**V** PBS (2013). *Latino Americans*. http://www.pbs.org/latino-americans/en/ An excellent documentary covering 500 years of history of the largest minority group in the United States. Told from the point of view of Latin@s themselves, the six-hour series recreates historical figures and pivotal events and features interviews with community leaders, authors, news commentators, politicians and performers. "We're trying to reconstruct a history that has not been written," says Professor of Ethnic Studies, David Montejano. "We had a blank slate that had to be recaptured and recovered." "Many people have this popular vision of Latinos as people who arrived the day before yesterday," says historian Vicki Ruiz. "But when you think about the first European settlement in what would become the United States—St. Augustine, in 1565! That predates Jamestown in 1607. The first European language spoken in what would become the United States—Spanish!" A positive, comprehensive introduction to the ethnic group that is instructive to non-Latin@ and Latin@ alike. The website gives Latin@ viewers the opportunity to submit their own videos about "what being Latino means to you"—who your role models are and how you celebrate your heritage.

**V** Sandoval, C., & Miller, P. (2009). *A class apart: A Mexican American civil rights story*. Video, 60 minutes. Distributor: PBS Home Video. Explores the history of Mexicans in the United States, and the incident that prompted Mexican American lawyers to challenge the racism, vigilantism, segregation, and exclusion that Latin@s endured in the 1950s. When a bar fight erupted in the little town of Edna, Texas, ending in the murder of one Mexican American by another, everyone knew that the crime would be tried before an "all-white" jury—that is, by a court system that had always excluded Latin@s on racial grounds. Yet Mexican Americans were legally classified as "white" by the state of Texas. The case of *Hernandez vs Texas*, which went all the way to the Supreme Court, argued that Mexican Americans were "a class apart," treated as inferior while being denied the legal protections due to "non-whites" that had been hard-won by blacks. Another great example of the social construction of race. The transcript of the film is available for downloading at http://www.pbs.org/wgbh/americanexperience/class/transcript/.

Anzaldúa, G. (1987). *Borderlands/La Frontera*. San Francisco: Aunt Lute Books. A powerful, creative, boundary-breaking work. This mélange of English and Spanish, poetry, narrative, mythology, and history challenges students' ideas of what writing should look like and how it should speak to the reader. About the Texas-Mexican border, but also about "the psychological borderlands, the sexual borderlands, and the spiritual borderlands [that] are not particular to the Southwest."

Chavez, L. R. (2008). *The Latino threat: Constructing immigrants, citizens, and the nation*. Stanford, CA: Stanford University Press. The Latino threat narrative, created by popular media and public discourse, portrays Latin@s as "an invading force from south of the boarder that is bent on reconquering land that was formerly theirs (the Southwest) and destroying the American way of life." This pervasive myth constructs Latin@s as different from previous generations of European immigrants: Latin@s are unable or unwilling to assimilate, they take what is rightfully "ours," they produce numerous offspring who are undeserving of citizenship or social benefits, and so on. Chavez counters these widely held beliefs though an empirical study of Latin@s' actual record of assimilation as well as their fertility and reproduction. Chavez shows how "media-infused spectacles"—white "patriots" defending the border with guns drawn; huge marches staged by Latin@s to claim social and cultural space—spark public discussion about the meaning of citizenship and the limits of equality. Even the debate over whether undocumented immigrants should receive organ transplants is ultimately about who is worthy of respect and for what price, Chavez says. When undocumented bodies are seen as undeserving of organ transplants from U.S. citizens, the value of their own bodies actually increases by "ensuring a net flow of organs from immigrants to citizen bodies." Fascinating stuff.

Foley, N. (2005). Becoming Hispanic: Mexican Americans and whiteness. In P. S. Rothenberg (Ed.), *White privilege: Essential readings on the other side of racism*. New York: Worth. This short piece explains how Mexican Americans throughout the nineteenth century fought legal battles to be called "white," though doing so did not necessarily grant them "the rights and privileges that whiteness bestowed." The video, *A Class Apart*, shows what happened when this contradiction was challenged. Use these two resources to start a discussion of the author's controversial claim that "[b]y embracing whiteness, Mexican Americans have reinforced the color line that has denied people of African descent full participation in American democracy."

Lui, M., Robles, B., Leondar-Wright, B., Brewer, R., & Adamson, R. (Eds.), (2006). *The color of wealth*. Ch. 4: Neighbors and fences: Latinos in the United States. New York: The New Press. Inequalities in home ownership, education, and economic mobility are traced to the history of grudging acceptance—and at times, outright rejection—of Latin@s by whites. A brief history of Latin@s in the United States that highlights exclusionary laws and policies, and a discussion of the creative ways Latin@s have organized to procure low-interest loans, buy needed goods, open businesses, and help each other build their own homes.

Magana-Salgado, J. (2014, May). Detention, deportation, and devastation: The disproportionate effect of deportations on the Latino community. http://www.maldef.org/assets/pdf/DDD_050614.pdf. This joint report of the Mexican American Legal Defense and Educational Fund, the National Day Laborer Organizing Network, and the National Hispanic Leadership Agenda details the Obama administration's immigration enforcement policies that have "resulted in historically unprecedented number of removals/deportations of immigrants living—in some cases, for decades—in the United States." Although undocumented immigrants come from many countries and continents, no community has felt a larger impact than Latin@s, says the report; in 2013, 96.7 percent of all deportations were to Latin American countries, primarily Mexico. Not only do Latin@s feel targeted by these practices, they are concerned that detention seems to have been designed expressly for profit. The federal government's decision to use private detention facilities has "spawned an entire lobbying industry designed to encourage Congress to detain more immigrants in private facilities and dramatically increase resources for immigration enforcement, as well as profits for the owners of private prisons."

Morales, M. (2012, July 22). What we mean when we call someone "white." *Thought Catalogue.* http://thoughtcatalog.com/2012/what-we-mean-when-we-call-someone-white/. This blog by student Mallory Morales explores the complexity of race, color, culture (including stereotypes about culture), social class, immigrant background, and privilege in the Latina experience. The piece is followed by some unusually thought-provoking ideas in the Comments section. Instructors can use perceptive online comments like these to encourage discussion in classes where students are reluctant to talk. Ask students to read the comments carefully and then indicate which ones they agree with, which they disagree with, which ones offended them, which ones they have questions about, and so on. In small groups, students share their reactions about the comments, saying why they feel the way they do. Their most pressing questions and common reactions can then be brought to the large group for general discussion.

Navarro, M. (2012, January 13). For many Latinos, racial identity is more culture than color. New York Times. http://www.nytimes.com/2012/01/14/us/for-many-latinos-race-is-more-culture-than-color.html?_r=0 "More than 18 million Latinos checked the 'other' box in the 2012 census ... an indicator of the sharp disconnect between how Latinos view themselves and how the government wants to count them." The U.S. Census counts people by race, rather than ethnicity, which obscures differences in culture, language, and the complex mixture of geographic or "racial" origins in most Latino families. Rather than acknowledging this difficulty, Navarro says, the Census Bureau wants to find better ways of persuading Latinos to choose a single race. But many Latin@s want the whole idea of racial categorization to be rethought. Are Latin@s as a whole "the equivalent of another race in this country," as some suggest? Should more Latin@s identify as "white" in order to gain the social and economic advantages this category has always granted? If the census disregards race altogether, will Latin@s have more—or less—political clout?

Ngai, M. (2004). *Impossible subjects: Illegal aliens and the making of modern America.* Princeton, NJ: Princeton University Press. This comprehensive history of immigration, amply documented and written with scholarly passion, discusses how the long-standing open-door policy changed and the concept of the "illegal" emerged as "the central problem in U.S. immigration policy in the twentieth century." As immigration became more restricted and regulated, new categories of racial difference were created and inscribed in law. Students will find fascinating new information in Chapter 3, "From Colonial Subject to Undesirable Alien: Filipino Migration in the Invisible Empire."

Oboler, S. (1997). "'So far from God, so close to the United States': The roots of Hispanic homogenization." In M. Romero, P. Hondagneu-Sotelo, & V. Ortiz (Eds.) *Challenging fronteras: Structuring Latina and Latino lives in the U.S.* New York: Routledge. Excellent scholarly account of how such a culturally and historically diverse group came to be characterized by a single ethnic label. Good background for instructors and important for students who are attempting to gain a deeper understanding of Latin@ cultures.

Stavens, I. (1995). *The Hispanic condition: Reflections on culture and identity in America.* New York: HarperCollins. Intelligent commentary on the history, literature, artistic expression, and political protest of the various Hispanic peoples in the United States. Lavish, poetic—anything but dry. For instructors and serious students. The first chapter, "Life in the Hyphen," makes a superb introductory text for courses that are in any way connected to the Latin@ experience.

United We Dream (no date) www.unitedwedream.org. This powerful grassroots action organization led by immigrant youth advocates for fair treatment of all immigrant teens and families regardless of their immigration status. Students who are immigrants themselves can find resources here that will help them fight deportation proceedings, obtain a work permit or driver's license, or continue their education. Allies can join the network and participate in stopping deportations and painful family separations, advocate for access to higher education, and support LBGTQ immigrant youth.

## Native Americans

**V** *11 Essential Native American films you can watch online right now.* (2014, November 28). http://indiancountrytodaymedianetwork.com/2014/11/28/11-essential-native-american-films-you-can-watch-online-right-now-158052 Praised by critics and film festivals alike, these feature length movies are available from a variety of online outlets such as itunes and vimeo. The films explore family ties, personal struggles, life on and off the reservation, faith and music, youthful love, isolation, and racial tensions. Unlike Hollywood depictions, these films portray life from a Native point of view, with Native heroes and villains, Native strengths and weaknesses, Native values, personalities, humor and turns of phrase. These films provide helpful background for any teacher who is faced with a curriculum that treats Native people as if they no longer exist.

**V** Grossman, R. (2005). *Homeland: Four portraits of Native activism.* Video, 88 minutes. Katahdin Productions. This award-winning film features activists from the

Northern Cheyenne, the Alaskan Gwich'in, the Navajo, and the Penobscot tribes working to protect their lands from environmental degradation. The second segment is especially engaging: not only does it show idealistic young people taking on politically powerful oil companies, it is also a love story set in the gorgeous Alaskan wilderness. All four of these portraits show Native people as strong, healthy, and accomplished rather than victims. Their devotion to preserving their cultural and environmental heritage, and their victories, large and small, can inspire students to think about their own life paths.

**V** PBS American Experience (2009). *We shall remain*. Five-part series, 90 minutes each on three CDs. Accommodation and resistance of Native people to European Americans, told from a Native American point of view, from first contact to the American Indian activism of the 1960s and 1970s. Part 1, *After the Mayflower*, tells the story of the Wampanoag of New England: their attitudes towards the newcomers, their attempts to avoid warfare, the treaty that ended in a devastating war. Part 2, *Tecumseh's Vision*, tells of the great Native American leader and strategist who created a Native confederation to resist what clearly had become a brutal invasion. Part 3, *Trail of Tears*, tells of a different sort of resistance as the Cherokee adopt white culture and win recognition of tribal sovereignty in the Supreme Court; Part 4, *Geronimo*, tells of the leader of the last Native American group to face the U.S. military with armed resistance. Part 5, *Wounded Knee*, shows the birth of modern Native American activism that protested the long history of broken treaties and abysmal living conditions on reservations.

**V** Poten, C., & Roberts, P. (2007). *Contrary warriors: A film of the Crow tribe*. Video, 60 minutes. Distributor: Direct Cinema Limited. Through the life of tribal elder Robert Yellowtail, we learn of the fight to protect Crow customs, language, lands, water, and mineral resources from attempts to destroy or appropriate them. These views of the land, the Native rituals, the social events and family ties add meaning and depth to historical readings such as Dee Brown's *Bury my heart at Wounded Knee* (1971).

**V** Rae, H. (2006). *Trudell*. Video, 78 minutes. Distributed by VisionMaker. John Trudell, a charismatic Native American activist, poet, and musician, was a central figure in the takeover of Alcatraz and the confrontation at Wounded Knee in the 1960s, and an organizer of the "Trail of Broken Treaties" caravan to Washington, D.C., protesting the exploitation and destruction of Native land by resource-hungry corporations. Trudell's mystical, romantic view of the Native past and his portrayal of Euro-American "civilization" as an immensely destructive force evokes the spirit of the 1960s. The first half of the film with its archival footage can be used in conjunction with readings from Johnson, Nagel, and Champagne's (1997) *American Indian activism*, which details the same era.

**V** Rosenstein, J. (1997). *In whose honor? American mascots in sports*. Video, 46 minutes. Distributor: New Day Films. Features Charlene Teters, a Spokane Indian who bravely picketed the stadium at the University of Illinois where she was a graduate student, despite ridicule by sports fans. Her activism began the day she brought her children to a basketball game where they were mortified by the ways that made-up versions of Native American dance, paint, regalia, and music were used "in honor" of a vanished tribe. Points of view of the university administration, football fans, legislators, other Native activists, and Teters herself add complexity to the issue. For an update on the issue, see Munguia (2014, September 5).

American Psychological Association. (2005). "APA Resolution Recommending the Immediate Retirement of American Indian Mascots, Symbols, Images, and Personalities by Schools, Colleges, Universities, Athletic Teams, and Organizations." http://www.apa.org/pi/oema/resources/indian-mascots.aspx A strong, clear statement that explains why mascots are damaging, both to Native Americans and to U.S. society as a whole. I assign this short document as preparation for the video, "In Whose Honor?" (Rosenstein, 1997).

Aragon, D. (2016, March 31). Groups campaigning to abolish UNM official seal over racism. *Daily Lobo.com*. http://www.dailylobo.com/article/2016/03/31-racist-seal Student activists at the University of New Mexico are protesting the design of the official seal, which appears on student diplomas. "The UNM [official seal] celebrates genocide and conquest—both are violations of basic human rights and belong in a museum of a bygone era," says the founder of the grassroots group, "Red Nation." Despite the cynicism of some members of the Native community about the utility of the students' action, they remain undeterred. They point out that they are asking not only for a cosmetic change in the drawing of the seal but substantial improvements to Native American students' lives on campus: "the reconstruction of the Native American cultural center, formation of a council of elders at the Board of Regents comprised of leaders from surrounding pueblos and the demand of tuition waivers for federally recognized tribes," as well as university-wide regulations against hate crimes.

Brown, D. (1971). *Bury my heart at Wounded Knee*. New York: Holt, Rinehart & Winston. A history of the American West from a Native American point of view. This classic history of resistance tells what Native leaders were thinking as they tried to adapt to or fight the invaders and how the people met the tragic threat to their existence bravely and with honor.

Crow Dog, M. (1991). *Lakota woman*. New York: HarperPerennial. The autobiography of a Sioux woman who grew up in the 1950s in a Native boarding school and came of age during the American Indian Movement and the siege of Wounded Knee. Wonderful, accessible, "suppressed history" that has often made my students angry. "Why wasn't I told about this?" is a typical reaction. This account can be enriched by online, historical documents that show the justification and rationalization for the boarding school system found at: www.twofrog.com/reqsch.html

Dunbar-Ortiz, R. (2015). *An indigenous peoples' history of the United States*. Beacon Press. "This is a history of the United States as experienced by its Indigenous inhabitants," says the author. "I wanted to set aside the rhetoric of race, not because race and racism are unimportant, but to emphasize that Native peoples were colonized and deposed of their territories as distinct peoples—hundreds of nations—not as a racial or ethnic group. 'Colonization,' 'dispossession,' 'settler colonialism,' 'genocide'—these are the terms that drill to the core of U.S. history, to the very source of the country's existence." Despite these extreme challenges, Native resistance, determination, and the preservation of history through story-telling have ensured their survival. A must-read for a serious study of the Native American experience, and indeed, of American history itself.

Fenton, D. A. (2015, April 22). Racism at core of Native teen suicides in Pine Ridge. *Colorlines*. https://www.colorlines.com/articles/racism-core-native-teen-suicides-pine-ridge On the Pine Ridge Reservation, site of the massacre of Wounded Knee, the hospital "treated 241 patients under 19 who actively planned, attempted or committed suicides" in a four month period. In this short piece, a high school English teacher and self-described "newcomer" to the reservation shows how racism from the white community—the slurs shouted at sports events, the disproportionate use of force in police encounters, the obliviousness of whites to dangers faced by reservation children send a clear message to Native youth: "Your lives are not valued. You do not have a place in the world beyond the reservation."

Johnson, T., Nagel, J., & Champagne, D. (Eds.). (1997). *American Indian activism: Alcatraz to the longest walk*. Urbana: University of Illinois Press. Recollections of the nineteen-month Native American occupation of Alcatraz Island (1969 to 1971) by men and women who took part in the action that sparked the American Indian Movement. Many points of view are expressed here, as participants from a great variety of backgrounds tell their own stories. I especially like Chapter 14, "The Eagles I Fed Who Did Not Love Me," in which the author likens his experiences in the Vietnam War with life on the Reservation.

Lakota People's Law Project. (2015, February). Native lives matter. http://www.docs. lakotalaw.org/reports/Native%20Lives%20Matter%20PDF.pdf Students may be surprised to learn that despite the attention given to black victims of police shootings, Native Americans are the racial group most likely to be killed by law enforcement. In addition, like African-Americans and Latin@s, Native Americans are targeted by a deeply discriminatory criminal justice system. Native men are imprisoned at four times the rate of white men and Native women at six times the rate of white women. This excellent report focuses on the Lakota Sioux but has implications for Native people all over the country, and for people of color generally. Reports of abuse sound sickeningly similar to those exposed by the Black Lives Matter movement: an 8 year old pinned to a wall by a police Taser for threatening a babysitter with a small paring knife; teens routinely incarcerated with adult prisoners; the use of "cruel and sadistic" punishments at a state "training school" rather than education and mental health services; dismissal of reports of sexual abuse in foster homes. "The roots of these problems are money and racism" says the report. Statistics bear out the shocking stories that so few outside Indian Country are talking about.

Lui, M., Robles, B., Leondar-Wright, B., Brewer, R., & Adamson, R. (Eds.), (2006). *The color of wealth. Ch. 2: Land rich, dirt poor: Challenges to asset-building in Native America.* New York: The New Press. Excellent resource that explains why the paternalistic arrangement set up by the U.S. government to "manage" tribal resources has resulted in wealth for outside corporations and poverty for Native Americans—the highest rate for any ethnic group. Includes a short history of colonization of Indian lands and the appropriation of Indian assets, attempts at judicial, legislative, and administrative reform, and challenges by Native American activists to corporate control.

Munguia, H. (2014, September 5). The 2,128 Native American mascots people aren't talking about. http://fivethirtyeight.com/features/the-2128-native-american-mascots-people-arent-talking-about/ This site explains the history of the controversy surrounding the Washington Redskins' refusal to change the name of the team that continues to demean Native American people. Yet while this high-profile conflict drags on, over two thousand U.S. sports teams—high school, college, pro, semi-pro and amateur—retain names that reference Native Americans in racially insensitive ways: Braves, Chiefs, Indians, Orangemen, Raiders, Redmen, Reds, Redskins, Savages, Squaws, Tribe and Warriors. Tribe names are also used without permission: Apaches, Arapahoe, Aztecs, Cherokees, Chickasaws, Chinooks, Chippewas, Choctaws, Comanches, Eskimos, Mohawks, Mohicans, Seminoles, Sioux and Utes. Maps showing where Native Americans live in contrast to where their names are being used as team mascots are telling. A useful update to the powerful film, *In whose honor?*

NCAI News. http://www.ncai.org/. The National Congress of American Indians website has a wealth of news reports on current political, social and economic issues in Indian Country. Students in my Human Rights class use this site to explore issues of their choice, then write letters to their members of Congress recommending action.

Peltier, L. (1999). *Prison writings: My life is my Sundance.* New York: St. Martin's Press. Archbishop Desmond Tutu calls this book "a deeply moving and very disturbing story of a gross miscarriage of justice." Imprisoned for life for the killing of an FBI agent during the modern-day siege of Wounded Knee, Peltier and his supporters still hope that he will one day regain his freedom. The International Leonard Peltier Defense Committee website offers background and opportunities for action on Peltier's behalf. You can also watch the 90 minute film produced by Robert Redford, *Incident at Oglala*, www.whoisleonardpeltier.info for free on the site.

Wilson, J. (2000). *The earth shall weep: A history of Native America.* New York: Grove Press. This beautifully written account, sympathetic to both Native and European worldviews, strives for a historical analysis that falls somewhere between the two sides of the political spectrum. "Liberals often seem more willing—or even eager—to accept that European settlement cost many millions of Native American lives," Wilson writes, "while conservatives tend to cling to the view that there was only a small, 'backward,' pre-Columbian population—an idea that not only seems to reduce the scale of the human tragedy, but also makes the triumph of European culture appear more inevitable, and, finally, more desirable." Although Wilson's "we" and "they" language clearly indicates that he is writing for non-Natives, his interest in understanding cultural differences makes this history more accurate than many. I especially like Wilson's first chapter, where he contrasts a Shastika (California) creation myth with the Book of Genesis—the "creation myth" of Western culture.

## Biracial, Multiracial, and "Mixed"

SV *Racial documentary–"Other" Mixed identity.* http://www.youtube.com/ watch?v=-5j4LkOz9C8U. Attractive, confident young adults discuss their multiple identities, their families, their life experiences, and how they deal with questions that range from the curious to the annoying: "What are you?" "Where are you from?" "What are your parents?" "Which side do you identify with more?"—questions that are never asked of whites, whose ancestry comprises a variety of European groups. Students who identify as biracial or multiracial will find something to identify with in this video, and all students can discuss the suggestion at the end of the piece, "Maybe if we didn't talk about race as much it wouldn't be a problem." Do Americans have an unhealthy fascination with race, or do they want to put the whole issue behind them—or both?

Alvarez, J. (1998). A white woman of color. In C. C. O'Hearn (Ed.), *Half and half: Writers on growing up biracial and bicultural*. New York: Pantheon. Novelist Julia Alvarez describes learning about race and racism within her own family growing up in the Dominican Republic, and how that was complicated by their immigration to the United States. She concludes that "ethnicity and race are not fixed constructs or measurable quantities. ... [They] evolve as we seek to define and redefine ourselves in new contexts." Good prompt for writing or discussion about how the ethnic identification of all our families has changed over the generations.

Burnley, M. (2015, February 8). My biracial life: A memoir. *Philadelphia.* http://www.phillymag.com/articles/my-biracial-life/ This funny, poignant piece gives students an idea of what it's like to lead a "racially ambiguous" life—if they're not doing so already. "I'm hard to stereotype," says the author. "But people still try. Recently, I've gotten Mexican, Pakistani, Italian, Brazilian. Countless cabdrivers have looked into the rearview mirror and spoken to me in another language, only to be disappointed that I can't reciprocate." Pictures of the author from infancy to the present show the various styles and identities he has tried out. "I've auditioned just about every hairdo in my life—from cornrows to uptown fades to the Afro—to close the gap between my perceived race and my actual ancestry. My hair became the crux of my racial identity, neither black nor white nor anything plainly recognizable to anyone. And I hated it." There's plenty for students to discuss here.

Code Switch (2013, May 12). *Checking more than one box: A growing multiracial nation.* http://www.npr.org/blogs/codeswitch/2013/05/12/183430945/checking-more-than-one-box-a-growing-multiracialnation? A segment of "All Things Considered" about the experiences of a Vietnamese mother and black father raising a multiracial young family. The mother, Thien Kim Lam, recalls being so offended at questions by strangers in the park where she took her children to play that she started a blog called "I'm not the Nanny: Raising biracial kids in a raceconscious world." http://www.imnotthenanny.com/. Nine million people in the United States now identify with more than one race, according to the U.S. census in 2000, the first year responders were allowed to check more than one box. "It's difficult to talk about multiracials as a group," this piece suggests, "because the issues each individual faces is different … and we only have the model of the black-white dynamic to work with." Does this mean we need "not just new categories, but perhaps a new way to talk about race?" What would that "new way" look like?

McBride, J. (1996). *The color of water: A black man's tribute to his white mother.* New York: Riverhead Books. A beautifully written memoir. Reporter James McBride intersperses interviews with his mother with his own memories of growing up in a large, impoverished, ultimately successful family. "Mommy's house was orchestrated chaos and as the eighth of twelve children, I was lost in the sauce, so to speak. … My brothers and sisters were my best friends, but when it came to food, they were my enemies. There were so many of us we were constantly hungry, scavenging for food in the empty refrigerator and cabinets. … Entire plots were hatched around swiping food, complete with doublecrossing, backstabbing, intrigue, outright robbery, and gobbled evidence." McBride manages to write with humor and compassion about a life few of his readers can imagine. If I had to assign only one text to a class of clueless, resistant, privileged white students, this would be it.

MSNBC. (2008, December 14). *Obama's true colors: Black, white … or neither?* http://www.msnbc.msn.com/id/28216005/. "A perplexing new chapter is unfolding in Barack Obama's racial saga: Many people insist that 'the first black president' is actually not black." Others claim that five previous U.S. presidents: Thomas Jefferson, Andrew Jackson, Abraham Lincoln, Warren Harding, and Calvin Coolidge also had African ancestry. A good discussion of the biracial and multiracial experience.

# Identity and Stereotyping

SV Obeidallah, D. (2013, April 24). *I'm a Muslim and I hate terrorism.* CNN: Opinion. http://www.cnn.com/2013/04/24/opinion/obeidallah-muslims-hate-terrorism/ "I'm not going to tell you, 'Islam is a religion of peace,'" says this political comedian and frequent contributor to television news programs, "nor will I tell you that Islam is a religion of violence. What I will say is that Islam is a religion that, like Christianity and Judaism, is intended to bring you closer to God. And sadly we have seen people use the name of each of these Abrahamic faiths to wage and justify violence." In this brief, informative piece, Obeidallah gives serious answers to three common questions: "Why do some Muslims commit terrorism?" "Why don't Muslims denounce terrorism?" "Why don't Muslims stop blowing stuff up?" An excellent piece for students who know little about Islam or harbor suspicions about people who appear to come from Muslim countries.

**SV** Race Forward. (no date) *#Race and.* https://www.colorlines.com/articles/video-part-2-raceand-explores-intersections-between-race-and-tribal-sovereignty-gender This 8-part video series explores intersectionality, or the ways in which an individual's race and other identities interact. In each video, an artist, activist, or commentator talks about how their race intersects with other aspects of their identity such as their gender, sexual orientation, disability, class, immigration status, tribal sovereignty, or religion. "Intersectionality" also refers to the ways racism, sexism, homophobia, ableism, classism, and xenophobia are interconnected and need to be studied simultaneously to see how oppressive systems work together. For an interesting discussion of the legal history of intersectionality see law professor Kimberlé Crenshaw's opinion piece in the Washington Post (2015, September 24), "Why intersectionality can't wait." https://www.washingtonpost.com/news/in-theory/wp/2015/09/24/why-intersectionality-cant-wait/

**SV** *Rant on Indian/South Asian stereotypes.* http://www.youtube.com/watch?v=8TwVj0Ixdik. A comical explanation by an attractive vlogger of how common stereotypes affect Indian American youth. This short, home-made video is funny and upbeat yet hits all the major stereotypes, accents, and strange ideas about Asian Indians ("You think we drink cow piss? Seriously, how do you guys come up with that stuff?"). The vlog provides an easy introduction to Indian and Indian American cultural practices and a mild reproof of viewers who ridicule what they don't understand.

**SV** *Strict Asian parents and stressed, pressured youth.* http://www.youtube.com/watch?v=3xz05GUU9I0. Asian parents and their high school age children discuss the pressure to be "a typical nerd" from an early age, and show through their conversations and actions—opening their college acceptance letters, for example—where the "smart Asian" stereotype comes from, and the results, both positive and negative, of the extreme pressure to excel. Though it doesn't set out to do so, this video dispels any idea that Asians are innately superior in math and science. Discussion might bring out a number of issues: the generation gap between immigrant parents and their children, the cultural values held by different ethnic or racial groups, or the effects of stereotyping Asian youth, even in a way that might seem complimentary.

Carbado, D. W. & Gulati, M. (2013). *Acting white? Rethinking race in post-racial America.* New York: Oxford University Press. "Being an African American in a predominantly white institution is like playing a small but visible part in a racially specific script. The main characters are white. There are one or two blacks in supporting roles. Survival is always in question. The central conflict is to demonstrate that one is black enough from the perspective of the supporting cast and white enough from the perspective of the main characters." The role is risky, with failure always just around the corner. Yet many black students and professionals play out this drama every day, since teachers and employers prefer "racially palatable blacks over racially salient ones." This book will fascinate many black students who may not have realized how pervasive this drama is, as well as students of other ethnicities who are not yet convinced that blacks (or any other group of color) face such challenges. My students love to talk about identity, idealized types, stereotypes, and who is authentically "X," be it black, Mexican, Native American, masculine, gay, or just plain "American." This text adds authority and complexity to the idea of performing an identity and can encourage reflection on students' own experiences.

Daily Nous (2015, June 15). Philosophers on Rachel Dolezal (updated). http://dailynous.com/2015/06/15/philosophers-on-rachel-dolezal/. Seven philosophers share their thoughts on the controversy surrounding Rachael Dolezal, the scholar and former head of the Spokane, Washington, NAACP who for years portrayed herself as African-American. Despite being "outed" as white by her parents, who produced photographs from their daughter's blond, blue-eyed childhood, Dolezal continues to maintain that she "is" black because she "feels black." The authors ask fascinating questions: If race is socially constructed rather than a biological reality, shouldn't it be reasonable for Dolezal, or indeed anyone, take on a black identity at will? Must a person's racial identity necessarily include their ancestral history and geographic origins? In claiming a particular minority identity, how important is it to have experienced subordination and exclusion? Is it possible to be "black" in some contexts and not in others? Why were antiracist allies so quick to mock and body-shame Dolezal for her decision to "pass" as black, seeing that "what we shame and dismiss one year we often come to understand and defend ten years later"? Do Dolezal's motives and social justice activism matter in our judgment of her attempt to pass as black? Should we even be asking the question, "Is Rachael Dolezal black or white?"

Fordham, S. (Spring 2010). Passin' for black: Race, identity, and bone memory in postracial America. *Harvard Educational Review*, 80(1), 4–29. In this challenging, mesmerizing text, an African-American anthropologist explains the concept of "passin' for black"—the almost universal choice (or rather, forced choice) of Americans with African ancestry to adopt a "black" identity rather than acknowledging their white ancestors. Fordham writes movingly about the pain of "trying to channel this country's romanticized notion of immigration: peoples from all over the world choosing to come to this land of liberty and unlimited opportunities." Instead, she cannot escape the "bone memory" of suffering her African ancestors endured in this country, and the added pain and frustration of being "compelled to disremember [the] traumatic past in order to authenticate a postracial America. When she began her research on girls' aggression and bullying she assumed that children of the people liberated by the civil rights movement would not be burdened by "the memories and denials that have scrambled previous generations." Yet her fascinating stories of two students, one denying her visual blackness, and the other, adopting a black persona regardless of the puzzled looks of everyone around her, show how slowly the past is receding. Students will have vastly different reactions to this piece, depending on their identity, their experiences, and their capacity for empathy.

New York Times (2015, June 16). How fluid is race? http://www.nytimes.com/roomfordebate/2015/06/16/how-fluid-is-racial-identity/race-and-racial-identity-are-social-constructs Six authors from a variety of ethnic backgrounds give their own short takes on race and identity in this excellent introduction to the basic concepts. Their essay topics: "Identity is your lived experience"; "Why we should embrace the racial chaos"; "Race and racial identity are social constructs"; "Racial fluidity complicates the value of race"; "Hispanic and Latino identity is changing"; and "Being able to negotiate identity is important." Each essay will bring up questions for discussion: When, if ever, will people of color be included the U.S. "melting pot?" Does "Hispanic" have a racial component, despite the US Census Bureau's current treatment of the category as an ethnicity, rather than a race? Does it make sense that a white person in an intimate relationship with a person of color would stop "feeling white" as he or she begins to see racism against their loved one more clearly? Who should get to define race, and why?

Obama, B. (1995). *Dreams from my father: A story of race and inheritance*. New York: Three Rivers Press. Barack Obama's detailed, honest account of growing up biracial in the 1960s and 1970s, his struggle to forge an identity, his longing to connect with his siblings and understand his absent father, and his foray into community organizing where he learns by trial and error how to work with the urban poor. My students found it interesting to compare this book with *The Autobiography of Malcolm X* (1992). They surprised me—and themselves—with the number of similarities they found between the two men, despite their vastly different life experiences.

Rankin, K. (2016, January 29). Study: Gender Impacts racial identity for biracial people. *Colorlines*. https://www.colorlines.com/articles/study-gender-impacts-racial-identity-biracial-people. The study by Stanford University researchers found that there were marked differences between the ways that men and women in the study identified themselves, with women identifying as biracial more than men. "It would seem that, for biracial women, looking racially ambiguous is tied to racial stereotypes surrounding femininity and beauty," says the study author. "So, biracial women are often seen as not fully white and not entirely minority, and they are cast as kind of a mysterious, intriguing 'racial other.' As a consequence, it may be easier for women to reside in multiple racial groups simultaneously. However, biracial men may be more likely to be perceived as 'people of color.'" The study also found that people who see themselves as religious tended to choose a single racial category rather than identify as biracial, and people of higher economic status tended to identify as white or multiracial, rather than as people of color.

Sen, R. (2007, July/August). Are immigrants and refugees people of color? *Colorlines*. www.colorlines.com. The author describes her transformation from an a-political "model minority" into a "person of color" who stands up for all oppressed people. Students who are coming to terms with their own identity, especially biracial and first-generation immigrant students, appreciate the author's conviction, even if they come to different conclusions about themselves.

Staples, B. (2005, October 31). Why race isn't as "Black" and "White" as we think. *New York Times*, Editorial Observer. African-American columnist Brent Staples reports on the surprising results of his own genetic tests and muses on the history of "mixed" race in America. Brings up topics such as the one-drop rule, "passing," and the social construction of race. This piece prompted me to send my own DNA for testing. Though I had fewer surprises than Staples, I did learn of the particular path my distant ancestors took out of Africa, and was moved to reflect on the resilience of the long line of human beings who made my life possible.

Steele, C. (2011). *Whistling Vivaldi: How stereotypes affect us and what we can do*. New York: W. W. Norton. Claude Steele, a renowned expert on stereotype threat, explains how invoking stereotypes of various identity groups affects individual performance. Steele writes in an engaging style about his decades of research that continue to surprise students (and faculty) who are unaware of how directly and immediately the reminder of a stereotype can affect an individual's performance on tests of ability. Whether they are black students facing the stereotype of inferior intellect to women reminded of the stereotype about their poor mathematical ability to white males told of their mathematical ineptitude compared to their Asian peers, students from all identity groups suffer an immediate and significant drop in test scores when reminded of their presumed inferiority. Significantly, stereotype threat has its greatest impact when students care the most about their performance. This finding has important implications for understanding the racial achievement gap in schools and colleges, where the highest achievers are affected more by stereotypical assumptions and judgments, even very subtle ones, than students who don't care. The author's friendly, straightforward language makes this a quick and easy read for students and an interesting way to complicate discussions of educational reform, affirmative action, and on-the-job performance.

Stuff white people like. http://stuffwhitepeoplelike.com/ Countless variations on this theme can be found on the internet, all of which prompt discussion about whether there is a "white culture," what it means to be "white," and whether whites can be hurt by stereotypes, either negative or positive, as much as people of color. This particular blog on the topic is more interesting and better written than most. According to the author, roller derbies, camping, getting drunk while watching the World Cup, vintage clothing, picking their own fruit, and the TED Conference all reveal very interesting characteristics of the white community. For example, since white people "like to feel smart without doing a lot of work," the simple, engaging TED talk is an ideal way for them to feel educated—and lord their knowledge over others. "So when a white person finds out that you have a PhD ... and attempts to engage you in a conversation about String Theory, you should know that all of their understanding comes from a twenty-minute talk they listened to while running on a treadmill. You should also be aware that the average white person considers their knowledge on the subject to be on par or superior to yours." White students will of course object immediately: "I'm not like that!" "That's stereotyping!" But is there some truth to the stereotype? Or do these observations only apply to a certain subgroup of white people? Or just the author's white friends? Parallels to stereotyping of blacks, immigrants, Native Americans, and others will come to mind.

Walker, Taté (2014, November 13). Free the fringe: 6 ways to destereotype Native American Heritage Month. *Everyday Feminism.* http://everydayfeminism. com/2014/11/free-the-fringe-6-ways-to-de-stereotype-native-american-heritage-month/ This short piece is written especially for teachers of young children. "Those paper Indians you're making with your students, or those paper headdresses kids will wear in the school play, and the stories told about the first Thanksgiving are doing little more than perpetuating harmful stereotypes and racism," says the author. Why? Because they treat Native people as if they are merely "neat props in romanticized timelines of US history," with no real problems, grievances, or authentic cultural identities. Ways to move past these harmful classroom lessons include highlighting Indian Country's heroes and leaders; checking out U.S. history from a Native perspective, playing contemporary native music in the classroom, having students watch Native performers online, research Native activists, and many other activities that celebrate Native resilience and humanity.

Wise, T. (2005). *White like me.* Brooklyn, NY: Soft Skull Press. In this chatty reflection on his youth in the U.S. South, Tim Wise explains his growing awareness of racism and his first small acts of resistance, his understanding of how he, and whites generally, collude with an unfair system, and his decision to work against his white privilege by becoming an antiracist activist. This book is gentler and more forgiving, both of himself and of other whites, than his shorter polemics—which are also excellent and can be found all over the internet. Wise's home page: www.timwise.org

X, Malcolm. (1992)[1965]. *Autobiography of Malcolm X.* New York: Ballantine Books. Classic account of the transformation of an intelligent, perceptive child to street hustler and pimp, to prison inmate, to Muslim minister and black nationalist community leader. As relevant today as in the 1960s for its brutal honesty about race and internalized racism in America. Malcolm's live speeches can be found on Google Videos and on YouTube. My students are intrigued by his talks and debates with college students of his day.

# Orientalism and Cultural Appropriation

Iqbal, N. (2016, May 22). Black lives matter. So does Islamophobia. Beyoncé in a sari? Not so much. *The Guardian.* http://www.theguardian.com/world/commentisfree/2016/

may/22/black-lives-matter-islamophobia-beyonce-cultural-appropriation. This piece argues that too much attention is paid to cultural appropriation that is simply "annoying and dumb," (as compared to "very real and very insensitive cases ... the most obvious being Native American headdresses—a sacred tradition regurgitated as cheap and crass festival costume fodder.") Calling people out for minor infractions ("co-opting henna and sari tops for that ethnic festival") detracts attention from much more serious issues, like people of color dying in police custody, the rights of Bangladeshi factory workers who produce some of these items, and the like. People of color "should not waste energy policing each other on issues such as who can enjoy certain music and certain fashion," says the author. An interesting argument that complicates the many pieces condemning cultural appropriation of any sort.

Johnson, M. Z. (2015, June 14). What's wrong with cultural appropriation? http://everydayfeminism.com/2015/06/cultural-appropriation-wrong/ This blog post avoids difficult questions about what exactly constitutes cultural appropriation by giving nine rather obvious examples: the "authentic Mexican food without the sketchy neighborhood"; the "Redskins" sports logo; the blond cornrows. However, the blogger's explanations of why these things are offensive are very helpful to the beginner. For example, a black woman has to avoid certain hairstyles, which, when she wears them, are deemed unprofessional, but may be seen as "cool" or fashionable on white women. Use this piece for high school and early college classes, or wherever cultural appropriation is misunderstood.

Lee, B. (no date). Orientalism in modern pop culture. http://modernorientalism.weebly.com/ This helpful site both illustrates and analyzes examples of Orientalism in film, music and video games in a sober, academic manner. The term as it is used today originated with author Edward Said, who defined it as "a collection of thoughts that is marked by a subtle and persistent Eurocentric prejudice against Arabo-Islamic peoples and their culture." The term has been broadened in popular use to mean exoticizing or "othering" any group of color. Excellent film clips of comedy and action films, interviews, and music from the 1970s to the present accompany the text.

Patheos.com. (2016, April 11). Cultural appropriation has nothing to do with "race". http://www.patheos.com/blogs/sermonsfromthemound/2016/04/cultural-appropriation-has-nothing-to-do-with-race/ Here, in a nutshell, is a definition of cultural appropriation: "[W]hen someone from a colonizing or culturally dominant culture takes a ritual or sacred or meaningful practice from a subjugated or devalued or colonized culture, lifting it out of context and draining it of meaning. And probably making money out of it." This blog post summarizes its key features: power difference and a history of oppression, loss of the original meaning of the object or practice, and economic gain for the appropriator. Examples illustrate subtle differences that sometimes exist between appropriating and appreciating various cultural practices. Is a Yoga practice that was appropriated by Europeans hundreds of years ago still offensive? Is the mimicking of Native American regalia cultural appropriation if done by

Asians for profit? Is it wrong to buy a pair of earrings from an African street vendor if the design is symbolic of a fertility rite practiced long ago? What about white tourists buying an authentic Nigerian tribal mask from a Nigerian trader and displaying it in their home?

Reappropriate. (2014, April 4). Hey, Air France your Orientalism is in the air. http://reappropriate.co/2014/04/hey-air-france-your-orientalism-is-in-the-air/ This popular blog post points out how an advertising campaign by Air France featuring white women in "cultural drag" turns "exotic" cultures around the world into "sensationalized, fictionalized" caricatures. "It's clear that your ad campaign may be running in the countries of my people, says the (presumably) Chinese writer, but you're not actually trying to sell Air France to my people. You're trying to sell my people to your people." Photos of the models in their Orientalist garb say it all. This site is really worth a look.

Reappropriate. (2014, April 17). What is Orientalism and how is it also racism? http://reappropriate.co/2014/04/what-is-orientalism-and-how-is-it-also-racism/ This post responds to the comments on the blogger's "Hey Air France" post above. "Recently," the blogger says, "I wrote a post about Air France's new ad campaign "France is in the Air"—which contains images that are both mundane and textbook examples of modern Orientalism—and have since been inundated by many tweets and comments arguing that the campaign is not racist." Other comments express genuine puzzlement about the term, or assert that the images in the ad campaign are harmless clichés or that they are attempting to honor various cultures. The blogger gives a lengthy, thoughtful response, complete with pictures, which will help students understand the concept and why its use is both disrespectful and racist.

# Anti-immigrant Attitudes

**SV** Scherer, M. (2013, February 14). Jose Antonio Vargas' emotional Senate testimony. Time. Swampland. http://swampland.time.com/2013/02/14/jose-anto-nio-vargas-emotional-senate-testimony/. In the short video on this site, Vargas, the grandson of Filipino American immigrants, speaks personally about his undocumented status at a Congressional hearing on Comprehensive Immigration Reform. He tells how he discovered that the green card his grandfather gave him was fake, how he thought he could not go to college because he could not apply for financial aid; how he secured a private scholarship from someone who believed in him, and how he became a well-known journalist. "How can they say I don't exist if my name appears in newspapers and magazines?" he asks. Vargas, "an American at heart," concludes that "an unjust law is no law at all." Students are moved by this eloquent testimony, and may be interested in the efforts of activist college students who are working for a more just immigration policy.

V Vargas, J. A. *Documented*. http://documentedthefilm.com. 90 minutes. Emotional and riveting, Vargas's story is a personal one. At age 12, he arrived from the Philippines not knowing he was undocumented, then "built his own American dream" by becoming a Pulitzer Prize winning journalist, and currently risks deportation by revealing his undocumented status to Congress and the wider public to make a point. Vargas wants the world to know that undocumented people "dream of a path to citizenship; they dream of contributing to the country they call home." This excellent film can currently be viewed online for the price of a paperback. The educators' version, usually bought by libraries, comes with an educational curriculum.

Alcarez, L. (2013, March 20). Gringos offended by the term "gringo" are actually pendejos. *Pocho: News y satire.* "'Gringo' is about as pejorative as 'Yankee' or 'Americano,' says Alcaraz. "In my vast experience as a long-time receiver of hate mail from anti-Latino Anglo Americans, the only 'gringos' who take offense to the term 'gringo' are anti-Mexican white nationalists looking to be offended." It is fear of becoming a minority that drives white people's objections to such racialized terms, says Alcarez. But they shouldn't worry. "No one is going to 'oppress' you, outlaw your language, ban your books, or send your parents back to Europe. In fact, everybody's gonna be nice to you. And we like your food, too!" Students can use this article and others written from the point of view of oppressed communities to reflect on the population shift in the United States, where "whites" will become a minority in 2050, the possibility that whites will become the new target of racism and exclusion, and the impact of racial terminology on various individuals and groups.

Bhatia, S. (2013, February 22). What does it mean to be American? *Psychology Today.* http://www.psychologytoday.com/blog/culture-the-move/201302/what-does-it-mean-be-american. This short piece makes the interesting distinction between legal U.S. citizenship (being born into or legally acquiring the status of a citizen) and cultural citizenship (being accepted as "American"). If immigration reform allows the 11 million undocumented immigrants to acquire legal citizenship, Bhatia points out, there is no guarantee that they will be perceived or accepted as "real Americans." This is already the case for many legal citizens in this country, who face bullying, hate crimes, and demeaning messages from authority figures and the media. When students question the idea that we have constructed different categories of American citizens, I ask them to close their eyes and think of a typical American. What does that person look like? Sound like? Dress like? Students always admit they see a white male, or maybe a blond, blue-eyed family arrayed on a suburban lawn. Where do these images come from? And how else do we decide who is a "real American"? Are these categories fixed, or do they depend on historical and cultural circumstances? You can complicate the discussion in interesting ways with piece below on "real" vs. "un-real" Americans that brings in political opinion, rural vs. urban lifestyle, and other cultural factors that divide white Americans from each other as well as from Americans of color. http://blogs.reuters.com/great-debate/2008/10/29/real-vs-unreal-americans/

Fox, C. (2011). *Three worlds of relief: Race, immigration, and the Welfare State from the Progressive Era to the New Deal.* Princeton, NJ: Princeton University Press. This scholarly book about the development of U.S. social welfare system punctures the myth that European immigrants made it on their own without government support, that blacks have always been on welfare, and that Mexican immigrants are opportunists, evading the law and using the welfare system to their advantage. In fact, as this book shows, "European immigrants were largely included within the contours of social citizenship, while blacks were largely excluded. Mexicans straddled the boundaries of social citizenship precariously until relief officials forced them out—expelled from the boundaries of social citizenship and the nation."

Hellerstein, E. (2016, March 10). A shocking glimpse inside America's privatized detention facilities for immigrants. http://thinkprogress.org/justice/2016/03/10/3757575/ secretive-world-of-privatized-immigrant-detention/ This piece begins with a poignant letter from a 29-year-old asylum seeker, Maribel Zelaya, who was locked up in the nation's only all-women's detention center, a former medium security prison in rural Texas. Zalaya had fallen into a deep depression and had finally joined a hunger strike, one of many at immigrant detention centers across the country. "I cannot bear this punishment any longer," she writes in Spanish. "I'm dying of desperation, of this injustice, of this cruelty. We are immigrants, not criminals. To treat us like this, it's as if they must not have hearts, as if we weren't human. They treat us like dogs." Indeed, private prison companies have found a lucrative market in the growing detention of immigrants. Today, nine of the ten largest detention centers in the country are run by for profit prison companies. A Congressional mandate requires that the Department of Homeland Security make more than 30,000 beds available every night for immigrant detention. Thanks to the 'bed mandate,' the total number of people in detention each year has risen dramatically. Federal oversight is dismal. A recent report by the National Immigrant Justice Center "found major flaws with ICE's inspection process of detention centers, including a culture of secrecy within the organization, lack of independent oversight, and a failure to adequately capture the true conditions for people inside the centers."

Hennessy-Fiske, M. & Carcamo, C. (2016, April 11). What happened in WWII is happening again: Immigrant detention centers through the eyes of a therapist. *Los Angeles Times.* http://www.latimes.com/nation/la-na-internment-detention-20160411-story.html When therapist Satsuki Ina visited immigrant detention centers along the U.S. border she found striking similarities to the Japanese internment camp where she had been held as a child during World War II. As she observed families for signs of trauma she found children troubled by nightmares, parents fearful of abuse by guards and worried about backlash for speaking out. Other effects of internment, even years later, include "an easily triggered startle response, extreme vigilance when [one is] the only person of color in a room and an anxious need for control in the face of uncertainty." The Obama administration has defended family detention, noting that detainees receive three square meals and clean housing. "That's what they said about us too," Ina says. "You have a roof over your head."

Mast, N. (2016, April 8). What we don't talk about when we talk about immigration. http://www.afsc.org/blogs/media-uncovered/what-we-don%E2%80%99t-talk-about-when-we-talk-about-immigration Major media underreport or ignore the human rights crisis of immigration detention and deportation, says the American Friends Service Committee (AFSC). While opinion polls on these topics are common enough, they tend to focus on vague or superficial questions such as whether 'illegal immigrants' take American jobs, whether English proficiency should be a stipulation of citizenship, or which groups of immigrants the U.S. government should allow to stay. These questions grossly oversimplify the issue, says AFSC. Why are pollsters only asking Americans whether immigration is inconvenient to them? Why not ask how they feel about immigration detention and deportation policies that tear families apart, undermine community cohesion, and erode public trust in law enforcement? How do they feel about the costs of such programs? Teachers can use this article and other background readings to get students started on constructing an opinion poll of their own on immigration as a group project. Students love this project. Some have thought of some interesting variations, such as filming respondents (with their permission) as they give their answers, and comparing answers from different populations such as the youth at their school vs elders in a retirement community, or between two self-identified ethnic groups.

Tavernise, S. (2013, May 29). For Medicare, immigrants offer surplus, study finds. http://www.nytimes.com/2013/05/30/health/immigrants-give-more-to-medicare-than-they-receive-a-study-finds.html. According to a Harvard Medical School study, "immigrants have contributed billions of dollars more to Medicare in recent years than the program has paid out on their behalf." In fact, even undocumented immigrants who use false social security numbers to secure employment have actually generated a surplus of about $12 billion for the Social Security Trust Fund because they are not able to collect the money they have contributed. This short piece challenges students' ideas about immigrant contributions (or lack thereof) to the U.S. economy and to the well-being of citizens.

Teaching Tolerance (no date). An educator's guide to the immigration debate. http://www.tolerance.org/magazine/number-47-summer-2014/feature/educator-s-guide-immigration-debate This brief historical guide provides enough background for a thoughtful discussion of some of the most pressing immigration issues facing the United Sates today. Many students believe that their European ancestors came to this country legally, in contrast to Mexican and Central American immigrants who sneak across the border to "take advantage" of our country's resources. But European American students may not realize that when many of their ancestors arrived in this country immigration was not regulated; almost anyone who could pay for passage could "take advantage" of American land, freedom, and work opportunities. The first immigration laws, passed in the 1800s through the 1920s, were meant to exclude people based on their "non-white" status, first the Chinese, and then southern and south-eastern Europans, who were not considered "fully white" at the time. "Congress made it clear: British, German, Irish, and Scandinavian immigrants were fine, but everyone else was more or less undesirable."

Teaching Tolerance (no date). 10 myths about immigration. http://www.tolerance. org/immigration-myths This fact sheet covers most of the misconceptions about immigration that young people hear from adults: undocumented immigrants bring crime; they pay no taxes but take advantage of our benefits; they take American jobs; they don't want to assimilate or learn English, and so on. Each myth comes with a paragraph that counters it with facts; some include questions that prompt students to think more critically. Suitable for middle school and up.

United We Dream. (2016, April 4). 4 things you should know about border patrol abuses. http://unitedwedream.org/blog/4-things-you-should-know-about-border-patrol-abuses/ For the 12 million people living along the U.S.–Mexico border, there is nothing shocking about the ways that the Customs and Border Protection (CBP) agency operates. They're used to it. Here is what the grassroots organization United We Dream wants the rest of America to know: Since 2010, border patrol officers have killed or brutalized dozens of people, including unarmed minors shot in the back and in the head. No one at CBP has been held accountable for abuse or excessive use of force in the 90 years of its existence. Despite U.S. Constitutional protection from arbitrary stops and searches, people who find themselves within 100 miles of any U.S. border are under the control of CBP, which can set up immigration checkpoints and stop people at will. CBP is extremely well funded and staffed. The agency received $13.2 billion a year. In 2016, President Obama requested an additional $720 million. Ask students to discuss in small groups how they think immigration should be regulated at the border, if at all. What would their ideal border crossing look like?

# "Whiteness" and White Privilege

V Brown, M. (2008). *The order of myths*. Video, 80 minutes. The Cinema Guild. Whites and blacks in Mobile, Alabama still host separate Mardi Gras carnivals, each with its own lavish floats, banquets, balls, and royalty. Whites have held these segregated celebrations since the first Mardi Gras in America was held in Mobile in 1703. Today, contradictions abound: The black mayor of Mobile hands the white royal couple the keys to the city. Whites explain the separate black celebration as "their own choice," while blacks make political speeches demanding recognition and respect. When the black king and queen show up at the coronation of the white royalty, whites treat them graciously, even going so far as to announce them by name and clapping politely as they enter the hall, but it is clear that Mobile's white celebrants are not ready to move further toward integration.

**V** Browne, K. (2008). *Traces of the trade: A story from the deep North*. Video, 86 minutes. Ebb Pod Productions. When filmmaker Katrina Browne discovers, to her horror, that her Rhode Island family's wealth and privilege had been built on the slave trade, she and a group of relatives decide to retrace the journey of the ten thousand men, women, and children their family had brought in bondage to America. Their visit to contemporary Ghana, Cuba, and the "fairy tale world of old New England" is profoundly disturbing to the family as well as to white viewers, who are forced to think about the ways they, too, may have reaped benefits from these practices. Viewers learn that it was actually the North that dominated the slave trade, and that slave labor benefited not only plantation owners, but cities, towns, and the surrounding farmlands all up and down the East Coast. The family's conversations with Africans and African-Americans along the way encourage them to reflect on important questions of guilt, shame, restitution, and reconciliation.

**V** Butler, S. (2006). *Mirrors of privilege: Making whiteness visible*. Video. 50 minutes. World Trust Educational Services. White antiracist activists including Peggy McIntosh and Tim Wise talk about the events and insights that brought them to their work. Their childhood memories, their feelings of guilt and shame, and their growing understanding of white privilege will help white viewers—from the well meaning to the firmly committed—understand what it means to be an ally.

**V** Henson, R. (1990). *Trouble behind*. Video, 56 minutes. Distributor: California Newsreel. Unlike most other southern towns, Corbin, Kentucky, home of Colonel Sanders of Kentucky Fried Chicken, had, in 1990, only one black family. In this film, local whites say that blacks "choose" to live elsewhere and claim there is no more prejudice in Corbin than in any other community in America. Through interviews of current residents and archival films and photos, the filmmakers investigate the events that led to the ethnic cleansing of the black population after the first World War. The frequent use of "nigger" by white folks young and old, their casual descriptions of terrorist acts against local blacks, and their denial of racism are shocking and eye-opening. Excellent discussion starter. What differences and similarities do students find between Corbin and other white localities and social gatherings they're familiar with?

**V** Turnley, D. (2012). *Shenandoah*. https://vimeo.com/43903604 (trailer) When Luis Ramirez was beaten to death by four star high school football players in this small, coal mining town in central Pennsylvania, many residents tried to cover up the crime. This documentary by Pulitzer Prize winning photographer David Turnley gives us the context: a hard-scrabble, working class town where life chances for whites are declining, and the arrival of Mexican immigrants looking for work at a local mattress factory set their teeth on edge. The film is unusual in its compassionate look at the perpetrators of a serious crime as human beings who are capable of reflection and growth, and at the town's European immigrant population as a community wrestling with its conscience. Beautifully filmed, with meticulous attention to detail.

**V** Wise, T. (2008). *Tim Wise: On white privilege.* Video, 57 minutes. Media Education Foundation. A lecture given at Mt. Holyoke College by white antiracist activist Tim Wise on topics ranging from white denial of the existence of racism, to facts and examples that demonstrate systemic injustice, to white guilt and responsibility. Wise is hard-hitting, stern, and immensely articulate, a style that can be overwhelming to students who are new to this topic. However, the video conveniently breaks up the talk into six segments which can be used for shorter discussions or as prompts for journal writing. Students can access many of Wise's speeches on www.youtube.com

**SV** *Whites think they suffer from racism more than blacks.* http://www.youtube.com/watch?v=GxenmFuNxjI. Sam Seder at Majority.fm briefly explains a Tufts University study that found that whites see themselves as targets of bias, discrimination, and race hatred by people of color more than the other way around. This short, confident, opinionated piece prompts discussion and debate on the meaning of the term "racism," how it is experienced by members of various ethnic groups, and why anti-white bias might be increasing.

Hartigan, J. Jr. (1997, September). Establishing the fact of Whiteness. *American Anthropologist, 99,* 495–505. Argues that the study of race should include a detailed study of how whites gained dominance and established a set of institutional routines and "white cultural practices" that create and maintain privileges. Whiteness is defined as "a core set of racial interests often obscured by seemingly race-neutral words, actions, or policies." A good summary of the field. Not for the beginner; white students, especially, need more of a basic understanding of the social construction of race, the concept of white privilege, and the suppressed histories of people of color before they are ready to entertain such a negative view of themselves and their ancestors.

Johnson, A. G. (2005). Privilege as paradox. In P. S. Rothenberg (Ed.), *White privilege: Essential readings on the other side of racism.* New York: Worth. Very short, accessible explanation of how privilege works. "I'm not race privileged because of who I am as a person. Whiteness is privileged in this society, and I have access to that privilege only when people identify me as belonging to the category 'white.'" A useful argument for students who claim they're not privileged because their family is working class or because their ancestors arrived in the United Sates after slavery ended.

Kincheloe, J. L., Steinberg, S. R., Rodriguez, N. M., and Chennault, R. E. (Eds.). (2000). *White reign: Deploying whiteness in America.* New York: Palgrave Macmillan. A good introduction to critical multiculturalism, the study of power relations that create racial, class, and gender inequalities and the resulting disparities in economic and social rewards. For instructors and advanced students who are already convinced that contemporary racism is real, that disparities exist, and that whites are advantaged by the system.

Kivel, P. (2011). *Uprooting racism: How white people can work for racial justice.* Third Edition. Philadelphia: New Society Publishers. "I am talking to you as one white person to another," begins the author. "Whatever your other identities you probably are not used to being addressed as white." Kivel talks comfortably and frankly about whiteness as an assumed norm, about the fiction of race, about white benefits and middle-class privilege, about the costs of racism to white people. Highly recommended for white students at either beginning or advanced levels of understanding. Use "Part I: What Color Is White?" for a short introduction to the issues in any class dealing with race and racism. Helpful preparation for white students who want to do community service in impoverished communities of color.

McIntosh, P. (1992) [1988]. White privilege and male privilege: A personal account of coming to see correspondences through work in Women's Studies. In M. L. Andersen & P. H. Collins (Eds.), *Race, class, and gender.* Belmont, CA: Wadsworth. The classic account of white privilege; a must for anyone wanting to understand differences in assumptions and treatment they do not ordinarily see. McIntosh lists forty-six "privileges" she has as a white person that are not granted to her colleagues of color: "I can swear, or dress in secondhand clothes, or not answer letters, without having people attribute these choices to the bad morals, the poverty, or the illiteracy of my race." "I can remain oblivious to the language and customs of persons of color who constitute the world's majority without feeling in my culture any penalty for such oblivion." And the one that white students remember most: "I can choose blemish cover or bandages in 'flesh' color and have them more or less match my skin." This article is often cited by white students as the one that changed their thinking about privilege.

Vera, H., Feagin, J. R., & Gordon, A. (1995). Superior intellect?: Sincere fictions of the White self. *Journal of Negro Education,* 64(3), 295–306. Sincere fictions constructed by whites about themselves are remarkably similar over time, say the authors. Whites believe they have superior intelligence, that they are hard working, objectively scientific, humble but heroic in the quest for truth, and friendly and benevolent toward people of color. This rationalization of white dominance and privilege harms everyone, including whites, because it effectively denies or suppresses other explanations for inequality, poverty, and poor school performance. Clearly written, with understandable references to Max Weber, Pierre Bourdieu (who developed the concept of sincere fictions), Gordon Allport, and Antonio Gramsci. The 1915 film, *Birth of a Nation,* made to justify the rise of the Ku Klux Klan, is an interesting visual accompaniment to this article. For advanced students.

# White Extremism

V Bolen, A., Rafferty, K., & Ridgeway, J. (1991). *Blood in the face.* 75 minutes. Distributor: First Run/Icarus. White supremacist hate groups are featured in speeches, nighttime cross-burning rallies, living room conversations, and picnics in rural Michigan. Old news clips of their heroes Adolf Hitler and George Lincoln Rockwell are interspersed with interviews of current leaders and youthful hangers-on. "We must not preach to the converted," a leader says. "There needs to be race-oriented comic books aimed at high school students." Among their targets: Jews, homosexuals, "coloreds," Mexicans, Filipinos, Asians, "foreigners" in general, and Christians who preach tolerance. This is the vicious, "old-fashioned racism" that was officially sanctioned in America not so long ago. I would not show this film to high schoolers, or large classes, or any group I didn't know well, since the groups consented to be filmed as a recruiting strategy. But for classes studying intolerance, this information is vital, if extremely scary. As an antidote, show the video, "Not in our town" (California Working Group, 1995) about a community's response to such groups.

**V** Kaye, T. (1998). *American history X.* 119 minutes. New Line Home Video. A young white supremacist, just out of prison for a vicious hate crime, attempts to save his younger brother from going down the same path. Scenes of brutal racist violence and displays of white power by charismatic leaders show the reality of many U.S. terrorist groups today. Not for the faint of heart.

**SV** PBS *As racial hate groups rise, strategies to shut them down.* http://www.pbs.org/newshour/bb/as-racial-hate-groups-rise-strategies-to-shut-them-down/. Excellent online interview with Heidi Beirich, leader of The Intelligence Project at the Southern Poverty Law Center, about the efforts of the SPLC to use the courts to put a number of Klan groups out of business. While these lawsuits have been extraordinarily successful, they have not made much of a dent in the 784 active hate groups catalogued by the SPLC in 2014, and that now number more than 1000. The newest trend in racist killings, says Beirich, is the so-called "lone wolf"—the young person who has been completely radicalized online. "That's exactly the same phenomenon that we see, for example, for people who are inspired by ISIS. They go onto Web sites where there's propaganda that's widely available. It enrages them for some reason. That kind of lone wolf terrorism is a big problem, and there's more of it today than it was 10 years ago, and we don't expect that to change."

Costello, N. (2016, March 17). Black lives matter and the Irish slave myth. *Al Jazeera English.* http://www.aljazeera.com/indepth/features/2016/03/black-lives-matter-irish-slave-myth-160315092722167.html Among the current attempts by whites to diminish or even ridicule the suffering of U.S. blacks under slavery is a new "fact" sweeping the internet: that the Irish were also slaves in the United Sates and "were treated worse than any other race." One online article that falsely equates indentured servitude or penal slavery with racialized slavery has been shared nearly one million times. "Historically, the majority of Irish prisoners of war, vagrants and other victims of kidnapping and deception thought to have numbered around 10,000 people were forcibly sent to the West Indies in the 1650s," says Irish historian Liam Hogan. "Those that survived were pardoned by Charles II in 1660. In contrast, the transatlantic slave trade lasted for four centuries, was the largest forced migration in world history, involving tens of millions of Africans who were completely dehumanised, and its poisonous legacy remains in the form of anti-black racism. So this neo-Nazi propaganda is false equivalency on an outrageous scale."

MSNBC. (2008, October 27). Plot by skinheads to kill Obama is foiled. http://www. msnbc.msn.com/id/27405681/ Not only did these two young white supremacists plan to kill Barack Obama, they also intended to murder eighty eight black high school students, fourteen of them by beheading. "The court documents say the two men met about a month ago on the Internet and found common ground in their shared 'white power' and 'skinhead' philosophy." One might ask why such individuals are not labeled "terrorists" by the U.S. government.

Purnell, B. (2015, July 1). Confederate flags in the Jim Crow North. *AAIHS* http:// www.aaihs.org/confederate-flags-in-the-jim-crow-north/. In this succinct piece, the African-American Intellectual History Society explains how the flag of the Civil War South has been used historically as a symbol of opposition to equality for blacks, both in the South and the North. "Perhaps now, in the 2010s, the Confederate flag means different things—heritage and sectional pride—than it meant in the past … Perhaps. But that flag's connection to the white nationalist terrorist's shooting of 9 Black people in Charleston, South Carolina, proves that the Stars and Bars still have a great amount of white nationalist, racist, segregationist meaning woven within its fabric."

Southern Poverty Law Center. (no date). Extremist files: David Lane. https://www. splcenter.org/fighting-hate/extremist-files/individual/david-lane. "Although he died in prison in 2007 at the age of 69, David Lane remains one of the most important ideologues of contemporary white supremacy," according to the SPLC. Lane was the author of the "best-known slogan of the U.S. white supremacist movement," the so-called '14 Words': "We must secure the existence of our people and a future for White children." Besides being an avid writer of hate literature, Lane was involved in the machine gun assassination of Jewish talk show host Alan Berg in Denver, Colorado, and the robbery of $3.6 million from an armored car in Ukiah, California. This alarming article may spark students' interest in discovering how widespread domestic terrorist groups have become in recent years. The Southern Poverty Law Center (SPLC) has maps, data, and stories at www.splc.org.

Tenold, V. (2015, July 26). The little Fuhrer: A day in the life of the newest leader of white nationalism. *Al Jazeera America*. http://projects.aljazeera.com/2015/07/ hate-groups/. This article profiles Matthew Heimbach, the leader and founder of a nationalist youth organization that believes that each ethnic group should form its own country. Unlike most other purveyors of hate, Heimbach believes in a certain measure of equality between the races and cultures, including the "traditional white culture" of poor and working class Christian whites. "I support white power, black power, brown power and yellow power," Heimbach says. "All races should be the dominant political force in their region. That is why America needs to be divided into smaller, ethnically and culturally homogenous states. In countries where races are mixed, one race will always dominate the others. That is why we need separation. Not because the white race is better than the black race. We need to stop the hate and separate." Is this a good idea? Students might consider whether racial, cultural, or religious separation is feasible and/or desirable. Ask them to take the idea seriously and list all the possible benefits and drawbacks that might result from separation. Has ethnic separation been tried in other historical periods or other parts of the world? What has been the result? How feasible would it be in the United States?

Viets, S. (2016, March 18). Meet White Lives Matter: The racist response to the Black Lives Matter movement. *Southern Poverty Law Center*. Hatewatch. www.splcenter.org/hatewatch/2016/03/18/meet-white-lives-matter-racist-response-black-lives-matter-movement. The idea that white lives matter (or alternatively, that all lives matter) is not racist in itself—just naïve. White lives have always mattered more than black lives, so the assertion that black lives are just as worthy as white lives should not be controversial. But across the country, hard-core racists are using social media to promote the catch phrase "White Lives Matter" (WLM) "to counter a message they believe is playing a part in the systematic devaluing of white culture—even orchestrating what they call a 'white genocide.'"

# Racial Socialization

V Films for the Humanities and Sciences. (2003). *How biased are you?* Video, 45 minutes. A Discovery Channel Production. An excellent film for students who believe they and likeminded peers are not prejudiced. The film begins with stark examples of bias by store clerks waiting on white and African-American customers. The rest of the film centers on tests of "hidden bias" created by researchers at the University of Virginia and the University of Washington, and other tests of bias designed for young children. The results are often surprising. Have students take the bias test at http://www.tolerance.org/Hidden-bias and discuss their results in class—or write about their score and their reactions to the test for your eyes only. Another set of implicit bias tests, created by Harvard University, can be found at https://implicit.harvard.edu/implicit/takeatest.html

V Yale University Films. (1985). *A class divided*. Video, 60 minutes. Distributor: PBS Video. A third grade teacher's dramatic demonstration of how racism can be quickly learned, internalized, and rationalized. Jane Elliott divides her all white class into two groups: the blue eyes and the brown eyes, telling the children convincingly that one eye color is better and more privileged than the other (then after a few days, switching the privilege to the other group). Children in the privileged group quickly take on bossy, nasty behavior, while those in the target group become tearful and passive, their test scores dropping dramatically within twenty-four hours. The second half of the video shows a similar exercise done with prison guards and parole officers, where employees who signed up to be in a "brown-eyed" group sit quietly as observers while the instructor stigmatizes and berates the blue-eyed group, who are initially unaware that this is only a role play. "Blue-eyed" employees soon begin to show the typical response to stigma: talking back, playing the fool, trying to "pass," and so on. A wonderful demonstration that such reactions are natural, human attempts to cope with marginalization, not "inborn" traits. Students of all ethnicities are very moved by this film, especially the work with children. A teacher's guide, transcripts, and readings can be found at: www.pbs.org/wgbh/pages/frontline/shows/divided/.

Blunt, J. (1995). Lessons in silence. In T. Jordan & J. Hepworth (Eds.), *The stories that shape us: Contemporary women write about the West*. New York: Norton. In this short, beautifully written memoir, Judy Blunt tells how she learned fear and disgust for her Native American neighbors as a child growing up in Montana. Used as a discussion starter or for written reflection, this story helps students think about the ways they learned society's racial rules.

Bonilla-Silva, E. (2003). *Racism without racists: Color-blind racism and the persistence of racial inequality in the United States*. Lanham, MD: Rowman & Littlefield. "How is it possible to have [a] tremendous degree of racial inequality in a country where most whites claim that race is no longer relevant? More important, how do whites explain the apparent contradiction between their professed color-blindness and the United States' color-coded inequality?" Interviews with college students show that "whites have developed powerful explanations—which have ultimately become justifications—for contemporary racial inequality that exculpate them for any responsibility for the status of people of color."

Ritterhouse, J. (2006). *Growing up Jim Crow: The racial socialization of Black and White Southern children, 1890–1940*. Chapel Hill: University of North Carolina Press. The traditional "racial etiquette" of the U.S. South was passed down by parents of both races, upheld as benign "tradition" by whites and a matter of survival by blacks. Long before the Civil Rights Movement, young blacks were challenging this social order, while white youth continued to enforce it by evermore elaborate rituals and practices. Videos that show contemporary forms of this behavior include "Trouble Behind" (Henson, 1990) (about Kentucky) and "The Order of Myths" (Brown, 2008) (about Alabama).

Southern Poverty Law Center. SPLC Survey: Presidential campaign leading to widespread fear, bullying in schools. (2016, April 13). https://www.splcenter.org/news/2016/04/13/splc-survey-presidential-campaign-leading-widespread-fear-bullying-schools An online survey of 2000 teachers nationwide, including 5000 comments from educators, found that the 2016 presidential campaign "is producing an alarming level of fear and anxiety among children of color and inflaming racial and ethnic tensions in the classroom. Many students worry about being deported … Muslim children are being called 'terrorist' or 'ISIS' or 'bomber.'" Teachers are choosing to avoid the issue by not teaching about the election, although The SPLC advises against this. "Use incidences of incivility as teaching moments," they counsel. Easier said than done, especially when an apparently successful and respected adult is instigating these racist reactions. This short piece makes it very clear that children learn racism not just from their family, but from the society around them.

# Racism: Contemporary Stories and Examples

V ABC News. (1996). *America in black and white: #2 How much is white skin worth?* Video, 23 min. Distributor: ABC News. Newscaster Ted Koppel asks an audience of whites the same question that Andrew Hacker has been asking his young white Economics students for twenty years: "How much money would you accept in compensation if you found out you had to live the rest of your life as an African American?" Their answers are eye-opening—considering that these folks believe racism is a thing of the past and that compensation to blacks for past injustice is unnecessary. The second shocker is the personal story of Greg Williams, Dean and Professor of Ohio State University College of Law, about growing up first "white," then "black" in 1950s America. Born in Virginia to ostensibly white parents, he enjoyed the privileges of other white children in the segregated South. When he was ten, his parents' divorce forced a move with his "Italian" father to Muncie, Indiana, where he discovered a loving black grandmother and the rest of his African-American relatives. His new status carefully noted on his high school record ("appears to be white, but father is colored—don't be fooled"), the same Greg Williams now suffered exclusion from social activities, low expectations by teachers, and other indignities that continued to follow him though his ultimately successful career. A vivid example of the social construction of race and the value of white skin in contemporary U.S. culture. Excellent for beginning students.

V ABC News. (1996). *America in black and white: #3 The color line and the bus line.* Video, 23 minutes. Distributor: ABC News. Puzzled by the different reactions of his white (indifferent) and black (outraged) colleagues to the death of seventeen-year-old Cynthia Wiggens in a traffic accident, Ted Koppel goes to Buffalo, New York to uncover "the insidious racism that whites don't acknowledge." Cynthia was flattened by a truck as she tried to make her way across a seven-lane highway to get to her job in an upscale mall in a white suburb. Blacks suspected immediately what whites generally didn't realize or want to acknowledge: irrational fear of low-income blacks who might come to the mall to work or shop had blocked the construction of a safe, convenient bus stop and highway crossing between the two communities. Koppel uncovers more subtleties for his mostly white audience: how the dearth of businesses in the inner city made it necessary for working-class blacks to cross the color line to in order to work at all; the regulations that prevent blacks from getting public sector jobs in the community that happens to be blessed with public services; the reasons why Cynthia wasn't safe in college becoming a pediatrician as she had dreamed (unreasonably, Koppel's tone suggests) but was instead a high school dropout struggling to support a beloved infant son. A memorable example of the complexity and insidiousness of institutional racism. Students remember these stories and repeat them, incredulously, to their friends.

**V** Cho, M. (1996). *Another America*. Video, 56 minutes. Distributor: Asian American Telecommunications Association. The filmmaker tells the story of his uncle's murder in downtown Detroit, where Koreans had long owned businesses that cater to African-Americans. The confession of the 17-year-old killer, and interviews with black and Korean business owners and customers show the complexity of relations between these groups. The film helps students understand both the resentment and the respect between Koreans and African-Americans and how white racism and neglect of urban neighborhoods contribute to the tension between communities of color.

**V** Dow, W., & Williams, M. (2003). *Two towns of Jasper*. Video, 83 minutes. PBS Home Video. In 1998, in the town of Jasper, Texas, three white men chained a black man to the back of their pickup truck and dragged him three miles to his death. Two film crews, one black, one white, document the reactions of the respective communities to the crime, the trials, and the effects of the brutal murder on race relations in east Texas. This "incident" was downplayed in the mainstream media at the time and/or explained as "complex" (because the black man was not seen as an upstanding citizen) to the outrage of communities of color.

**V** Lee, M. W. (1994). *The color of fear*. Video, 90 min. Distributor: Stir-Fry Productions. Men of different ethnicities come together in Ukiah, California to talk about their experience of racism. Contains great quotes for class discussion: "America doesn't incorporate all of us." "Why can't you people just be individuals?" "Racism is basically a white problem." "American, white and human have become synonymous." "It's a white responsibility to eliminate racism." Also discusses Asian, black, and Latin@ prejudices against each other:
"Asians take their cues from whites." "I'm afraid of [blacks'] misplaced rage." The experience is very hard on the clueless white male, who finally comes to appreciate the other men's perspectives. This video is much appreciated by students of color because of the eloquent, emotionally intense explanations of racism and exclusion. White students will benefit most if they have already had a solid introduction to issues of race, racism, and identity.

**V** Warnock-Graham, O. (2006). *Silences*. Video, 22 minutes. New Day Films. This crisp, provocative documentary about a white family's refusal to talk about a son's evident African heritage exposes the shame and guilt around "race mixing" and the denial of racism in U.S. life. Excellent discussion starter.

**SV** A&M *views: Hispanic Americans* https://www.youtube.com/watch?v=2m1WD-VojR Students at Texas A&M ask their peers on campus a simple question: "What are some of the stereotypes you may have heard about Hispanic Americans?" Their answers are remarkably candid. This video not only opens up discussion about stereotypes of immigrants, undocumented immigrants, and Latin@s in general, it also suggests a way that students can spread their conversations about race and racism beyond the classroom.

**SV** ABC News. *What would you do? AntiSemitism and Jewish discrimination.* https://www.youtube.com/watch?v=BRX31HOikws At a bakery, a couple asks to post a flier about a job fair at their Temple synagogue. The actor playing the clerk lets fly familiar invective: "You Jews are all alike; you want to control the banks, crash the economy, and steal the jobs. We're not supporting Jews here!" Unlike most of the other segments in this series, customers speak up immediately, Jews and nonJews alike. The producer later points out that non-Jews, including a Christian pastor, were even angrier than the Jewish customers. Students may be interested in exploring why they think this is so. Lessons learned from World War II? Residual guilt for not speaking up during the Holocaust? Shame that the United Sates denied asylum to Jews seeking refuge? Students also may want to explore the effects of peer pressure on bystanders. Does voicing opposition to racist or anti-Semitic sentiments encourage others to speak up? What effect does moral outrage have on the perpetrators?

**SV** ABC News. *What would you do? Latino hate crime episode.* http://www. youtube. com/watch?v=ru1F29vuVKI. On a downtown Newark, New Jersey street, a group of young thugs attack a Latino immigrant, pummeling him and shouting, "Speak English!" Will anyone come to his rescue? Passers-by are unaware that the scene is staged and that their reactions are being recorded on hidden camera. Of the 99 people who witnessed the event, 67 did nothing. Producer John Quinones interviews both the silent bystanders and the few courageous people who try stop the beating. Surprisingly, it was not only the large, confident males who stepped up. For an in-depth look at some of the individuals who perpetrate these kinds of assaults, show the full-length film, *Shenandoah*, that tells the story of the high football stars in central Pennsylvania who beat a Latino resident to death for the same apparent reason—refusing to speak English. (See *Shenandoah* in "Whiteness and White Privilege")

**SV** ABC News. *What would you do? Muslims in America.* https://www.youtube.com/watch?v=XvIDqgyK8fw. At a small, roadside bakery near Waco, Texas, hidden cameras catch an opinionated shopkeeper refusing to serve a Muslim woman in a headscarf, both of them actors for ABC Primetime News. The "shopkeeper" blatantly insults the "customer," using crude epithets and stereotypes: "Americans don't wear towels on their heads." "Get back on the camel and go back to wherever you came from." The announcer tells us that Muslims hear these crude epithets all the time and that for many Muslim women it is a daily battle to prove their apparel makes them no less American. In this case, however, more customers are outraged at the shopkeeper's language than approve of it. Many leave the store angrily, saying they'll no longer shop there, while others try to explain to the shopkeeper why such discrimination is wrong. Still, most customers say nothing. The emotional reactions of people on both sides of the issue prompt class discussion: What makes a person a "real American"? What does patriotism mean in an age of terrorism?

**SV** ABC News. *What would you do? Racism and illegal immigration.* https://www.youtube.com/watch?v=plaqunpTzvM. While an immigrant worker watches, actors portray a Spanish-speaking day laborer trying to get a cup of coffee from a cashier in a New Jersey restaurant. "We don't speak Mexican here." "We don't want illegal aliens." "No English, no service," are common responses by customers who aren't aware of the hidden camera. John Quinones, the producer of the series for ABC News, reveals to the audience that he is Mexican American and a former migrant worker. So strongly does he identify with the laborers in this scene that he steps in to play the part of the immigrant seeking service. At the end of the day, he comforts the real immigrant worker who has watched the continual rejection of the actor and who is now reduced to tears. "I don't know why they discriminate against us," he says. "We're human, same as them." A compelling start to a discussion of illegal immigration.

**SV** ABC News. *What would you do? Shopping while black.* https://www.youtube.com/watch?v=8Z4fNFtbmGo. In this ABC Primetime short, actors portray a confrontation between a white sales clerk and an African-American shopper in an upscale New York City boutique while bystanders comment, sometimes furtively, sometimes in collusion with the clerk, about the motives of the shopper and the store's apparent need for her surveillance. Producer John Quinones then confronts the shoppers outside the store to ask them why they reacted as they did. This powerful video provokes discussion about people's willingness to act in defense of those who are being unfairly treated, and can encourage students' reflection on their own willingness to be allies.

**SV** ABC News. *What would you do? Sikh being refused a job at a restaurant.* https://www.youtube.com/watch?v=B7wO8SI0ucQ Ever since 9/11, there has been an increase in hate crimes against Sikhs, although this religious group has no connection with Islam or in fact, any Arab nation (Sikhism originated in the Punjab region of what is now India in the sixteenth century; its male adherents wear turbans as a religious mandate). In this segment of "What would you do?" an actor playing a restaurant manager appears to be having a conversation with a well-qualified Sikh who is applying for a job. As the conversation turns into an argument, the manager tells the applicant that he must agree to take off his turban during working hours, despite the fact that doing so would violate a principle of his religion. "I can't hire you looking the way you look," says the manager. "It's threatening." Bystanders do not speak up, not realizing, perhaps, that discrimination based on religion is against the law. As this issue is a bit different from outright refusal of service to an ethnic or religious minority, it is bound to spark discussion about what limits, if any, there should be on mandating equality.

Bakalar, N. (2009, June 23). Vital signs, perceptions: A customer bias in favor of white men. *New York Times*, D6. "A new study suggests that people give higher customer satisfaction ratings to white men than to women and members of minorities, even when their performance is the same." College students were the "people" in this University of Wisconsin study. Three groups of students were shown three videotapes of customer interactions with salespeople in a book store where every detail of the encounter was identical—down to the camera angles—except race and gender. A second, larger study had HMO customers rate their doctors' performance. The number of follow-up e-mail messages sent by doctors to patients increased their ratings—but only when the doctor was a white man.

Barnes, R. (2014, April 22). Sotomayor accuses colleagues of trying to 'wish away' racial inequality. *The Washington Post*. https://www.washingtonpost.com/politics/sotomayor-accuses-colleagues-of-trying-to-wish-away-racial-inequality/2014/04/22/e5892f90-ca49-11e3-93eb-6c0037dde2ad_story.html. When the Supreme Court upheld Michigan's constitutional amendment banning the consideration of race in public university admissions, Justice Sonia Sotomayor, the Court's first Latina Justice, read her lengthy dissent aloud to her colleagues, accusing them of trying to "sit back and wish away" racial inequality. "We are fortunate to live in a democratic society," she began. "But without checks, democratically approved legislation can oppress minority groups. For that reason, our Constitution places limits on what a majority of the people may do." Her colleague John Roberts disagreed, saying that she should not criticize what is simply a difference of opinion among the justices. Sotomayor's personal experience growing up in a housing project and reaping the benefits of affirmative action makes her a passionate defender of the practice. Her eloquent dissenting opinion can be found here in full: https://supreme.justia.com/cases/federal/us/572/12-682/dissent7.html.

Bidgood, J. (2016, January 26). Amherst College drops 'Lord Jeff' as mascot. *New York Times*. http://www.nytimes.com/2016/01/27/us/amherst-college-drops-lord-jeff-as-mascot.html?_r=0. "You will do well to try to inoculate the Indians by means of blankets, as well as to try every other method that can serve to extirpate this execrable race." So wrote Lord Jeffrey Amherst in a postscript to a letter in 1763. The British military commander in the French and Indian War was so admired during the Colonial period that a number of towns and a prestigious college were named after him. But as Amherst College became one of the most diverse private colleges in the nation, students persuaded the trustees to choose a different mascot. Students covered the campus with fliers depicting the army handing a "gift" of smallpox infected blankets to Native Americans. "This is Jeff," said the flier. "We aren't Jeff." This particularly successful student protest is one of many that have been staged on college campuses in recent years about issues ranging from insensitive Halloween costumes at Yale http://time.com/4106265/yale-students-protest/ to political posters at Emory http://college.usatoday.com/2016/03/24/emory-students-protest-pro-trump-slogans-say-they-dont-feel-safe/ to objections to Woodrow Wilson's name on the Public Policy school at Princeton https://www.washingtonpost.com/news/grade-point/wp/2015/11/23/after-protests-princeton-debates-woodrow-wilsons-legacy/. An overview of the most prominent (and controversial) protests can be found here: http://www.theatlantic.com/education/archive/2016/04/campus-protest-roundup/417570/.

Drexler, M. (2007, July 15). How racism hurts—literally. *Boston Globe*, E1. More than 100 studies now show that the chronic stress of racism negatively affects one's physical health. This short article can be used in conjunction with excerpts from California Newsreel's video series, "Unnatural causes: Is inequality making us sick?" (2008)

Harwood, S. A., Choi, S. Orozco, M., Huntt, M. B. & Mendenhall, R. (2015). Racial microaggressions. University of Illinois, Urbana-Champagne. http://www.racialmicro-aggressions.illinois.edu/files/2015/03/RMA-Classroom-Report.pdf This helpful report of a survey of 4800 students of color at the University of Illinois, Urbana-Champagne describes a number of ways these students have experienced microaggressions on campus. These include feeling unwelcome, overhearing racist conversations, being subjected to offensive lecture content, being stereotyped in the classroom (over half the students reported this), not being taken seriously by peers or the instructor, feeling excluded and harassed in group projects, and being "steered" to less challenging courses and majors. Quantitative data and quotes from the surveyed students give credibility and immediacy to these issues. Important for future teachers, faculty discussions, and administrators.

Holloway, K. 2015, March 4). 10 ways white people are more racist than they realize. *Salon*. http://www.salon.com/2015/03/04/10_ways_white_people_are_more_racist_than_they_realize_partner/ This piece summarizes a number of studies that reveal blatant racism and/or implicit bias among whites, who generally believe that racism is no longer a problem today. Emergency room personnel are less likely to give black and Latin@ children medication for severe pain than white children. Whites are more likely to use illegal drugs than blacks or Latin@ but are far less likely to go to jail for it. White college professors respond more positively to questions they believe were asked by white males. These classic studies are excellent for class discussion, especially if they are paired with tests of the students' own implicit bias. (https://implicit.harvard.edu/implicit/takeatest.html)

Loller, T. (2007, January 26). Study says skin tone affects earnings. http://www.washingtonpost.com/wp-dyn/content/article/2007/01/26/AR2007012601202_pf.html A study of new immigrants to the United Sates shows that regardless of race or country of origin, those with lighter skins earn eight to fifteen percent more than those who are darker. Because of employer discrimination, "on average, being one shade lighter has about the same effect as having an additional year of education." What do your students think is the cause of this phenomenon? What can be done about it?

Lorde, A. (1984). *Sister outsider*. Freedom, CA: The Crossing Press. An important, short chapter, "The Uses of Anger: Women Responding to Racism," explains the reasons behind the angry feelings of some women of color toward white women who claim to be their allies. White liberals may hear themselves in her quotes. A good background piece for advanced students in multicultural classrooms, and an important reflection piece after "race breaks out." Relieves students of color of the need to reveal some of their deepest feelings, while exposing sympathetic whites to perspectives they might not "get" on their own.

Microaggressions.com http://www.microaggressions.com/about This fascinating site lets social media savvy students follow blog posts that describe microaggressions they've experienced, ask questions, respond, and learn from one another. The project's purpose is "NOT about showing how ignorant people can be" but rather, to show how insensitive comments "create and enforce uncomfortable, violent, and unsafe realities onto people's workplace, home, school, childhood/adolescence/adulthood, and public transportation/space environments." Although the term's original meaning pertained to racial slights and insults, this site expands the concept to other identities such as sexuality, class, religion, and education level. Students can choose threads that discuss one or several of these identities, follow the project on Twitter, send in their own experiences, and send ideas to the editors. After students have followed the blog for a week or so, they can report on what they learned, how their ideas may have changed by reading the experiences of others, and what can be done to improve the community climate.

Miller, M. E. (2016, May 25). White high school football players in Idaho charged with raping black, disabled teammate with a coat hanger. *Washington Post.* https://www.washingtonpost.com/news/morning-mix/wp/2016/05/25/white-high-school-football-players-in-idaho-charged-with-raping-black-disabled-teammate-with-a-coat-hanger/. Not only was this young man viciously raped, but the attack followed months of racist abuse by white students that was ignored or even encouraged by staff. The apparent ringleader of the rape was a "large and aggressive male who had been sent to live with his relatives in Idaho due to his inability to keep out of trouble in Texas." Yet he was able to bring out the most horrific sort of violence in his white teammates and teachers, and because of his family connections and athletic ability, managed to escape notice for his behavior. Ask students to imagine how the media might react if this same behavior had occurred in a largely African-American high school, with black students and faculty as perpetrators and a lone white mentally disabled teen as victim.

Nigatu, H. (2013, December 9). 21 racial microaggressions you hear on a daily basis. https://www.buzzfeed.com/hnigatu/racial-microaggressions-you-hear-on-a-daily-basis?utm_term=.gvvXrKjX0#.nqZlex2lA. Although the term, "microaggression" was coined in the 1970s, it has gained currency only recently, when high school and college students of color began using it to spread the word about the racial climate at their schools. Columbia Professor Derald Sue defines microaggressions as "brief and commonplace daily verbal, behavioral, or environmental indignities, whether intentional or unintentional, that communicate hostile, derogatory, or negative racial slights and insults toward people of color." In this short piece, 21 photos of students at Fordham University hold up hand-lettered signs describing common microaggressions they experience on campus. "Just because I'm Mexican that doesn't mean I should be the automatic 1st choice for the role of Dora the Explorer in the high school skit" says one. "No, you're white," says another sign held by a visually white student. "'So what does your hair look like today?' she said as she pulled off my hat without my permission," says another. Some of these are obvious slights; others are more thought-provoking. They all will get students talking about the microaggressions they have experienced or heard, how they've reacted to them (as a target or an ally), and how they might respond to people who say that students are just too sensitive these days. The piece may even inspire a group project.

Powell, K. (no date). Utne Reader. Will racism ever end, will I ever stop being a nigger? http://www.utne.com/community/kevin-powell-will-racism-ever-end-zl0z16sz-sau.aspx. Writer of twelve books, public speaker, world traveler, activist Kevin Powell has lived the near mythological American Dream, coming up from the projects, abandoned by his father, fighting depression violence, abuse and fear to become a world famous personality. But regardless of his achievements, Powell tells us, he is still seen as a "nigger," or almost worse, the object of "that nutty game of the 'special' black person handpicked to represent the rest of us [which is] as old and tired as racism itself. This hard-hitting piece challenges even the most knowledgeable white allies. "If you refuse to hear me," Powell says, "if you refuse to read this essay to the very end, if you refuse to acknowledge that my history is your history, too," then there's no way we can have a "courageous conversation" about race and racism in America, period.

Powell, T. (2014, July 24). My son has been suspended five times. He's 3. *The Washington Post.* https://www.washingtonpost.com/posteverything/wp/2014/07/24/my-son-has-been-suspended-five-times-hes-3/. African-American op-ed columnist Tunette Powell describes her concern and puzzlement when her three-year-old was repeatedly suspended from preschool. What could she have been doing wrong? Her family lived a comfortable life. Her husband was an "amazing father." And the little boy had given them few problems; even babysitters reported nothing unusual. The suspensions were all the more worrisome to her as she recalled her own expulsion from school, and the lasting effect the teacher's disparaging words had on her self-esteem. If only she had been a model preschooler, she thought, this never would have happened to her child. But her chance remark about her son's suspensions to other mothers—all white—at a children's birthday party changed her mind. As she related what her son had done to get suspended, the mothers were shocked. Their own children, it turned out, had done similar things or worse at the preschool but none had been suspended. "My son threw something at a kid on purpose and the kid had to be rushed to the hospital," said one parent in disbelief. "All I got was a phone call." It turns out that Powell's little boy is not alone in being singled out for suspensions. Black children make up

18 percent of all preschool enrolment, but receive 48 percent of those receiving more than one suspension. How is this happening? This piece should be in the course pack of every aspiring teacher of pre-K and elementary school children. Students might also read a UCLA study showing that white female undergraduates viewed black boys as older and less innocent than their white peers. That study can be found here: http://www.apa.org/news/press/releases/2014/03/black-boys-older.aspx.

Richmond, E. (2013, June 11). Schools are more segregated today than during the late 1960s. *The Atlantic.* http://www.theatlantic.com/national/archive/2012/06/schools-are-more-segregated-today-than-during-the-late-1960s/258348/. How is it possible that school segregation is worse today than forty years ago? John F. Kennedy lamented the racial segregation of his era, yet today, the U.S. is facing the same challenges. Poverty, ethnicity, language, "housing patterns" (where people live, voluntarily or out of necessity) neglect of inner city schools, funding cuts, and a Supreme Court that ruled against race-based remedies for segregation based on school zoning all contribute to the problem.

Staples, B. (2009, February 27). The ape in American bigotry from Thomas Jefferson to 2009. *New York Times*, Editorial Observer. http://www.nytimes.com/2009/02/28/opinion/28sat4.html Attempts by whites to dehumanize blacks by comparing them to apes have been "central to our national history"—and not only in the bad old days, says op-ed writer Brent Staples. During the Obama campaign, "[m]onkey T-shirts were sold through the mail. Monkey dolls showed up at Republican political rallies. The most instructive image, which was spread over the Internet, depicted the presidential plane, Air Force One, renamed 'Watermelon One.' It carried the smiling face of a monkey holding, what else, a slice of watermelon." Even high-fashion images play on this theme, says Staples. The cover of *Vogue* featured basketball player LeBron James "roaring at the camera while dribbling a basketball with one hand and embracing the white fashion model Gisele Bündchen in the other" in an unabashed reference to King Kong. Yet whites continue to deny or downplay the significance of these degrading, demoralizing images.

Swaine, J., Laughland, O., & Lartey, J. (2015, June 1). Black Americans killed by police twice as likely to be unarmed as white people. *The Guardian.* http://www.theguardian.com/us-news/2015/jun/01/black-americans-killed-by-police-analysis. According to a database complied by *The Guardian*, 32% of blacks shot dead by police in the first half of 2015 were unarmed, as compared to 25% of Latin@s and 15% of whites. By the newspaper's calculations, the number of people killed by law enforcement, regardless of ethnicity, is far greater than the findings of the federal government's official public record. The Guardian's interactive database, called "The Counted," includes age of the victim, precise location where they died, their gender and ethnicity, whether the person killed was armed, and which police agency was responsible. Students can access the database here: http://www.theguardian.com/us-news/ng-interactive/2015/jun/01/the-counted-police-killings-us-database.

Tchekmedyian, A. & Chang, C. (2016, April 27). *Los Angeles Times*. Top L. A. County sheriff's official sent emails mocking Muslims, blacks, Latinos and women. http://www.latimes.com/local/california/la-me-sheriff-burbank-emails-20160427-story.html. "Jokes" that run from racially insensitive to downright racist are considered "cool and witty" among white high school and college students these days, despite the pain they cause to their friends of color. The normalizing of these jokes then spills into the workplace, where the stakes are higher against speaking up. In this particularly blatant example, the Chief of Staff of the Burbank Police Department sent around "jokes" by email ridiculing the profiling of Muslims, the high incarceration rates in minority communities, and the supposed stupidity of people of color, including Mexicans, his own ethnic group. Ironically, he had been hired to "reform a department reeling from allegations of police brutality as well as racism and sexual harassment within its ranks."

Terkel, S. (1992). *Race: How Blacks and Whites think and feel about the American obsession*. New York: The New Press. Terkel's interviews make great background material. Some of my favorites are Maggie Holmes, an outspoken black domestic worker who grew up in the segregated South, Tasha Knight, a black writer for a trade magazine who describes office prejudice, and especially, Peggy Terry, a reformed white racist who grew up poor in the South and later joined the Civil Rights Movement. After your class has gotten to know each other pretty well, ask them to interview each other about their experiences with race. Develop a list of questions together that everyone in the class can use.

Thomas, E. (2013, February 21). Forest Whitaker falsely accused of shoplifting: How do I explain racism to my son? *The Washington Post*. https://www.washingtonpost.com/blogs/therootdc/post/forest-whitaker-falsely-accused-of-shoplifting-how-do-i-explain-racism-to-my-son/2013/02/21/164886d2-7c65-11e2-a044-676856536b40_blog.html Despite a father's efforts to protect his seven-year-old from racism, the child happens to watch the news on a day off from school, and his disturbed questions begin. "Why would a father not want any black nurse to save his baby at the hospital? He only wanted white nurses? Why would that matter?" This short piece can be startling to white students who believe that the lives of their friends of color are no different from theirs. They are not aware that many of their black friends have had "the age old discussion that every black parent eventually has to have with their kids." They never had to be instructed on how to remain calm if the police stop them on a pretext. They never needed to be reminded to get a receipt at a store in case they're suspected of shoplifting. They never had to learn that some teachers will underestimate them, even if they're the smartest kid in the class. A good piece to start discussions of the prevalence of everyday racism in our "postracial" society.

University of Texas at Austin. Texas theory wiki. Name discrimination. http://wikis.la.utexas.edu/theory/page/name-discrimination. Several studies on whether or not a "black-sounding name" carries a burden are summarized here, each with different conclusions. One study of 16 million births in California over forty years concludes that a black-sounding name had "no significant effect on how someone's life turns out," that is, their overall economic circumstances. Another study looked at the likelihood of getting a particular job, and found that fake resumes with black-sounding names were 50 percent less likely to get a callback than comparable resumes with white-sounding names. Another study concluded that even when higher quality resumes were used, applicants with black sounding names got significantly fewer callbacks than those with white sounding names. Interestingly, the amount of discrimination did not vary by occupation. "Federal contractors and employers who list 'Equal Opportunity Employer' in their ad discriminate as much as other employers."

Wessel, D. (2003, September 4). Racial discrimination still at work. *Wall Street Journal*. http://www.wsj.com/articles/SB106262466678910800 Though whites believe that racial minorities have equal job opportunities these days, studies show that "the disadvantage carried by a young black man applying for a job as a dishwasher or a driver is equivalent to forcing a white man to carry an 18-month prison record on his back."

Wise, T. (no date) #WhiteLiesMatter. http://www.timwise.org/category/essays/page/2/. In his usual hard-hitting style, antiracist activist Tim Wise refutes right-wing claims about people of color in this series of short essays and Facebook posts. A few of his examples: black teen pregnancy is not a "growing crisis" (in fact, the fertility rate for this group is down by 81 percent); blacks do not have the "job edge" over whites (recent black college grads are twice as likely to be unemployed as their white peers); Asian success does not prove that racism is dead (in fact, Asians are not as successful in employment as whites); most blacks do not live in public housing (only 2.8 percent do). Links to studies and data sets are provided for students to do more detailed exploration of these myths.

Young, D. (2016, March 17). 35 types of postracial racism. *The Root*. http://www.the-root.com/articles/culture/2016/03/_35_types_of_post_racial_racism.html "In post-racial twenty-first-century America, no one actually wants to admit to being racist," says the author of this provocative blog. "They'll do racist things, say racist words, think racist thoughts, support racist businesses, vote for racist politicians and even willingly benefit from racist policies and business practices, but the moment you actually bring up racism, they're like, "Who, me? Never!" The blogger lists the kinds of racism that he's encountered: "'I'm not a racist; I'm a realist' racism"; "'Look how cool and witty and ironic I am when I do this remarkably offensive thing' racism"; "'Are we sure he's not a Muslim?' racism"; "'Although my test scores were pretty aggressively and demonstratively average, I'm going to the Supreme Court because there's no reason why these black kids should have been accepted instead of me' racism." This piece is guaranteed to get things hopping. To avoid mayhem, especially in mostly white classes, I ask students to individually label each type of racism in one of four ways: 1) I've experienced this. 2) I've heard someone make this argument. 3)

I get it, even though I've never heard it before. 4) I don't understand this. Why is it racist? Students discuss their reactions in small groups, then bring their questions and comments to the larger group for more discussion. This way, everyone engages with the material and is more likely to have their say.

# Psychology of Racism

**SV** American Anthropological Association. *A girl like me.* http://www.understandingrace.org/lived/video/index.html. A young African-American filmmaker, Kiri Davis, reproduces the "doll test" with African-American preschoolers, asking them their preferences between black and white dolls and the reasons for their choices. This short, painfully honest video clearly shows that whatever adults may say about a "postracial" society, for these youngsters, racism—and internalized racism—is alive and well. An excellent discussion starter for students who are reluctant to talk about race, or for any students at the beginning of the semester. The young children are so frank and honest about their preferences that students are compelled to believe them. And since the children prefer white dolls almost exclusively, students have to ask themselves how that could be. Discussion of how children learn racism, especially against their own group, will follow. To broaden the discussion to the ways children from the dominant group learn to exclude others, show the excellent film, *A class divided.* (See: Racial Socialization)

Carten, Al. (2015, July 27). How the legacy of slavery affects the mental health of black Americans today. *The Conversation.* https://theconversation.com/how-the-legacy-of-slavery-affects-the-mental-health-of-black-americans-today-44642. Effects of the hardships of the slave system on mental health can be transmitted from generation to generation. They range from posttraumatic stress, the effects of unresolved trauma, and the burden of forgiveness expected by one's religion, to a spike in suicide rates. Yet these observed effects have not yet made their way into mainstream mental health literature. Slavery is hard to talk about, this social work practitioner explains. For blacks descended from enslaved people "the subject evokes feelings of shame and embarrassment associated with the degradations of slavery. For whites whose ancestry makes them complicit, there are feelings of guilt about a system that is incongruent with the democratic ideals on which this country was founded."

Gaertner, S. L., & Dovidio J. F. (1986). The aversive form of racism. In J. F. Dovidio & S. L. Gaertner (Eds.), *Prejudice, discrimination and racism: Theory and research.* Orlando, FL: Academic Press. Aversive racism, according to the authors, "describe[s] the type of racial attitude that ... characterizes many white Americans who possess strong egalitarian values." It explains the ambivalence liberals sometimes feel between what they would like to believe about minorities and the reservoir of "discomfort, uneasiness, and sometimes fear" they feel in their presence. The article summarizes the authors' experiments conducted since the 1970s. Excellent background material for instructors, or for students interested in psychology or education.

Kunstman, J. W., & Plant, E. A. (2008). Racing to help: Racial bias in high emergency helping situations. *Journal of Personality and Social Psychology, 95*(6), 1499. Anti-black bias inhibits whites' helping behavior when victims need help the most, this study finds. "Aversive racism theory contends that contemporary prejudice is the result of White people's ambivalent attitudes toward Black people. Although White people affirm cultural values like fairness and equity, they have also internalized negative attitudes about Black people that evoke aversion and lead them to discriminate under certain conditions." In an emergency, whites are less likely to concentrate on appearing unbiased, and their aversion to close contact with blacks becomes more apparent.

Lewis, T. (2016, March 10). There's a disturbing effect of discrimination that no one's talking about. *Business Insider.* http://www.businessinsider.com/new-stress-poll-from-the-american-psychological-association-2016-3. In the 2015 survey of "Stress in America" conducted by the American Psychological Association (APA), the focus was on the effects of discrimination on health. Blacks, Asians, Latin@s, and Native Americans reported that "race was the number-one type of discrimination they faced." Overall, more than 60 percent of the individuals surveyed reported experiencing day-to-day discrimination "such as being treated disrespectfully or being harassed or threatened." A link to the APA fact sheet http://www.apa.org/topics/health-disparities/fact-sheet-stress.aspx provides summaries of current research: African-Americans, Native Hawaiians, and Latin Americans suffer hypertension and diabetes due to the chronic stress of discrimination; the stress of racism can contribute to "adverse birth outcomes;" and "perceived discrimination" plays a role in mental health disorders of African-Americans and Asians.

PBS Frontline. (1995–2008). Secrets of the SAT. Interview: Claude Steele. http://www.pbs.org/wgbh/pages/frontline/shows/sats/interviews/steele.html Interview with Claude Steele, professor of social psychology at Stanford University and the pioneer researcher who showed how "stereotype threat" can help explain the gap between blacks and whites in IQ and SAT scores. Steele's research shows that negative societal perceptions about the abilities of a racial or gender group (women taking math tests also are affected by this phenomenon) create tension and distraction that can result in less than optimal performance. Steele discusses other explanations of the test gap as well in this wide-ranging, comfortable interview. Also on this website is a discussion of race-sensitive admissions to universities, and interviews with scholars arguing many sides of this issue, including Derek Bok, former president of Harvard, Henry Chauncey, first director of the Educational Testing Service, and John Yoo, former law clerk to conservative Supreme Court Justice Clarence Thomas. A superior resource for discussions of affirmative action.

Poussaint, A. F. (1999, August 26). They hate. They kill. Are they insane? *New York Times,* A21. A noted African-American psychiatrist discusses America's reluctance to label racism as a mental health problem, despite strong evidence that emotionally disturbed patients "project their own unacceptable behavior and fears onto ethnic minorities, scapegoating them for society's problems." Short op-ed piece that can raise interesting questions for discussion: If racism is confined to the mentally ill, does that absolve the rest of us from responsibility? Or are we all crazy?

Rooks, N. M. (2012, April 9). Trayvon Martin: The problem with the "Some of my best friends are black" defense. *Time*. Ideas. http://ideas.time.com/2012/04/09/ theproblem-with-the-my-best-friend-is-black-defense/. When a white suspect in the shooting of a black teenager defends himself in front of the media, it is useful to have a black friend. George Zimmerman's black friend, Joe Oliver, has told the world that their friendship is proof that Zimmerman's crime could not have been racially motivated. What's the problem with this defense? Studies show that having a black friend or family member does not make one immune to racism, says Rooks. Unconscious and even conscious racial bias by whites against blacks has been demonstrated in video game simulations and public opinion polls for years, and the presumption of black male criminality has been reinforced and exaggerated further by the media. A 2011 study showed that whites with black friends worry even more about local crime than whites without such relationships. "It would seem as if there are many more George Zimmermans in the world than we may be comfortable admitting," says Rooks. "Some murder. Some use racial epithets. Some do things even more subtle, like pass over black candidates for jobs or educational opportunities." See also a short *Time* op-ed, "Inside the racist mind," that takes this idea a bit further (http://ideas.time.com/2012/04/19/inside-the-racist-mind/) These pieces, along with a little background on the Trayvon Martin killing, will challenge non-black students' beliefs about themselves and encourage reflection about personal bias on the part of all students.

Staats, C., Capatosto, K., Wright, R. A., & Contractor, D. (2015). http://kirwan-institute.osu.edu/wp-content/uploads/2015/05/2015-kirwan-implicit-bias.pdf. In this extensive report, authors at The Kirwan Institute explain the latest cognitive science research "about our hidden biases that can shape our judgments and decision-making without our conscious awareness." Written to educate the general public, the report begins with "Mythbusters," a short section that refutes common objections: that implicit bias is not truly unconscious—people are simply hiding what they feel in an effort to be politically correct; that having friends of different races makes one unbiased; that people from targeted ethnicities cannot have biases against their own group, and that "having implicit bias makes me a bad person." Trends in the field are then discussed, followed by the research on implicit bias in the fields of criminal justice, health, employment, education, and housing. A final section on "debiasing" suggests that implicit biases can be gradually unlearned and replaced with "new mental associations."

Unzueta, M. M., & Lowery, B. S. (2008, November). Defining racism safely: The role of self-image maintenance on White Americans' conceptions of racism. *Journal of Experimental Social Psychology* 44(6), 1491–1497. This study suggests that whites find it easier to see racism in the prejudiced acts of individuals than in persistent racial inequalities rooted in societal institutions. The reason? Acknowledging institutional racism requires an awareness of white privilege, which is threatening to whites' self-image. Believing that people of color will only encounter racism if they come into contact with bigots is easier for well-meaning whites, since it does not remind them of their race privilege. This interesting study may shed some light on the resistance of white students to learning about white privilege and institutional racism and the guilt that they feel when it dawns on them.

# History of Racism

V Griffith, G. W. [1915] (1998). *Birth of a nation*. Video, 187 minutes. Distributor: Image Entertainment. Originally produced as a silent film in 1915, this classic, racist portrayal of the Civil War, Reconstruction, and the rise of the Ku Klux Klan is a chilling depiction of the blatant racism, both interpersonal and institutional, that plagues U.S. history. This is a frightening film, both for students of color and for white students who believe in the essential goodness of America.

V Williams, M., & Harris, M. (2007). *Banished*. Video, 84 minutes. California Newsreel. History textbooks rarely mention ethnic cleansing in the United States. Nevertheless, "thousands of African Americans were driven from their homes and communities by violent racist mobs in the late nineteenth and early twentieth centuries." Three of these towns—which remain all-white today—are featured in this film: Forsyth County, Georgia, Pierce City, Missouri, and Harrison, Arkansas. These interviews with local residents and the reflections of African-Americans who try to find their former property and the graves of their ancestors create the opportunity for a classroom discussion of reparations. The casual racism of some of the older residents is revealing to some students.

SV Wise, T. (2016, March 14). Racism as divide and conquer, from the 1600s to Donald Trump. http://www.timwise.org/2016/03/racism-as-divide-and-conquer-from-the-1600s-to-donald-trump-tim-wise-presentation-to-the-california-federation-of-teachers-san-francisco-march-2016/. In this 3 minute clip from a presentation to the California Federation of Teachers, Tim Wise explains how the idea of the "white race" was invented by wealthy colonial landowners to trick poor European immigrants into thinking that their interest and the interests of the powerful coincided. By giving poor whites power over blacks as slave patrollers (a direct antecedent, says Wise, of police departments today), the upper class created the notion that "you may not have much, but at least you are white." Both the system of enslavement and the union movement work against people of color, Wise says, but they also work against the economic interests of working class whites. The full 45 minute presentation can be found here: https://www.youtube.com/watch?v=477QqWOVBHw.

Blee, K. M. (1991). *Women of the Klan: Racism and gender in the 1920s*. Berkeley: University of California Press. A startling description of the involvement of a half million women in the "second wave" of Klan activity, organized, ironically, during the campaign for female suffrage. This incarnation of the Klan attracted housewives who were eager for participation in the larger society as well as "the better people": judges, physicians, social workers, political reformers and feminists. "Poison squads" and whispering campaigns against Catholics, Jews, and blacks were righteously defended as reasonable methods to battle vice and immorality and uphold traditional moral standards. Children were drawn into the "fun, secret club" with its costumes, parades, church suppers, and county fairs. It all collapsed rapidly after the public exposure of corruption, only to reappear in the 1930s and 1940s in a new guise, this time without any visible female participation. A unique and important addition to Women's Studies courses; good background reading for students researching modern hate groups.

Fredrickson, G. M. (2002). *Racism: A short history*. Princeton, NJ: Princeton University Press. Can racism be defined as the prejudice that any ethnic group might feel "naturally" towards another? Or should we use the word to describe something more organized, single-minded, and brutal? The origin of the belief in "permanent, unbridgeable" difference, plus the power to dominate and exclude groups that are considered inferior is explored in this short, accessible volume. Students may be surprised to learn that racism originated in religious rather than ethnic notions of difference, that the term "racism" was coined to describe the treatment of the Jews in Nazi Germany, and that early peoples were more apt to welcome strangers and assimilate them into the tribe than shun them as "other."

Gates, H. L. Jr., & Stauffer, J. (2009, January 18). A pragmatic precedent. *New York Times*, Op-Ed. What would Abraham Lincoln have thought of President Barack Obama? Though he opposed slavery and ultimately ended it, Lincoln was a "man of his times" when it came to his thinking about racial equality. He made frequent demeaning references to blacks in his speeches, and did not consider any black his intellectual equal until he met Frederick Douglass. "The truth is that successful blacks were almost total strangers to Lincoln, born as he was on the frontier and raised in a state settled by white Southerners. From this perspective, then, Lincoln most probably would have been shocked, perhaps horrified, by Mr. Obama's election. Like the majority of Northern whites, Lincoln had a vision of America that was largely a white one."

Gould, S. J. (1981). *The mismeasure of man*. New York: W. W. Norton. Stephen Jay Gould's classic explains, in extremely clear language, the rise of scientific racism, from craniology to intelligence testing. Gould says, "Appeals to reason or to the nature of the universe have been used throughout history to enshrine existing hierarchies as proper and inevitable. The hierarchies rarely endure for more than a few generations, but the arguments, refurbished for the next round of social institutions, cycle endlessly." Helpful introduction to the subject of racism for scientifically minded students who believe, naively, that science has always been "a search for truth."

Halford, J. M. (1999, April). A different mirror: A conversation with Ronald Takaki. *Educational Leadership, 56*(7), 8–13. In this friendly, accessible interview of the late

Asian American scholar Ronald Takaki, some surprising facts turn up: "How many Americans really know why slavery was established in what would become the United States?" Takaki asks. "Many people have this notion that slavery just began when the first 20 Africans were landed by a Dutch slave ship in Jamestown Virginia, in 1619. But actually, those first 20 Africans were not slaves. They became indentured servants." In fact, he adds, slavery was not seen as profitable until fifty-five years later when white indentured servants, whose right to bear arms had been granted by the English Crown, took up an armed rebellion against their masters. At this point, planters decided to shift to African labor, since Africans had no rights they were required to respect.

La Sorte, M. (1996). Italians and Americans. In G. Ibieta & M. Orvell (Eds.), *Inventing America: Readings in identity and culture*. New York: St. Martin's Press. "An Italian was not an Italian. He was a wop, dago, duke, gin, tally, ghini, macaroni or spaghetti or spaghetti bender. He was also Hey Boy or Hey Youse, or he was given a generic name: Joe, Pete, Tony, Caro, Dino, Gumba. ... A day did not pass that the Italian was not vilified in one manner or another. The Americans laughed at his speech, his clothes, his customs, and where and how he lived. Such treatment caused Italians to be wary of all Americans." Helps students understand that ridicule and put-downs were suffered by many ethnic groups as they struggled to make their way in America and can lead to deeper discussions of why people who have been targets of prejudice sometimes turn around and target others.

Rattansi, A. (2007). *Racism: A very short introduction*. New York: Oxford University Press. This book by British sociologist Ali Rattansi illustrates the difficulty of using simple definitions or examples to define racism today. In its original form, racism was a set of beliefs about inherent physical, mental, and moral deficiencies in "non-white" populations. Such claims of immutable characteristics are relatively rare today, yet beliefs and "proofs" of cultural and personal deficiency have been added to explain and sometimes defend the original hierarchy of differences. Rattansi introduces readers to various forms of intolerance in ancient societies, the origin of the term "racism" (coined in the 1930s as a response to Hitler's ethnic cleansing of the Jews), the ways scientific racism justified colonial expansion and the slave trade, the continuing racial disparities in the United Sates today and the growing support for racist movements. My students found this book challenging because of the sheer number of ideas and the lack of certain answers. However, I found it an excellent model for discussion of complex issues. Its scope, clarity and brevity provided a way into key concepts and the historical background that so many of our students lack.

Snowden, F. M. Jr. (1983). *Before color prejudice: The ancient view of blacks*. Cambridge, MA: Harvard University Press. Written accounts of contacts between African blacks and Mediterranean whites from the time of the Egyptian pharaohs clearly show that racism as we know it today was absent from the ancient world. A good antidote for students who despair that racism will always be with us because it is "human nature." Assign it to a multiethnic group of students to read and report orally to the class.

Wise, T. (2015, June 20). Heritage of hate: Dylann Roof, white supremacy and the truth about the Confederacy. http://www.timwise.org/2015/06/heritage-of-hate-dylann-roof-white-supremacy-and-the-truth-about-the-confederacy/. Is the Confederate flag a racist symbol? Many whites in the South say no. Even though the flag is displayed by perpetrators of hate crimes such as Dylann Roof, the 21 year old South Carolina man who killed nine African-American members of the Emanuel African Methodist Episcopal Church https://mic.com/articles/121060/dylann-roof-s-terrifying-manifesto-has-been-discovered-here-are-the-shocking-excerpts#.3ThrBwofv, the "Stars and Bars" more often depicts the "heritage" of the South, they say, rather than hate. Yet it is clear from historical writings that this heritage had racism at its core. The Confederacy was founded on "the great truth that the negro is not equal to the white man, that slavery, subordination to the superior race, is his natural and moral condition." The "immediate cause and the late rupture and present revolution" of the Southern states against the North, proclaimed the Vice President of the Confederacy, was "our peculiar institution"—African slavery. Many quotes throughout this short essay support this notion. Tim Wise, a white Southerner himself, concludes that the Confederate culture of white supremacy needs to be destroyed—not by retribution or hate, but "by our resistance to its logic, our opposition to its policies, and our insistence that we can and must do better."

# Institutional Racism

## Government

V Lee, S. (2006). *When the levees broke: A requiem in four acts.* Video, 256 minutes on four disks. Distributor: HBO Home Video. A thorough treatment of the 2005 Hurricane Katrina disaster, when thousands of people of color were flooded out of their homes in New Orleans' Lower Ninth Ward. Interviews with survivors, some of them resigned, some irate, some energized and ready to rebuild, show emotions and points of view rarely captured by the news media. The callousness and incompetence of national and local authorities and how those attitudes and actions were interpreted by local people provide much insight into the enduring poverty of African-Americans. Beautiful clips of a jazz funeral and interviews with trumpeter and composer Wynton Marsalis give depth and meaning to the disaster.

Advancement Project. Expanding democracy for all people. (2013, September 18). http://www.advancementproject.org/blog/entry/expanding-democracy-for-all-people "Most Americans would probably be surprised to learn that there is no provision of the Constitution or federal law that explicitly and affirmatively guarantees all citizens the right to vote ... In fact, the U.S. is one of only 11 of the 119 democratic countries in the world that do not explicitly provide the right to vote in their Constitutions. What's more, the U.S. Supreme Court decision in *Shelby County vs. Holder*, which acknowledged the existence of persistent discrimination in voting, opened the door for new barriers to voting to emerge in states across the country." North Carolina is a case in point. Dozens of changes to existing laws have made it harder for youth, working class people, and people of color to register to vote and to access polling booths.

Fox, H. (2015). *Fractured: Race relations in "post-racial" American life*. New York: Peter Lang. Chapter 6: Racism as a complex system. The shooting of the African-American teenager Michael Brown by a white police officer in Ferguson, Missouri in August, 2014 looked to many like a classic example of racism in law enforcement. But this tragic case was more than that. Ferguson police department practices combined with both interpersonal and institutional racism in government, media, education, and employment to create a toxic complex system. By studying the Michael Brown case in detail, students can clearly see how institutional racism works, and how it is maintained by both blatant racism and implicit bias by well-meaning people.

Katznelson, I. (2005). *When affirmative action was white: An untold history of racial inequality in twentieth century America*. New York: W. W. Norton. Students are surprised and troubled to discover that affirmative action began long before the issue of race-based admissions was raised on college campuses. New Deal and Fair Deal programs of the 1930s and 1940s were not only deeply discriminatory against people of color, but gave whites the economic and educational boost that propelled large numbers of them into the middle class. Whites were provided with low-interest home loans, free college educations, and a comprehensive social safety net that was denied to farm laborers and house cleaners—the only jobs available to many Latin@s and blacks in that era. Helps students see how the effects of discriminatory practices are passed down through the generations and why individual effort isn't enough for most hardworking people to overcome these powerful forces.

# Criminal Justice

**V** Herrman, C., & Whalen, K. (2008). *Tulia, Texas*. Video, 58 minutes. Distributor: California Newsreel. When forty-six people were indicted for selling cocaine in the small town of Tulia, Texas, residents of "black town," the neighborhood on the proverbial "other side of the tracks," were shocked to discover that their community had been all but emptied of its young adults. Those who decided to fight the charges in court were given unusually severe sentences: sixty, even ninety-nine years for selling small amounts of powered cocaine to a white undercover agent. When big city lawyers got involved, they discovered that the agent himself was guilty of multiple crimes in other towns and perjured himself repeatedly during his own trial. This story reveals the racism that permeates the criminal justice system, not only in small Texas towns, but in localities all across the United Sates.

**V** Smith, A. D. (2000). *Twilight Los Angeles*. Video, 76 minutes. Distributor: PBS Home Video. Anna Deavere Smith transforms herself into the people she interviewed after the 1992 Los Angeles riots—some of the worst in U.S. history—that erupted after Rodney King was brutally beaten by white police. Her mesmerizing performance (she does great accents and facial expressions) is interspersed with historical footage: videotapes of King's beating; the shooting, caught on tape, of a black teenager by a Korean store owner for allegedly stealing a bottle of orange juice; the fires consuming neighborhoods of color; the looting of stores by people of all races. The beauty of this piece is that it tells the same story from a variety of points of view; an activist, a gang member, a Korean store owner, a juror, a bystander, and many others are given their say without analysis or judgment. Brings up issues of police practices, legitimate and illegitimate protest, relations between groups of color, and racism in the justice system.

Advancement Project. (2009). Ending the schoolhouse to jailhouse track. http://www.advancementproject.org/issues/stopping-the-school-to-prison-pipeline/pages/stories-and-victories "Through a combination of harsh discipline policies and increased security, our schools are funneling many students into a 'schoolhouse-to-jailhouse track.' Suspensions, expulsions, and in-school arrests have increasingly made schools into gateways to the criminal justice system. The harsh reality is that the burden of this criminalization falls disproportionately on students of color. Students of color are suspended and arrested at far higher rates than their white classmates." The Advancement Project analyzes why this is happening and what should be done about it. Advancement Project. Telling it like it is: Youth speak out on the school-to prison pipeline. Power U Center for Social Change. http://www.advancementproject.org/resources/entry/telling-it-like-it-is-youth-speak-out-on-the-school-to-prison-pipeline An extremely informative, short, graphic "novel" about the disenfranchisement of urban youth of color from the point of view of high school students themselves. Features three characters who talk about their experiences with their school's zero tolerance policy, the targeting of youth of color for suspension, expulsion, and arrest, the economic and social costs of school surveillance, and how youth activists are working creatively for change. Text boxes give additional facts and figures. An inviting, in-depth look at the interaction between schools and the criminal justice system that draws students in, and, as a bonus, provides an excellent model of an argument that considers sensible objections and gives informed, straightforward replies. For more on this topic see Fact sheet: How bad is the school to prison pipeline? http://www.pbs.org/wnet/tavissmiley/tsr/education-under-arrest/school-to-prison-pipeline-fact-sheet/

Alexander, M. (2012, September 3). The myth of desegregation. Time. Ideas. http://ideas.time.com/2012/02/03/the-myth-of-desgregation/ In this opinion piece, author Michelle Alexander questions the conclusion of a study by a conservative think tank: that black segregation has declined by 80% since the Civil Rights era. Although it cannot be denied that many blacks were able to leave inner city communities where they had been confined before residential segregation officially came to an end, Alexander asks us to consider the people who were not counted in the study: prisoners. "In a sense, mass incarceration has emerged as a far more extreme form of physical and residential segregation than Jim Crow segregation. Rather than merely shunting people of color to the other side of town, people are locked in literal cages—en masse. Bars and walls keep hundreds of thousands away from mainstream society—a form of apartheid unlike the world has even seen." Since most prisoners come from neighborhoods that are still extremely segregated, and since many of these people were imprisoned by a racially biased criminal justice system, we cannot say that the era of segregation is over.

Alexander, M. (2010). *The new Jim Crow: Mass incarceration in the Age of Colorblindness.* New York: The New Press. This book has quickly become a classic in sociology and urban studies courses that deal with the criminal justice system. Its alarming thesis, that, even as Barack Obama's election heralded a new, positive chapter in race relations, the majority of black men either languish behind bars or are labeled felons for life, has made both scholars and students rethink their idea of our nation's progress toward equality. We used to think overt disenfranchisement of people of color was a thing of the past. But with this new analysis, we are forced to consider that all the discriminatory laws and practices that were abolished with the end of Jim Crow segregation have again become perfectly legal when applied to prisoners and, in many states, ex-convicts. Racial exclusion from education, housing, social services, voting, and jury service are all practiced with impunity. Yet because felons are disproportionately people of color, and because they became felons through blatantly discriminatory criminal justice practices, the system effectively reinstitutes the racial caste system, all under the guise of a color-blind or "postracial" America. An important analysis, extremely well argued.

Cahill, T. (2009). *A saint on death row: The story of Dominique Green.* New York: Nan A. Talese. A moving account of how race, poverty, and a biased criminal justice system affected one man and how his case inspired grassroots political activism, including a United Nations resolution condemning the death penalty. Green's intense spirituality caused Archbishop Desmond Tutu to remark, "Who could have expected that Texas Death Row would be made into an avenue of divine grace?" Students can search the website of the Death Penalty Information Center at www.deathpenaltyinfo.org and Amnesty International USA www.amnestyuse.org for other reports and analyses of race-based criminal justice issues.

Chiles, N. (2014, August 8). Study: the more whites are told criminal justice system unfair to blacks the more they like it. *Atlanta Black Star.* http://atlantablackstar.com/2014/08/08/study-whites-told-criminal-justice-system-unfair-blacks-like/ The headline says it all. "The study by researchers from Stanford University, published in Psychological Science, found that even when whites believe current sentencing laws are too harsh, they're less likely to support changing them if they're reminded that the current U.S. prison population is disproportionately Black." This piece describes two "clever experiments" where two groups of California commuters watched different versions of a video, one where the number of black inmates shown was proportional to the actual number of blacks in the prison population

(25%), while the other showed the number of blacks imprisoned under the three-strikes law (45%), which at the time was under review. After agreeing that the "three strikes" law was too harsh, commuters were asked to sign a petition to change the law. But if they had seen the video with the larger number of black inmates they were less likely to sign than those who had seen the version with the smaller number of blacks.

Coates, T. (2015, October). The black family in the age of mass incarceration. *The Atlantic*. http://www.theatlantic.com/magazine/archive/2015/10/the-black-family-in-the-age-of-mass-incarceration/403246/ In this brilliant article, Ta-Nehesi Coates explains how Daniel Patrick Moynihan's 1965 report, "The Negro Family," helped create the largest incarcerated population in the world—even though that was not its intent. Beginning with Moynihan's own tragic childhood, his fear of looking like a "sissy" in his adolescence, and his rise to stardom in the Washington elite, Coates traces the origins of Moynahan's influential report to Congress. "[Moynihan] was, it might be said, a conservative radical who disdained service programs such as Head Start and traditional welfare programs such as Aid to Families With Dependent Children, and instead imagined a broad national program that subsidized families through jobs programs for men and a guaranteed minimum income for every family." But his recommendations for ending poverty were ignored, and the press publicized his report as "an expose of 'the breakdown of the Negro family' with its high rates of 'broken homes, illegitimacy, and female-oriented homes.'" Mass incarceration of blacks began to skyrocket shortly thereafter. As Coates says, "America had an app for that."

Infographic: Racism in the criminal justice system. http://www.arrestrecords.com/infographic-racism-in-the-criminal-justice-system/ This searchable site contains arrest records for African-Americans state by state, showing that blacks in the United States face overwhelming prejudice within the criminal justice system. Some conclusions: Blacks comprise 12.6% of the population but 37.1% of inmates. Blacks are overrepresented on death row. Blacks who killed whites were sentenced to death 22 times more frequently than blacks who killed blacks, and 7 times more frequently than whites who killed blacks. Black children also conform to this general racial trend. Students who are looking for statistics for research projects and reports will find much information here.

Hudson, R. (2015, May 28). I'm a black ex-cop and this is the real truth about race and policing. http://www.vox.com/2015/5/28/8661977/race-police-officer "On any given day, in any police department in the nation, 15 percent of officers will do the right thing no matter what is happening, fifteen percent of officers will abuse their authority at every opportunity, and the remaining 70 percent could go either way depending on whom they are working with." This from an ex-police officer who served in the St Louis Police Department for five years. Students will find it sobering that 70% of officers are estimated to be "highly susceptible to the culture in a given department," and who, in the absence of any real effort to challenge department culture, become part of the problem. The shocking personal stories the author tells make this piece very convincing.

King, A. E. O. (1997, September). Understanding violence among young African American males: An Afrocentric perspective. *Journal of Black Studies, 28*(1), 79–96. "Contrary to traditional European and European American social science theory, the violent behaviors exhibited by many young African American males were practically nonexistent in Africa prior to the Atlantic slave trade. ... If this is true, then how might we explain the intraethnic and intragender violence that has been so much a part of the African American male experience?" Given the violence of American slavery, the lynchings and castrations after slavery ended that were occasion for "massive celebrations" by whites, and the police brutality and capital punishment that disproportionately affect black males today, black violence and self-destructive behavior seem almost inevitable. A must-read for any student who wants to understand why many young black men are still angry.

New York Civil Liberties Union. (2007, March). http://www.nyclu.org/publications/report-criminalizing-classroom-2007 Report: Criminalizing the classroom. "Since the NYPD took control of school safety in 1998, the number of police personnel in schools and the extent of their activity have skyrocketed. At the start of the 2005–2006 school year, the city employed a total of 4,625 School Safety Agents (SSAs) and at least 200 armed police officers assigned exclusively to schools. NYCLU's report thoroughly documents and abuses and offers suggestions for reform.

Washington Post (2010, September). Top-secret America. http://projects.washingtonpost.com/top-secret-america/ "The top-secret world the government created in response to the terrorist attacks of Sept. 11, 2001, has become so large, so unwieldy and so secretive that no one knows how much money it costs, how many people it employs, how many programs exist within it or exactly how many agencies do the same work." A two-year investigation by the Washington Post uncovers a tangled network of national security and intelligence agencies, many targeting people from the Middle East and Central Asia. Though the program's ostensible mission is "defeating transnational violent extremists" it is unclear, according to the report, that Americans are safer because of it. Students can explore the locations of the various programs and the connections between agencies in a searchable database, and read articles on the findings of the report. Although much of the information focuses on the scope and complexity of the program, its expense, its secrecy, and the sheer volume of reports generated for no apparent purpose, one can easily see why many Arab Americans and Muslims, whether new immigrants or U.S. citizens, are worried about being targeted by law enforcement.

# Health

V California Newsreel. (2008). *Unnatural causes: Is inequality making us sick? Episode 1: In sickness and in wealth.* Video, 56 minutes. This surprising documentary shows how health and longevity are tied directly to socioeconomic class. People with the most access to power, resources, and opportunity live longer, healthier lives than the middle class, who in turn have better health than the poor. This is not simply about access to health care. People with higher incomes than the level below them experience more control over their jobs and living environments, more respect, more access to healthy foods and enjoyable exercise, and more resources to help them handle life's difficulties. As income drops, stress increases, resulting in the excess production of stress hormones which raise blood pressure and increase vulnerability to illness. Daily encounters with racism amplify this burden on the body. The website for the series provides transcripts, a discussion guide, podcasts, and opportunities for action. http:// www.unnaturalcauses.org/

V California Newsreel. (2008). *Unnatural causes: Is inequality making us sick? Episode 2: When the bough breaks*. Video, 29 minutes. Why do African-American infants die at twice the rate as those born into white families? Even more perplexing, why do well-educated black women have worse birth outcomes than white women who haven't finished high school? Two neonatal physicians examine the cumulative effects of racism on pregnancy and birth.

V California Newsreel. (2008). *Unnatural Causes: Is inequality making us sick? Episode 3: Becoming American*. Video, 29 minutes. Latin@ immigrants arrive in the United Sates with a "health advantage," despite their low education and income levels. But the longer they stay, the more their health and longevity deteriorate. Social exclusion and loss of the "protective shield" of family, tradition, and community take a measurable physical toll.

V California Newsreel. (2008). *Unnatural causes: Is inequality making us sick? Episode 4: Bad sugar*. Video, 29 minutes. As Native Americans lost land and water resources, first to white settlers, then to the U.S. government, and most recently, to white-owned agro-businesses, diabetes rates have soared. Forced dependence on government handouts caused changes in diet, with white flour, lard, and large quantities of sugar replacing natural foods. Poverty, racism, disempowerment, and loss of language and culture magnify the stress on the body. Reclaiming some of what was lost is an important step toward better health.

American Public Health Association (APHA) (2015, July 21). The impact of racism on the health and well-being of the nation. https://www.apha.org/events-and-meetings/webinars/racism-and-health Four webinars are available on this site, one how to name and address racism, the second about preventing violence, the third on disparities in access to quality care, and the fourth on the effect of racism on high school dropout rates. Slides shown in these comprehensive academic presentations are available for download.

Benson, L., Yuen, L. (2014, January 30). 'Structural racism' blamed for some of state's severe health disparities. http://www.mprnews.org/story/2014/01/29/

structural-racism-blamed-for-states-health-disparities This short, informative piece helps explain why African-American babies in Minnesota are twice as likely as white babies to die in their first year, a disparity that is "the worst in the country." While overall, Minnesota's health system is quite good, the report says, it is failing many people of color who live in low-income neighborhoods because of "structural racism and white privilege." Lack of access to high quality care, insufficient cultural awareness on the part of medical personnel, a "bootstraps mentality" at neighborhood clinics, and the lack of political will for structural change all contribute to the poor health outcomes. The full report can be accessed from this site.

Eligon, J. (2016, January 21). A question of environmental racism in Flint. http://www.nytimes.com/2016/01/22/us/a-question-of-environmental-racism-in-flint.html?_r=0 An excellent introduction to environmental racism through the water crisis in the city of Flint, Michigan. Low income residents, mostly black and brown, were exposed to lead-contaminated water while city officials stalled, denied, and ignored the problem. Although Governor Rick Snyder would not discuss the role race may have played in the crisis, many residents and activists wondered, "If Flint were rich and mostly white, would the city have responded more quickly and aggressively to complaints about its polluted water?"

Skloot, R. (2010). *The immortal life of Henrietta Lacks*. New York: Crown Publishers. A remarkable look at the life and surviving family of the poor Southern tobacco farmer whose cervical cells (HeLa cells) have helped scientists all over the world fight polio, understand the workings of cancer, and advance our knowledge of viruses, in vitro fertilization, cloning, and genetic screening, not to mention making billions of dollars for the biotechnology industry. Yet because Ms. Lacks was black and poor, her cancer cells were taken without her knowledge or consent, and neither she nor her family was ever thanked or compensated. Science writer Rebecca Skloot tells this story in such agonizing emotional detail and with such homage to the family that readers are both entranced and horrified. What does this mean for medical science, scientific discovery, and our country's history of race and class? What caused otherwise good people to ignore such obvious ethical problems in their research? Have these practices been eliminated?

Washington, H. A. (2006). *Medical apartheid: The dark history of medical experimentation on Black Americans from colonial times to the present*. New York: Doubleday. How African-Americans' mistrust of the medical establishment has developed from the plantation days when remedies were both tried out on slaves and withheld from them because of their supposed biological differences, to the Tuskegee experiment from the 1930s to 1972, where scientists coldly studied the progression of syphilis in black men without offering them either treatment or cure; to the experiments on black children without their parents' fully informed consent; which, shockingly, continued into the late 1990s. This carefully documented account explains the reluctance of many blacks today to participate in research that would benefit them, and their resistance, at times, to following "doctor's orders."

Williams, D. R., & Mohammed, S. A. (2009, February). Discrimination and racial disparities in health: Evidence and needed research. *Journal of Behavioral Medicine* 32(1), 20–47. This review of the literature clearly shows the relationship between racism and health outcomes. While restricted access to economic advancement and quality medical care indirectly affects health, the trauma of stigma and "perceived discrimination" also takes its toll. The authors call for more research, and the need to "measure [racism] comprehensively and accurately, assessing its stressful dimensions, and identifying the mechanisms that link discrimination to health." Students who are headed for the health professions will be interested to know that such research exists and is finally being taken seriously by mainstream scientists.

## Urban Neighborhoods

**V** Broadman, R. (2005). *Brownsville, Black and White*. Video, 80 minutes. Berkeley Media. A fascinating, well-documented case study of the Brownsville section of Brooklyn where impoverished Jews and blacks lived, worked, and played together in the 1940s, and how the trust and camaraderie broke down in the 1960s with the advent of a conceptually flawed policy of "urban renewal." While this film is about how policy decisions regarding housing and infrastructure destroyed a neighborhood, it also addresses ethnic identity movements, grassroots advocacy for education, and community control. The interviews, old footage, and narration of the history of the period help students analyze race relations and institutional racism in depth.

**V** California Newsreel. (2003). *Race, the power of an illusion. Episode 3: The house we live in*. Video, 56 minutes. "Today, the net worth of the average Black family is about 1/8 that of the average white family. Much of that difference derives from the value of the family's residence." This film explains how these differences arose, from the construction of the "white" category that reserved certain advantages for groups who successfully argued they should be considered white, to the programs and practices that built up whites' net worth. The PBS website provides supplementary readings about the topic, as well as hundreds of other resources on race in general at http://www.pbs.org/race/000_General/000_00-Home.htm

**V** California Newsreel. (2008). *Unnatural causes: Is inequality making us sick? Episode 5: Place matters*. Video, 29 minutes. During World War II, towns like Richmond, California employed large numbers of people of all ethnicities in the defense industry. When the war ended, so did the jobs, and people of color were left in impoverished, polluted, and increasingly violent neighborhoods as whites moved to the suburbs, taking advantage of the federally funded "whites only" home loans. Recent Asian immigrants to these former boom towns suffer the same effects of poverty and ill-health—asthma, diabetes, and low life expectancy—as do the descendents of the people left behind.

**V** Falconer, D. (2010). *Deforce*. Video, 86 minutes. Detroit Documentary Productions. http://www.deforcemovie.com/. This film shows the connection between historical events and current racial and economic realities, between the clandestine world of city politics and the lives of the most impoverished. Detroit's past glory as the automobile capital of the world, its history of racism, its rebellions against police brutality, its gross mismanagement, its abandoned neighborhoods and drastically shrinking population, and above all, the politics that have both kept the city together and torn it apart are featured in this fast-paced look at a failing American city. The unique focus on race and racism in this film is essential for students to understand urban decay, failing schools, incarceration rates, and joblessness. I find it particularly useful for students who come from either the impoverished urban core or the wealthy suburbs created by the "white flight" of the 1960s and 1970s. When their own city looks like a war zone yet no one explains how it got that way, even the most progressive students are bound to question the character and will of the people who continue to live there. This film introduces them to both the hidden history of such a city and the complexities of enduring poverty.

V Palast, G. (2007). *Big Easy to Big Empty: The untold story of the drowning of New Orleans*. Video, 30 minutes. Investigative reporter Greg Palast explains how "reckless negligence" caused fifteen hundred deaths in New Orleans' Lower Ninth Ward when poorly constructed levees were unable to hold back the rising waters of Lake Pontchartrain in the aftermath of Hurricane Katrina in 2005. In one of the most memorable scenes, Palast helps a woman break into her own apartment, which, despite the lack of hurricane damage, had been boarded up and slated for demolition to make way for lucrative business interests. Students will either be as outraged as Palast or skeptical that the U.S. government could allow such things to happen. Either way, discussion will be lively.

Coates, T. (2014, June). The case for reparations. *The Atlantic*. http://www.theatlantic.com/magazine/archive/2014/06/the-case-for-reparations/361631/ In this immaculately detailed piece, African-American journalist Ta-Nehesi Coates traces generations of theft of land, possessions, educational opportunities, homes, and neighborhoods from black Americans, by means ranging "from legal chancery to terrorism." "Some of the land taken from black families has become a country club in Virginia ... oil fields in Mississippi, and a baseball spring training facility in Florida." The tens of millions of dollars collectively lost by the black community should be cause for reparations, Coates argues. An interactive map shows how redlining created impoverished black neighborhoods in Chicago and other inner cities. Today, the wealth gap remains, even between upper-middle class income blacks and their white counterparts. "The implications are chilling," Coates writes. "As a rule, poor black people do not work their way out of the ghetto—and those who do often face the horror of watching their children and grandchildren tumble back."

National Commission on Fair Housing. (2008, December). *The future of fair housing*. http://www.nationalfairhousing.org/Portals/33/reports/future_of_fair_Housing.pdf A six-month, cross-country investigation reveals that "despite strong legislation, past and ongoing discriminatory practices in the nation's housing and lending markets continue to produce extreme levels of residential segregation that result in significant disparities between minority and nonminority households, such as access to good jobs, quality education, homeownership and asset accumulation. This fact has led many to question whether the federal government is doing all it can to combat housing discrimination. Worse, some fear that rather than combating segregation, HUD and other federal agencies are promoting it through the administration of their housing, lending, and tax programs."

## Education

V Independent Lens/PBS (2011). *Precious Knowledge.* Video, 75 minutes. Producer: Dos Vatos Films. This film portrays the 2010 banning of a high school Mexican American studies program by the Tucson Unified School District, despite the fact that Latin@ students who took these courses succeeded in school and in life far beyond anyone's expectations. The film raises questions about whose knowledge should be taught, who benefits and who suffers from a "whitewashed" curriculum, and how white privilege works in politics and education. I introduce this film by providing some background on the Mexican American civil rights movement and some of the issues faced by low income Latin@ students whose neighborhoods and lives are compellingly shown in the film. In class discussion, my students were surprisingly divided on the question of how the suppressed histories of U.S. minorities should be taught. Should these stories and events be integrated more fully into the general history curriculum, or should they be aimed specifically toward minority students? Should cultural terms from languages other than English be used in a social studies program? Should politicians, educators, or the people themselves control the curriculum? What are the benefits and drawbacks of classes that teach U.S. history from the point of view of the oppressed? For an update on the controversy, see http://www.azcentral.com/news/politics/articles/20130311 arizona-ethnic-studies-ban-ruling.html

Adams, D. W. (1996). Fundamental considerations: The deep meaning of Native American schooling, 1880–1900. In T. Beauboeuf-Lafontant and D. S. Augustine (Eds.), *Facing racism in education,* second edition. Harvard Educational Review. Reprint Series (28). Cambridge, MA. Devastating exposé of the racism, greed, and arrogance that drove the campaign to establish Native American boarding schools. Protestant ideology, the "civilization-savage paradigm," and the desire to dispossess the Native Americans of their few remaining lands destroyed cultures, languages, religion, livelihoods, and self-worth. A student who did well on an examination question ("Tell me something of the white people") wrote: "The Caucasian is away ahead of all of the other races—he thought more than any other race, he thought that somebody must made the earth, and if the white people did not find that out, nobody would never know it—it is God who made the world."

Berlak, H. (2001, Summer). Race and the achievement gap. *Rethinking Schools Online*, 15(4). http://www.rethinkingschools.org/archive/15_04/ Race154.shtml. Research suggests "three related explanations for the race gap in academic achievement and in test scores. First, are students' perceptions of the opportunities in the wider society and the realities of 'making it.' Second, are the educational opportunities available in the educational system itself—within school districts, schools, and each classroom. Third, are the cumulative psychic and emotional effects of living in a social world saturated with racist ideology, and where racist practices and structures are pervasive and often go unnamed."

Brownstein, R. (2015, September 04). Report highlights racial disparities in school discipline—once again. *Southern Poverty Law Center*. https://www.splcenter.org/ news/2015/09/04/report-highlights-racial-disparities-school-discipline-%E2%80%93- once-again A University of Pennsylvania study reveals that in 13 Southern states, black children are suspended and expelled up to five times more frequently than white students, often for minor infractions of school rules such as being in the hall without a pass, tossing a penny on a school bus, or violating the school's dress code by wearing an untucked shirt. For these "crimes," say the authors, some black students are being violently arrested and jailed in ways that "shock the conscience." Links to the study and other helpful materials are found throughout the article.

Fordham, S. (1996). Racelessness as a factor in black students' school success: Pragmatic strategy of pyrrhic victory? In T. Beauboeuf-Lafontant and D. S. Augustine (Eds.), *Facing racism in education*, second edition. Harvard Educational Review. Reprint Series (28). Cambridge, MA. Explores the attempts of some high-achieving black students to ignore or downplay their race and to cut themselves off from the black community, explicitly disparaging its culture, language, and values in order to resist peer pressure to do poorly in school. This influential study by an African-American ethnographer helps explain the complex forces behind the achievement gap between blacks and whites. Helps future teachers understand why blacks have created and maintained an oppositional culture that undermines their success in the larger society, and the personal and emotional price that high achievers often pay for rejecting that culture.

Ochoa, G. L. (2008, Summer). Pump up the blowouts. Rethinking Schools online, 22(4). http://www.rethinkingschools.org/archive/22_04/pump224. shtml. "[I]n March 1968, over 10,000 East Los Angeles students walked out of their schools protesting a system of educational inequality. Carrying Chicano Power and Viva La Raza placards, students had a list of nearly 40 grievances and demands for the Los Angeles school board. At a time when about half of Mexican American students did not complete high school, students shifted the debate from theories blaming students and families to one that centered on institutional injustices. They demanded bilingual and bicultural education, more Mexican American teachers, relevant curriculum, accurate textbooks, and the end of curriculum tracking and prejudiced teachers who steered Mexican American students into vocational classes." The author argues that teaching about such nonviolent protests, most of which are ignored or trivialized in standard curricula, is empowering to students.

West, C. (1997). Diverse new world. In S. Maasik & J. Solomon (Eds.), *Signs of life in the USA*, second edition. Boston: Bedford Books. Short, pithy article by Cornel West on how African-Americans (and others) can take charge of their own education by supplementing works of Western civilization with those that affirm black humanity. Use for classes with students of color and white allies who have already been introduced to the idea of ethnocentrism. This article is also superb for faculty discussions of how (or whether) to revise Eurocentric curricula. "Don't just read Voltaire's great essays on the light of reason," advises West, "—read 'The Peoples of America,' in which he compares indigenous peoples and Africans to dogs and cattle. Don't read just Kant's 'Critique of Pure Reason,' read the moments in 'The Observations of the Sublime,' in which he refers to Negroes as inherently stupid. It's not a trashing of Kant. It's a situating of Kant within eighteenth-century Germany, at a time of rampant xenophobia, along with tremendous breakthroughs in other spheres."

U.S. Department of Education. (2014, January 8). U.S. Departments of Education and Justice release school discipline guidance package to enhance school climate and improve school discipline policies/practices. http://www.ed.gov/news/press-releases/us-departments-education-and-justice-release-school-discipline-guidance-package-enhance-school-climate-and-improve-school-discipline-policiespractices Students of education are often more interested in solutions than a continual stream of bad news about the difficulties of being a teacher. This helpful report provides resources for creating safe and positive school climates, which are essential for boosting student academic success and closing achievement gaps. A "Dear Colleague" letter describes how schools can meet their legal obligations under federal law while avoiding discrimination by race, color, or national origin. Other components of this package include principles for best practices, and guides to resources and state regulations regarding discipline.

Zinn Education Project. www.zinnedproject.org/node/7. Howard Zinn, a progressive historian, provides resources for teachers that will "introduce students to a more accurate, complex, and engaging understanding of United States history than is found in traditional textbooks and curricula. ... 'A People's History of the United States' emphasizes the role of working people, women, people of color, and organized social movements in shaping history. Students learn that history is made not by a few heroic individuals, but instead by people's choices and actions and therefore students' own choices and actions also matter." Zinn writes in strong, positive language that students connect with immediately. The website also provides a link to excellent books for further reading, lesson plans and activities for teachers, and a video with the engaging title, You Can't Be Neutral on a Moving Train (Ellis & Mueller, 2004), that details Zinn's life work.

# Language

V Booth, M., Young, K. (2014). *Pidgin: The voice of Hawaii.* http://pidginthevoiceof-hawaii.com/ Prospective teachers of Language Arts will be interested in this lovely film that chronicles Hawaiian Pidgin, "the language of Hawai'i's working people in its rise from plantation jargon to a source of island identity, pride, and controversy." Part English, part Hawaiian, with other languages mixed in, Pidgin is "the language of the heart." But Pidgin speakers face stigma and discrimination. Why is the language ridiculed and its speakers shamed and ostracized? Is Pidgin a "real language" or only a faulty version of English? Are culture, heart, and soul as important as "getting up in the world"? Are there ways to honor Pidgin while teaching its more "respectable" cousin? Lots of questions for a lively discussion here. Interested students can also delve into the ways Pidgin is used by Hawai'ian novelists. See this *Atlantic* profile of writer Lois-Ann Yamanaka for ideas. http://www.theatlantic.com/magazine/archive/1999/02/this-hawaii-is-not-for-tourists/377458/

Alim, H. S., & Smitherman, G. (2012). *Articulate while Black: Barack Obama, language, and race in the U.S.* New York: Oxford University Press. Two linguists analyze how Obama's "mastery of Black cultural modes of discourse was crucial to his being elected America's forty-fourth president." From his first campaign speeches, Obama used black language to connect with racially diverse crowds, poke fun at his critics, and exhibit his sense of kinship with the black community. Language is central to racial politics in the United States, the authors point out. And it was Obama's skilled use of black language and style that made his unusual name, his interracial family history, and his unique international upbringing familiar to the people who were crucial to his electoral win. The book explores how Obama used language in speeches, interviews, and everyday interactions, from his "eloquent" "poised," "educated" speeches, to his ability to codeswitch to a relaxed, downhome vernacular when talking to predominantly black audiences, using an intonation and style that signal his comfort and sense of belonging in any African-American community. The authors' own use of code switching throughout the book is interesting to students and causes many of them to think more deeply about the common conviction that blacks should have sense enough to keep the vernacular out of professional life.

Linguistic Society of America. www.lsadc.org/ This website has short texts of several interesting LSA Resolutions, one on African-American Vernacular English (sometimes called Ebonics), another titled "Opposition to all discrimination and political sanctions against scholars on the basis of religion or ethnicity," and a third on language rights. The LSA Resolution on the Oakland "Ebonics" issue contradicts what many students have learned at home, i.e., that any version of English other than what is taught in school is "slang," "ungrammatical," or "wrong"; that dialects have simpler structures and less developed vocabularies than "languages"; that multilingual nations have trouble understanding each other and are prone to violent ethnic rivalries, and so on. See "Resolutions, Statements, and Guides" at http://www.lsadc. org/info/lsa-res.cfm

Lippi-Green, R. (1997). *English with an accent*. New York: Routledge. In Chapter 4: Language ideology and the language subordination model, linguist Rosina Lippi-Green reminds us of a form of prejudice that many people don't ordinarily think of: accent discrimination. "We do not, cannot under our laws, ask people to change the color of their skin, their religion, their gender, but we regularly demand of people that they suppress or deny the most effective way they have of situating themselves socially in the world. 'You may have dark skin,' we tell them, 'but you must not sound Black.' 'You can wear a yarmulke if it is important to you as a Jew, but lose the accent.' 'Maybe you come from the Ukraine, but can't you speak real English?' 'If you didn't sound so cornpone, people would take you seriously.' 'You're the best salesperson we've got, but must you sound gay on the phone?'" Essential topic for any English major or anyone interested in language and power.

Smitherman, G. (1977). *Talkin and testifyin: The language of Black America*. Boston: Houghton Mifflin. Chapters 1 and 2 introduce students to the idea that Black English is a distinct language with a complicated grammar that is derived from West African speech patterns. "In a nutshell: Black Dialect is an Africanized form of English reflecting Black America's linguistic-cultural African heritage and the conditions of servitude, oppression and life in America." Written in a joyful mix of academic English and African-American Vernacular English, these two chapters challenge students' ideas about language and power, and who gets to say what is "proper" English. I give this article to peer tutors who are learning to help other students with their writing. Unless they have taken Linguistics classes, students find these ideas completely new.

## Media and Popular Culture

SV *7 Native American Indian Comics*. Lolflix.com https://www.youtube.com/ watch?v=-h0bVpXYWUc This site features comedians Charlie Hill, Jim Ruel, Larry Omaha, Daniel Liddle, and others. Both funny and political, these snippets of Native American humor are interspersed with bits of history, culture, and spirituality. Thought-provoking segments show how non-native comedians can unwittingly perpetuate Native stereotypes, while Native comedians challenge the assumptions of their white audiences, bringing "a sense of humanity to a culture that some people only know through their sports team, their cartoon characters, or their video games." Worth watching, even if you're not intending to teach about Native Americans. The content of the humor is suitable for high school age and older.

SV *Arab American Comedian Amer Zahr*. https://www.youtube.com/watch?v=oSlw-ZCk1ELQ Speaking to a mostly Arab audience in this ten-minute segment, Palestinian American comedian Amer Zahr is amusing even when he pokes fun at non-Arab viewers on their fear of terrorism and their common stereotypes about his culture. His jokes about his immigrant parents, their very formal uses of English, and their inexperience with voice mail will help introduce non-Arab students to the warm family relations so common in Arab American immigrant families. Zahn's performance is followed by a fascinating piece by Korean comic Won Ho Chung speaking in fluent Arabic, and at times, in English, to an Arab audience in Dubai. Subtitles and the vast amusement of the audience make watching this clip an enjoyable, stereotype-busting experience. Students can easily find more video clips of comedians from various ethnic backgrounds on the internet. One of the most thought-provoking student presentations in my college class on race relations was an exploration of the boundaries between ethnic humor, racial stereotyping, and downright offensiveness.

**SV** Demby, G. (2013, April 8). *How code-switching explains the world.* http://www.npr.org/blogs/codeswitch/2013/04/08/176064688/how-code-switching-explains-the-world. A light, amusing look at a topic many monolingual students are curious about: the ability of Americans who speak more than one language or dialect to switch back and forth, depending on the social context. Short videos include President Obama responding to a clerk in a black-owned restaurant, a young child speaking to his parents in French, English and Indonesian, and most engagingly, a Comedy Central skit by two African-Americans passing each other on the street and switching dialects on their cell phone calls according to their assumptions about each other. Hilarious!

**V** Adachi, J. (2006). *The slanted screen: Asian men in film and television.* (See: Asian Pacific Americans.)

**V** Chris Rock: *Good Hair.* (2009). Video, 95 minutes. Distributor: HBO Films. This highly entertaining yet informational film on the history, psychology, economics, and politics of the industry that provides hair products and services to black women opens with Chris Rock at home, trying to answer his preschool daughter's poignant question, "Daddy, how come I don't have good hair?" To discover what "good hair" is all about, Chris Rock takes us on a journey to a hairstyling contest, to barbershops and salons where people divulge the amount they spend on hair products, to high-profile corporations where industry magnates gloat over their profits, to Indian temples where girls sacrifice their hair that is then made into wigs for African-American women. I use excerpts from this film to initiate a discussion of internalized racism and its effects on people in all target groups. I need to explain very explicitly that seeing (or experiencing) the African hair type as "bad" is not just a simple observation about the time and trouble it requires for its care or its tendency to frizz in the rain. Quoting Malcolm X's autobiography on black men "conking" their hair in order to look white (X, 62–65), and showing a brief, online video of Malcolm asking a female audience, "Who taught you to hate yourself?" http://www.youtube.com/watch?v=gRSgUTWffMQ provides helpful historical and cultural background. To take the point further, one might ask, "Why isn't white skin considered to be 'bad skin' in our society?" Objectively, white skin (like African hair) can be problematic. It burns easily, requiring costly suntan lotion. It looks ridiculous when sunburned and even worse when it starts to peel. It puts one at risk for skin cancer. It shows pimples blatantly. For women, pale skin can require layers of make-up to remove blotches and hide unsightly pores. Yet despite all this, pale skin is considered superior to all shades of tan, chocolate, or ebony. Why?

**V** Clift, R. A. (2010). *Blacking up: Hip-Hop's remix of race and identity.* Video, 57 minutes. Created by African-American youth in the 1980s, hip-hop reflects the lives and struggles of young blacks trapped by poverty in the urban ghetto. Yet this genre has been ardently embraced by white suburban youth, who buy the albums, dress like their favorite rappers, and imitate their style. This film asks whether white rappers reflect a new level of racial understanding or simply reinforce America's ugly history. Why are some blacks angry or disgusted by what they see as white appropriation of black culture? Who benefits economically from this multimillion dollar business? Whites and blacks give varying opinions on these and many other questions in this provocative, insightful, and engrossing film. Randall Kennedy's book (*Nigger*) adds depth to this discussion if read previous to watching the film. Students love this topic and are quick to contribute online videos that further illustrate the question of whether whites can adequately express black culture. See for example, Harlem Reacts to Harlem Shake (http://www.youtube.com/watch?v=IGH2HEgWppc). (To see the kinds of moves that the Harlemites in the video are reacting to, see Harlem Shake—White People Style http://www.youtube.com/watch?v=ImfKbAf-Fpg.) This discussion can lead to an exploration of the difference between cultural appropriation and cultural appreciation. What is the fine line between them? What happens when a style started by an oppressed group becomes so popular that it spreads globally? For example, Korean performers have borrowed cultural styles from African-American rap artists, yet have created a style and audience all their own. (See examples of Korean rap here: https://www.youtube.com/watch?v=TmNo8B3CD44) Does such borrowing count as cultural appropriation? Or is it only appropriation when whites do it—and make money from it?

**V** Films for the Humanities & Sciences. (2008). *Racial stereotypes in the media.* Video, 42 minutes. While current interpersonal racism is not nearly as overtly paternalistic and insulting as in the past, racial attitudes behind many production decisions are still pervasive and destructive. TV and film clips, with background information and results of studies provided by the narrator, clearly show how this bias operates. Although the film is a bit pedantic and may be too elementary for some groups, it can provide hard evidence for what many students already suspect. Showing this film could precede a research project where students look for evidence of bias in the media they most often read or watch.

**V** Hurt, B. (2006). *Hip-Hop: Beyond Beats & Rhymes.* Video, 60 minutes. Distributor: Independent Lens. This amazing film comments on a wide range of racial, cultural, and gender issues: violent masculinity, misogyny, homophobia, the military, the prison experience, the influence of Hollywood, the economics and politics of the rap music industry, and much more. The film manages to present cultural theory in mesmerizing detail and provides thought-provoking arguments on U.S. culture in general. I show this film near the end of the semester when students are feeling comfortable arguing with each other about race, class, and gender issues. In one of my classes, the discussion of the female perspectives shown in the film divided students along gender lines rather than racially. Suddenly white women and women of color were making exactly the same arguments, and men of color and white men were defending themselves as a group. At a critical moment, a white woman who had been trying with only limited success to understand black perspectives all semester experienced the frustration of trying to voice a minority opinion. Addressing a black male with whom she had been arguing for weeks, she asked him to look at how he was dismissing the perspectives of the women in the room in the same way he had been accusing her of dismissing him. The exchange was pointed, passionate, clear, and caring—dialogue at its best.

**V** Lee, S. (2000). *Bamboozled*. Video, 136 minutes. Distributor: New Line Cinema. In this smart, fast-paced, satirical film, a black, Harvard-educated screenwriter, disgusted by the behavior of his white boss, tries to get himself fired by writing a blatantly racist modern-day minstrel show for a live television audience. To his dismay, the show is a huge success. I show clips of this film to stimulate students' thinking about the boundaries of ethnic humor. Some historical context is necessary, since few students are aware of the ways in which blacks have been exploited for white entertainment or how white actors caricatured blacks by "blacking up" their own faces and performing stereotypical, degrading characterizations of black life. A montage of this genre in Hollywood film beginning in the early twentieth century is included at the end of *Bamboozled*, and can be shown separately.

**V** Shaheen, J. (2007). *Reel bad Arabs: How Hollywood vilifies a people.* (See Arabs, Arab-Americans, Middle-Easterners and Muslims.)

Butler, P. (2009). *Let's get free: A hip-hop theory of justice*. New York: The New Press. "Imagine criminal justice in a hip-hop nation. Believe it or not, the culture provides a blueprint for a system that would enhance public safety and treat all people with respect. ... Who would have thought that hip-hop—the most thuggish art—could improve law and order?" Paul Butler, Harvard Law graduate and former federal prosecutor tells his own story: how he became disenchanted with prosecuting the poor and vulnerable, how he discovered, through being arrested, that the system is stacked against people of color. In straightforward, sensible, argumentative style, he lays out his creative ideas to change it. When the criminal justice system is exposed as unbalanced and unfair, when criminals—mostly African-American and Latino men—are not glorified but still treated with love and respect, when punishment is used less frequently and more effectively, all of which, Butler says, are characteristics of hip-hop culture, the interests of all of society will be served. Students enjoy this book for its fresh ideas, its personal stories, and its understandability.

Cho, M. (2002). *I'm the one that I want*. New York: Ballantine Books. Comedian Margaret Cho's memoir addresses painful issues of race and identity and the othering of Asian Americans, gays and lesbians, and anyone else that doesn't fit in. In her honest, compelling journey to self-acceptance, Cho reveals the intense engagement with others that drives talented performers to critique culture through comedy. See her in live performance at http://www.dailymotion.com/video/x3hodr9

DeLeon, C. (2007, March–April). The segregated blogosphere. *Colorlines*. http://www.colorlines.com/article.php?ID=195. White liberal and left writers, who dominate the blogosphere, marginalize concerns of people of color. "They won't talk about the racial element of anything that's been deracialized by mainstream media. They're not going to talk about affirmative action, about the racial element of the immigration issue. ... Whenever issues of race come up, it's seen as a distraction." This has resulted in a separate blogosphere inhabited by people of color—which, in turn, has "emboldened racists hiding behind the mask of virtual reality." Students can check out both blogospheres and report on what they find.

Ferris State University. Jim Crow Museum of Racist Memorabilia. http://www.ferris.edu/jimcrow/. Museum artifacts and accompanying texts give students a comprehensive understanding of the kinds of blatant, brutal racism that were common in past generations, and some that can still be found today in advertisements, figurines, media characters, T-shirt messages, cartoons, and more. The "selected videos" page is especially instructive. This astonishing virtual museum should be viewed by anyone who, like most students today, has little awareness of the array of "hateful things" produced, sold, and displayed—often as "a joke"—by otherwise normal people.

Gaskins, B. (1996). The world according to *Life*: Racial stereotyping and American identity. In G. Ibieta and M. Orvell (Eds.), *Inventing America: Readings in identity and culture*. New York: St. Martin's Press. Photographer and writer Bill Gaskins looks at the ways blacks have been represented in *Life* magazine from 1936 to the present. Excellent analysis; short, very readable. The writing assignment suggested by the authors works well: Ask students to study a recent issue of *People* magazine or *Cosmopolitan* and write several paragraphs describing how often and in what ways blacks are portrayed, both in text and in pictures. Then do the same for a magazine written by and for African-Americans, such as *Ebony, Jet, or Essence*. How are the stories in each magazine slanted to give readers a particular notion of African-American life?

Joseph, B. (2007, November 16). The 9 most racist Disney characters. Cracked.com. www.cracked.com/article_15677_9-most-racist-disney-characters.html. Excellent site with video clips of the worst offenders: In The Little Mermaid, a Jamaican-sounding crab declares that it's better under the sea because you don't have to get a job; the strange "red skin" of Native Americans is explained in Peter Pan; a nearly naked black child polishes the hoofs of an aloof Aryan centaur in the initial version of Fantasia. As one proceeds down the list of film clips, the films get older and the racism becomes even more blatant. You can project these clips on screen in a wired classroom or ask students to view them and write their reactions to them before they come to class.

Kennedy, R. (2003). *Nigger: The strange career of a troublesome word*. New York: Vintage Books. Harvard Law professor Randall Kennedy discusses the history of the "N-word" (the term I always use in class), its contestation in court, the pitfalls of fighting its use, either as an epithet or a term of endearment, and his opinion on whether to try to appropriate the word or ban it. The book provides a range of reasonable arguments on all these issues, which helps students sort out their ideas and come to their own conclusions. It also provides excellent background for discussion of the use of the N-word in the current music scene, which frequently comes up both in general class discussion and in films and texts on popular culture. In my classes, there has been a stronger difference of opinion on this issue, both among African-American students and among students of other ethnicities, than on almost any other. Discussion is passionate and heated, and with good-natured reminders, can remain respectful of various points of view.

Lee, R. G. (1999). Orientals: Asian Americans in popular culture. Philadelphia: Temple University Press. The author presents six historical images of the "Oriental" in U.S. culture: pollutant of white culture, coolie laborer, effeminate deviant, yellow peril threat, model minority, and gook. Helps students of all ethnicities to understand how popular culture elaborates and extends the racism against these groups.

Thurston, B. (2012). *How to be black*. New York: HarperCollins. Baratunde Thurston, a young, African-American intellectual and stand-up comedian, discusses this topic with tongue-in-cheek humor, providing insight into issues such as "How to Be the Black Friend"; "How to Speak for All Black People"; "How to be the Black Employee," and "How to be The Angry Negro." My students love this book. Several white students have overheard amusing comments made by their roommates or by passers-by in the library since the book's title is displayed in large, prominent print. One white student commented, "People I didn't even know did a double take—someone even took my picture!" Using humorous texts and videos to approach sensitive issues can set a positive tone for class discussion. Enjoying a good comedian makes it easier for students to laugh together and, occasionally, to laugh at themselves.

Watkins, M. (2002). *African American humor: The best black comedy from slavery to today*. Chicago Review Press. A comprehensive look at the history of African-American comedy from the 1800s to the present. There are plenty of examples here: sketches, jokes, poems, and stories from stage, radio, and early television to the routines of contemporary stand-up comedians. Commentary from a variety of authors explains how slaves used metaphors, subtle language, and seemingly innocuous stories to aim veiled critique at whites, and how demeaning roles that blacks played for white audiences in the early days of popular media paved the way for the biting humor of Chris Rock and Dave Chappelle today.

Wisniewski, K. A. (2009). *The comedy of Dave Chappelle: Critical Essays*. Jefferson, NC: McFarland Books. Twelve essays examine Chappelle's work through critical race theory, showing us how comedy shapes culture by making us laugh at racial situations that would otherwise make us uncomfortable, silent, confused, or angry. Authors explore ideas such as racial inversion in language, race loyalty, black authenticity, cultural co-optation, and more. A serious, intellectual look at a deceptively light medium. See video clips of Dave Chappelle in live performance on various topics. I particularly like a segment called "The Racial Draft," https://vimeo.com/61499874, which makes fun of ethnic identity categories.

Bell, W. (2016). *United shades of America.* http://www.cnn.com/shows/united-shades-of-america In this acclaimed CNN television series, African-American comedian and social critic W. Kamau Bell explores corners of America that few outsiders experience. The first episode, The New KKK, will have students talking and thinking for a long time. How does Bell keep his cool in the company of such outright racists? And for their part, how can the KKK members welcome Bell so genuinely and answer his questions so honestly when their public speeches are so filled with hate?

# "Postracial" Culture, Politics, and Economics

SV *Spent.* http://playspent.org/ This unique, entertaining, and challenging online game asks players to imagine they're an unemployed single parent: their savings are gone, their house has been repossessed, and they are down to their last $1000. Can they make it through the month? Students can play this short, revealing game before class or even during a five-minute break. Discussion of the choices they made, how well they made it through the month, and what they learned from the exercise can help students with no experience of living on the edge understand the stark choices so many people face. The specific outcomes of various options are particularly instructive. Looking for a temp job? See if you can pass the typing test. Trying for a restaurant server position? Remember to factor the cost of a uniform and health insurance into your monthly budget. You might also ask for students' critique of the game (I wondered how realistic it was to suggest that an impoverished person has a "last $1000" in the bank at all). The discussion may then lead to a reconsideration of the common perception that poor people are responsible for their own misfortune or that people whose families have been impoverished for generations can make it into the middle class with nothing more than pluck and endurance. Since this game doesn't mention race, it can be instructive to pair it with a reading on the racial wealth gap (See Kochar, Fry & Taylor, below).

SV *Unequal opportunity race.* http://www.youtube.com/watch?v=eBb5TgOXg NY. This short, animated, must-watch video illustrates why many ethnic groups still lag behind whites, suggesting reasons for the economic, social and educational gaps and stressing the need for affirmative action. A provocative way to introduce students to inequalities in wealth, education, and outcome for people who are trying as hard as they can to succeed. A short article that gives figures for wealth disparities (such as Kochar, Fry & Taylor), or longer pieces that explain the inequalities in more depth (such as chapters from Lui et al., *The color of wealth*) should accompany this animation.

Dávila, A. (2008). *Latino spin: Public image and the whitewashing of race*. New York University Press. This fascinating book explains how the marketing of Latin@s as a fresh, new, uniquely American group serves political and corporate interests while at the same time, nativist and anti-immigrant groups are depicting Latin@s as law-breakers who undercut "real" American workers, threaten familiar values, and refuse to assimilate. So are Latinos ruining America, Dávila asks, or are they "on the road to whiteness," "coming of age," and "blending in"? Dávila explains this paradox as conservative nostalgia for an old-fashioned America: patriotic, respectful of family values, conventionally religious, and comfortingly white. Since the values and beliefs of many Hispanics tend to be opposed to homosexuality, divorce and abortion, and since the growing Hispanic middle class is oriented toward hard work and the pleasures and responsibilities of family, "at this time of uncertainty, Latinos can give America back to America." Yet this narrative is itself misleading, Dávila suggests, as it leaves out their diversity in terms of race, class, education, citizenship and nationality, as well as the ways they are racialized and racialize their own group. Some are able to assimilate and move up, others assimilate yet move down in status, depending on their perceived race, education, and parental background.

Fox, H. (2015). *Fractured: Race relations in "post-racial" American life*. New York, NY: Peter Lang. My latest book, based on in-depth interviews across the country, describes in both personal and historical terms why race relations are so fraught today despite claims that the worst of our country's racist history is behind us. From the book description: "What do you think is meant by the term 'post-racial' and how far do you think we've come, as a country, toward achieving it?" Helen Fox, a white teacher and scholar, asked variations of this question to eighty-seven high school and college students, educators, administrators, community organizers, international visitors, and tribal leaders across the country. Their stories reveal how far we are from a "post racial" ideal even in the most liberal of communities. Despite her long experience as an antiracist educator, Fox was surprised to learn how deeply the lives of people of color continue to be shaped by race, and how hard they have to work to ignore or overcome the assumptions, remarks, exclusion, and at times, blatant hostility from whites. The kinds of racism they experience depend on their gender, their religion, their geographical location, their skin tone, their forms of speech and expression, their socioeconomic class, their aspirations, their determination to be outspoken or stoic, the kinds and amount of contact they choose to have (or can't escape having) with whites, and of course, their ascribed race. Despite our nation's "postracial" climate, racialized assumptions, beliefs, and denials affect everything, from the reach of the national media down to the smallest community: the street where one lives, the friends one attempts to make, the social club, the study group, the classroom. As an art educator remarked, "The 'post-racial' reminds me of the post-modern—the fracturing of things. It's not like our society has finally come together—unless we've come together as a fractured society and we're feeling the prickliness of the broken shards." Works well for college and high school classes, book clubs, and community discussions about race.

Higginbotham, F. M. (2013). *Ghosts of Jim Crow: Ending racism in post-racial America.* New York: New York University Press. A well-written, reader-friendly book that speaks personally and knowledgeably about how to achieve a truly "post-racial" society, that is, a society free from notions of white superiority and black inferiority, from "black separation and white isolation," and from black victimization—"the harm imposed due to feelings of hopelessness." Understanding the history of black and white relations is critical to this project, the author says, and changing laws and practices that maintain institutional racism will also help move us in a post-racial direction, "but only by changing hearts and minds can the paradigm be permanently altered." A high-profile African-American lawyer and law professor, Higginbotham begins the book with his personal journey. As an A student with a successful, supportive family, who experienced no trace of racism or even race consciousness in his integrated neighborhood, Higginbotham gradually comes to understand this country's racial problems as he enters an exclusive private school, observes the behavior of the parents of his white friends, and follows the national news. His conclusion: successful blacks have become prominent despite racism, not because it has largely disappeared. Although some students, particularly African-Americans who grew up in poverty, may object to his simplistic suggestions about what blacks can do to better their own circumstances (focus more on education, speak standard English, provide positive role models, and avoid using poverty as an excuse for personal irresponsibility), all students are interested in his detailed suggestions for what the larger society can do to help increase economic, educational, and political empowerment for blacks. Students may question why the book concentrates exclusively on the black-white paradigm, a justified criticism. Yet it can be argued that the history of black-white relations in this country underlies all other forms of racial discrimination that Americans practice. Food for thought.

Jeter, J., & Pierre, R. E. (2009). *A day late and a dollar short: High hopes and deferred dreams in Obama's "post-racial" America.* New York: Wiley. Two *Washington Post* journalists write about the "state of the Black Union" on the eve of Barack Obama's first election. The book is engagingly written, and includes their own personal anecdotes, stories of individuals they interviewed, and in-depth reporting on the institutional racism faced by blacks in education, the criminal justice system, the military, and the health care system. The inequalities both between blacks and whites and within the black community are presented in gripping detail.

Kochar, R., Fry, R. & Taylor, P. (2011, July 26). Wealth gaps rise to record highs between whites, blacks, Hispanics. *Pew Research, Social & Demographic Trends.* http://www.pewsocialtrends.org/2011/07/26/wealth-gaps-rise-to-record-highs-between-whites-blacks-hispanics/ "The median wealth of white households is 20 times that of black households and 18 times that of Hispanic households," says a Pew Research Center study. The 2008 recession hit minority households much harder than it did whites. As a result, the typical black household held $5,677 in wealth; the typical Hispanic household held $6,235 while the typical white household held $113,149. Before assigning this piece to students you might ask them whether they think there is a racial wealth gap and how great they think that gap is. Students can then read the Executive Summary of the piece or delve into the detailed report.

Lui, M., Robles, B., Leondar-Wright, B., Brewer, R. & Adamson, R. (2006). The *Color of Wealth: The story behind the U.S. racial wealth divide.* New York: The New Press. "For every dollar owned by the average white family in the United States, the average family of color has less than one dime. Why do people of color have so little wealth? Because for centuries they were barred by law, by discrimination, and by violence from participating in government wealth-building programs that benefited white Americans." This first paragraph of the book says in a nutshell what almost all students are surprised to learn: throughout history, whites have benefitted from government programs that excluded people of color, and those economic losses continue to affect people of color today. Each chapter tells the story of a different ethnic group: Native Americans, blacks, Latin@s, and (to the surprise of many), Asian Americans. Each gives facts, figures, and histories of how the racial wealth divide became so skewed toward the powerful white majority at the expense of each group in turn. After students have learned how this happened they can discuss the question of the personal responsibility of the poor with more insight. Yet it is still challenging to help students make connections between what happened in the past to the behavior of individuals they come across today. Students can easily point to irresponsible behavior of a panhandler on the edge of campus and conclude that he has simply made bad life choices. Reflecting on how history affects the life chances of individuals and groups today is both a challenge and a responsibility.

Roberts, D. (2011). *Fatal invention: How science, politics, and big business re-create race in the twenty-first century.* New York: The New Press. An erudite, scathing history of scientific and philosophical racism in European and American history prefaces Roberts's argument that the new science of genomics, which was supposed to have demonstrated once and for all that race is a political category, not a scientific one, is creating new ways to validate old ideas of race. Roundly discredited "race science" is being repackaged, sometimes willfully, often unthinkingly, into a new version of "America's enduring racial order." Roberts gives convincing examples of how the pharmaceutical and biotechnology industries are "converting the new racial science into products that are developed according to race," and how solid social science research is being ignored and/or selectively reported to convince people to buy racial science, both metaphorically and in the marketplace. The first two chapters should be a staple of social science courses that trace the history and great ideas of the Enlightenment.

Sugrue, T. J. (2012). *Not even past: Barack Obama and the burden of race*. Princeton, NJ: Princeton University Press. In one of his speeches on race, Barack Obama makes a point about the saliency of past discriminatory policies in understanding today's racial inequalities by paraphrasing William Faulkner: "The past is not dead; it is not even past." This book looks at Obama's racial politics as they evolved throughout his life and through this lens, comments on America's understanding of race in the "post-racial" America that Obama's election has helped create. Sugrue's refreshingly clear, straightforward prose illuminates an exceedingly complex topic.

Wise, T. (2010). *Colorblind: The Rise of Post-Racial Politics and the Retreat from Racial Equity*. San Francisco, CA: City Lights Books. In this short, pithy book, anti-racist activist Tim Wise lays out an excellent argument against so-called "colorblind" politics. He begins with a critique of Barack Obama's first speech to a national audience in 2004 ("There's not a black America and a white America and Latino America and Asian America, there's the United States of America") and goes on to show the impact of Obama's presidential victory on the nation's ability to tackle issues of race and racism. While at the beginning of the semester most of my students are certain that "post-racial" does not accurately describe the United Sates today, none is really able to say why. This book gives them reasons. A PBS interview with Tim Wise by African-American social critic Tavis Smiley can be found here: www.pbs.org/wnet/ tavissmiley/interviews/anti-racist-activist-tim-wise/

## Activism

**SV** BBC (2016, January 7). *Meet the young female Arab-American activists*. In this short clip, three Arab American, Muslim women who are leading the protest against anti-Muslim rhetoric in the United Sates discuss their experiences as activists. High school and college students will relate to these upbeat, youthful leaders, whose experiences with their audiences and with their parents may leave them wanting to know more. They can find background, context, and stories of activism told in intimate detail in Nadine Naber's book, *Arab America: Gender, cultural politics, and activism* (2012), New York University Press.

**SV** Wise, T. (2015, January). *Tim Wise on white allyship and solidarity*. The King Center, Atlanta, GA. http://www.timwise.org/2016/03/tim-wise-on-white-allyship- and-solidarity-the-king-center-atlanta-ga-january-2015/ This clip from a longer speech sums up what white, antiracist activist Tim Wise has learned from being an ally: "Listen to people of color. The vast majority of white Americans have persistently, consistently, every generation of this country's history been unwilling to hear black and brown truths. Trust that people know their life better than you know their life. That's what we never—ever—understood."

**V** Tejada-Florez, R., & Telles, R. (1996). *The fight in the fields: Cesar Chavez and the farmworkers' struggle*. Video, 116 minutes. Distributor: Paradigm Films.

Archival footage, newsreel and interview document the inspirational life of Mexican American union organizer, Cesar Chavez, the most important Latino leader in this country's history. Most students don't know this history or anything much about labor in this country. A good, if detailed, introduction.

Advancement Project. www.advancementproject.org/ Students will be inspired by this group: "an innovative civil rights law, policy, and communications 'action tank' that advances universal opportunity and a just democracy for those left behind in America." News, reports, events, and long-term projects for "building a multiracial social justice movement" are detailed here.

Black Lives Matter. http://blacklivesmatter.com Founded by women of color Patrisse Cullors, Opal Tometi, and Alicia Garza, the #BlackLivesMatter organization is an "online forum intended to build connections between Black people and our allies to fight anti-Black racism, the spark dialogue among Black people, and to facilitate the types of connections necessary to encourage social action and engagement." The movement was started in 2012 after the shooting of Trayvon Martin, an unarmed African-American teenager on his way home from the corner store, by a hypervigilant neighborhood watch "commander." The movement aims to move beyond traditional male-centered black nationalism to "affirm the lives of Black queer and trans folks, disabled folks, black-undocumented folks, folks with records, women and all Black lives along the gender spectrum." It is unapologetic about its insistence that black people are "intentionally left powerless at the hands of the state," depriving them of their basic human rights and dignity. College and mature high school students of all ethnicities and political orientations can learn from this site and use it as a starting point for research. Why is this strident political rhetoric emerging at this point in our nation's history? Why does the movement blame state violence, rather than interpersonal racism for persistent black poverty, high rates of incarceration, and marginalization of various identities? What about the movement do they agree with or affirm?

Dunlap, L. (2007). *Undoing the silence: Six tools for social change writing.* Oakland, CA: New Village Press. Louise Dunlap, a writing teacher and activist, encourages students and community people to write by confronting the ways U.S. culture silences dissent. Convinced that all of us "have powerful voices somewhere inside," Dunlap shows us how to let go of self-judgment, generate and deepen our ideas, analyze our audiences, and start writing groups to provide feedback and mutual encouragement. This practical, inspiring book can be used in high school or college classrooms as well as by community activists who want to extend their voices.

hooks, b. (2012). *Writing beyond race: Living theory and practice.* New York: Routledge. Acclaimed black feminist author bell hooks brings together notions of race, class, gender, politics, history, and popular culture in this excellent collection of her own essays. How can we as a society challenge existing hierarchies and systems of oppression? Students want the answer to this burning question, especially after a long semester of study of the demoralizing realities of race relations in this country, and bell hooks provides some answers—or at least some thoughts for deep reflection. We must accept that our nation was founded and still functions on the premise of white supremacy if we are ever to understand the system we want to change. We need to "name what hurts," yet move past blame by identifying all the systems of oppression and understanding how they work together. We should question the presumed cultural good of assimilation (because "the dominant culture is also dominator culture"), reimagine the past, including the lives of our cultural icons, and find new ways to enact everyday resistance. Above all, we should follow hooks's model of thinking and writing beyond the boundaries that keep us all "overracialized." As always, bell hooks is thought-provoking, original, and comfortable being herself.

Horton, M. (1990). *The long haul.* New York: Doubleday. Myles Horton's autobiography documents his life as an educator of community leaders to work for social justice, from labor organizers in the 1930s to teachers and activists (including Rosa Parks) during the Civil Rights Era. Students need models of white activists who have done antiracist work all their lives. Horton's story appeals to them: he is anti-authority without being anti-intellectual; he thinks deeply and passionately; he figures things out for himself; and he makes his own life matter.

Lee, G. (2003, June 1). The forgotten revolution. http://hyphenmagazine.com/ magazine/issue-1-premiere-summer-2003/forgotten-revolution This brief history of the Asian American civil rights movement will help students understand why a high-achieving "model minority" would, like other oppressed groups, need a social movement to gain self-confidence and respect in the United States. It explains why the term "Asian American" was so radical fifty years ago, where it came from, and why it persists, despite criticism from youth today who point out that lumping together people from so many different backgrounds, life experiences, languages, and cultural traditions can be counterproductive. "Instead of feeling ashamed of being Asian, we began to feel proud," says the author about the beginning of the movement in the 1960s and 1970s. "In this sense, Asian pride was antiracist and politically progressive. We began to feel as if we were all a part of one larger community, but it also brought us closer to Blacks, Puerto Ricans, Chicanos and Native Americans, groups I would not have ordinarily felt close to."

Lorde, A. (1993). There is no hierarchy of oppressions. In R. Cleaver & P. Myers (Eds.), *A certain terror: Heterosexism, militarism, violence and change.* Chicago: Great Lakes Regional Office of the American Friends Service Committee. Very short, still-relevant piece by African-American poet Audre Lorde: "... I have learned that oppression and the intolerance of difference come in all shapes and sexes and colors and sexualities; and that among those of us who share the goals of liberation and a workable future for our children, there can be no hierarchies of oppression. I have learned that sexism (a belief in the inherent superiority of one sex over all others and thereby its right to dominance) and heterosexism (a belief in the inherent superiority of one pattern of loving over all others and thereby its right to dominance) both arise from the same source as racism—a belief in the inherent superiority of one race over all others and thereby its right to dominance." Excellent handout when students get to arguing about which groups are "really" oppressed and which are not. This piece can also be found on numerous blogs online.

Mock, B. Mainstream green is still too white. (2013, April 2). *Colorlines*. https://www. colorlines.com/articles/mainstream-green-still-too-white This article comments on a problem that white students sometimes notice in their campus organizations: the lack of diversity. This is not because people of color are uninterested or immune to the environmental crisis, says Mock; on the contrary, poor communities of color are more directly affected by climate change than neighborhoods where most white activists live. Reasons for the lack of people of color in mainstream environmental groups range from inept engagement tactics, to difficulty understanding the values and priorities of the communities most directly affected, to the use of language that can have different meanings to different groups. Smart student activists can use this article to think more deeply about their own tactics.

Nichols, W. J. (2013). *The DREAMers: How the undocumented youth transformed the immigrant rights debate*. Stanford University Press. "On May 17, 2010, four undocumented students occupied the Arizona office of Senator John McCain. Across the country a flurry of occupations, hunger strikes, demonstrations, and marches followed, calling for support of the DREAM Act that would allow these young people the legal right to stay in the United States." When this movement began, it drew a bright line between "good immigrants," the "thoroughly American" youth who were brought to the United Sates as children and grew up pursuing their "American Dream" (sometimes not knowing they were undocumented until it was time to apply for college) and other immigrants, often working class adults, who made a conscious decision to cross the border illegally, work under the table, and maintain financial and emotional ties to their home countries. In 2013, the organization expanded its platform to include the families and communities of DREAMers, and now advocates for a path to citizenship for 11 million undocumented Americans and "fair treatment for all." Students can also learn about the organization by exploring its website http://unitedwedream.org

Teaching Tolerance. On the front lines. www.tolerance.org/toolkit/front-lines. This short, succinct list of suggestions from activist educators tells newcomers what they need to consider as they work to promote equity in their classrooms. Ways to be a role model, examining one's own biases, and considering the costs of fighting alone in a hostile department are mentioned. The overall *Teaching Tolerance* website is a gold mine of ideas, lesson plans and classroom stories especially for teachers at the elementary and junior high levels.

Zinn Education Project. Native American activism: 1960s to today. http://zinned-project.org/materials/native-american-activism-1960s-to-today/ This history lesson includes the occupation of Alcatraz Island, Mt. Rushmore, and Plymouth Rock, the "Trail of Broken Treaties Caravan" and many other highlights of Native activism in the 1960s and 1970s. Educators looking for resources on this important period can explore the larger website, *The Zinn Education Project*, which promotes and supports the teaching of people's history in middle and high school classrooms across the country. Lesson plans, stories, reading materials for various levels, films, archival news clips, and many other free resources are available for download on this comprehensive site.

## Questions about the Purpose(s) of Colleges and Universities

Norm Denzin,
Shirley R. Steinberg
*General Editors*

What are the purposes of higher education? When undergraduates "declare their majors," they agree to enter into a world defined by the parameters of a particular academic discourse—a discipline. But who decides those parameters? How do they come about? What are the discussions and proposed outcomes of disciplined inquiry? What should an undergraduate know to be considered educated in a discipline? How does the disciplinary knowledge base inform its pedagogy? Why are there different disciplines? When has a discipline "run its course"? Where do new disciplines come from? Where do old ones go? How does a discipline produce its knowledge? What are the meanings and purposes of disciplinary research and teaching? What are the key questions of disciplined inquiry? What questions are taboo within a discipline? What can the disciplines learn from one another? What might they not want to learn and why?

Once we begin asking these kinds of questions, positionality becomes a key issue. One reason why there aren't many books on the meaning and purpose of higher education is that once such questions are opened for discussion, one's subjectivity becomes an issue with respect to the presumed objective stances of Western higher education. Academics don't have positions because positions are "biased," "subjective," "slanted," and therefore somehow invalid. So the first thing to do is to provide a sense—however broad and general—of what kinds of positionalities will inform the books and chapters on the above questions. Certainly the questions themselves, and any others we might ask, are already suggesting a particular "bent," but as the series takes shape, the authors we engage will no doubt have positions on these questions.

From the stance of interdisciplinary, multidisciplinary, or transdisciplinary practitioners, will the chapters and books we solicit solidify disciplinary discourses, or liquefy them? Depending on who is asked, interdisciplinary inquiry is either a polite collaboration among scholars firmly situated in their own particular discourses, or it is a blurring of the restrictive parameters that define the very notion of disciplinary discourse. So will the series have a stance on the meaning and purpose of interdisciplinary inquiry and teaching? This can possibly be finessed by attracting thinkers from disciplines that are already multidisciplinary, for example, the various kinds of "studies" programs (women's, Islamic, American, cultural, etc.), or the hybrid disciplines like ethnomusicology (musicology, folklore, anthropology). But by including people from these fields (areas? disciplines?) in our series, we are already taking a stand on disciplined inquiry. A question on the comprehensive exam for the Columbia University Ethnomusicology Program was to defend ethnomusicology as a "field" or a "discipline." One's answer determined one's future, at least to the extent that the gatekeepers had a say in such matters. So, in the end, what we are proposing will no doubt involve political struggles.

For additional information about this series or for the submission of manuscripts, please contact Shirley R. Steinberg, msgramsci@gmail.com. To order other books in this series, please contact our Customer Service Department at: (800) 770-LANG (within the U.S.), (212) 647-7706 (outside the U.S.), (212) 647-7707 FAX, or browse online by series at: www.peterlang.com.

# Also by Helen Fox

## Fractured: Race Relations in "Post-Racial" American Life
June 2015 | 188 pages

**978-1-4331-2369-6 (pb)**
CHF SFr.24.00 | EURD €20.95 | EURA €21.10 | EUR €19.20 | GBP £16.00 | USD $22.95

**978-1-4331-2370-2 (hc)**
CHF SFr.139.00 | EURD €123.40 | EURA €126.80 | EUR €115.30 | GBP £92.00 | USD $149.95

**978-1-4539-1619-3 (ebook PDF)**
CHF SFr.39.00 | EURD €36.53 | EURA €36.84 | EUR €30.70 | GBP £25.00 | USD $39.95

**978-1-4541-9788-1 (epub)**
CHF SFr.39.00 | EURD €36.53 | EURA €36.84 | EUR €30.70 | GBP £25.00 | USD $39.95

"What do you think is meant by the term 'post-racial' and how far do you think we've come, as a country, toward achieving it?" Helen Fox, a white teacher and scholar, asked variations of this question to 87 high school and college students, educators, administrators, community organizers, international visitors, and tribal leaders across the country. Their stories reveal how far we are from a "post-racial" ideal—even in the most liberal of communities. Despite her long experience as an anti-racist educator, Fox was surprised to learn how deeply the lives of people of color continue to be shaped by race, and how hard they have to work to ignore or overcome assumptions, remarks, exclusion, and at times, blatant hostility from whites. The kinds of racism they experience depend on their gender, their religion, their geographical location, their skin tone, their forms of speech and expression, their socioeconomic class, their aspirations, their determination to be outspoken or stoic, the kinds and amount of contact they choose to have (or can't escape having) with whites, and of course, their ascribed race. Despite our nation's "post-racial" climate, racialized assumptions, beliefs, and denials affect everything, from the reach of the national media down to the smallest community: the street where one lives, the friends one attempts to make, the social club, the study group, the classroom. As an art educator remarked, "The 'post-racial' reminds me of the post-modern—the fracturing of things. It's not like our society has finally come together—unless we've come together as a fractured society and we're feeling the prickliness of the broken shards."

## Table of Contents

**Order _Fractured_ directly from Peter Lang Publishing via the web: www.peterlang.com; email: customerservice@plang.com; phone: 800-770-LANG/212-647-7706; or fax: 212-647-7707.**